Public Purse, Public Purpose

Autonomy and Accountability
in the
Groves of Academe

Public Purse, Public Purpose

Autonomy and Accountability
in the
Groves of Academe

edited by

James Cutt
and
Rodney Dobell

The Institute for Research on Public Policy/
L'Institut de recherches politiques

Canadian Comprehensive Auditing Foundation

Canadian Cataloguing in Publication Data

Main entry under title:

Public purse, public purpose

Proceedings of a conference held in Ottawa, Ont., in November 1990.
Co-published by: Canadian Comprehensive Auditing Foundation.
Prefatory material in English and French.

ISBN 0-88645-129-9

1. Educational accountability—Canada—Congresses.
2. University autonomy—Canada—Congresses.
3. Universities and colleges—Canada—Finance—Congresses.
4. Higher education and state—Canada—Congresses.
I. Cutt, James, 1937- II. Dobell, Rodney, 1937-
III. Institute for Research on Public Policy.
IV. Canadian Comprehensive Auditing Foundation

LC67.68.C3P82 1992   379.71   C92-098552-1

Camera-ready copy and publication management by

PDS Research Publishing Services Ltd.
P.O. Box 3296
Halifax, Nova Scotia B3J 3H7
(902) 494-3865

Published by

The Institute for Research on Public Policy/
L'Institut de recherches politiques
P.O. Box 3670 South
Halifax, Nova Scotia B3J 3K6

and

Canadian Comprehensive Auditing Foundation
The Carriageway
55 Murray Street, Suite 210
Ottawa, Ontario K1M 5M3

Contents

Foreword

The role of universities in Canada has never been more important than it will be over the difficult adjustment period of the last decade of this century. The products of universities—educated and trained people, information derived from research, and a collective sense of identity and direction—will be decisive to the success and civility with which Canada weathers the period of change.

There is broad agreement that universities can best fulfil their appointed role if they continue to enjoy substantial autonomy in decision making. However, there is also increasing agreement—certainly outside universities and increasingly indeed among the more realistic in the groves of academe—that continued enjoyment of the self-regulatory model of university funding and governance must be earned by the external demonstration of accountability. Autonomy is to accountability as rights are to responsibilities. But what is meant by accountability? And who is to determine and report on it?

Public concern for accountability includes but goes beyond the traditional concern for integrity in the use of public resources. It extends to a requirement for assurance that universities are actually achieving what they claim to be pursuing in teaching, research, and public service and, furthermore, that they are doing so as efficiently as possible within their unique circumstances.

ix

Universities have, quite properly, expressed reservations about the determination of their accountability by external evaluators or auditors unfamiliar with those circumstances. But the accountability imperative must be addressed, and it will be imposed by governments or legislative auditors unless universities rise to the challenge themselves. And they must rise to that challenge, not only to keep governments and legislative auditors at bay, but also to compete successfully with other demands, particularly from the health sector, on scarce public resources.

There is broad agreement that only universities themselves can do the job of representing the subtlety and complexity of their objectives and operations in teaching, research, and public service. Much of the information will be descriptive and qualitative, and it will take time for a thorough framework of university accountability to evolve. But there is no escaping the issue and no doubt that the information produced will only be an adequate representation of the university story if universities tell it themselves.

In such a framework of external representations on accountability, auditors can play their traditional and appropriate role of attesting to, and thus providing assurance about, these representations. The accountability relationship exists between public funding sources and universities. The onus is on universities to demonstrate their accountability; the onus then on auditors is to lend credibility to that demonstration.

From recognizing these general propositions to finding all the necessary information is, of course, a substantial leap. Participants in the discussion summarized in this volume were fortunate to have not only the financial support of the Canadian Comprehensive Auditing Foundation (CCAF) but also the active involvement of a number of its members in the discussion.

Given the importance of finding agreement not only on a philosophical stance and a general approach but also on an operational process for cutting through a thicket of indicators and numbers, the CCAF joined with the Institute for Research on Public Policy (IRPP) to sponsor the accountability workshop and to publish jointly these proceedings. Both organizations gratefully acknowledge financial support from the British Columbia Ministry of Advanced Education, an early commitment that was crucial in establishing the feasibility of the project, and a grant from the Social Sciences and Humanities Research Council (SSHRC) in support of the workshop. The editors wish also to acknowledge with deep appreciation the insightful and conscientious support of Heather Neufeld and Ruby Day in bringing the record of this meeting from raw tapes to camera-ready text.

As all orders of governments give increasing emphasis to social investment in learning and increasingly recognize the social purposes of universities in building a competitive economy, the views set out here themselves assume critical importance in the development of post-secondary education in the new Canadian federation. The IRPP and the CCAF hope that this volume will contribute to some progress in a field where progress is crucial to the nation's future.

J-P Boisclair
Executive Director
Canadian Comprehensive
  Auditing Foundation

Monique Jérôme-Forget
President
Institute for Research on
  Public Policy

January 1992

Avant-propos

Le rôle des universités n'a jamais été aussi important que celui qu'elles seront appelées à jouer durant la difficile période de remise en ordre de la dernière décennie du siècle. Les services que l'on attend d'elles, essentiellement dans les domaines de l'éducation et de la formation, dans la publication des résultats de leurs recherches et dans la formulation d'une identité et d'objectifs communautaires, seront indispensables au Canada, si celui-ci veut s'adapter avec succès et sans trop de perturbations aux changements qui s'imposent.

Dans l'ensemble, on reconnaît que, pour être en mesure de remplir le rôle qui leur a été attribué, les universités doivent continuer à bénéficier d'une autonomie appréciable en matière de prise de décisions. Toutefois, à l'extérieur des universités surtout, mais également dans les secteurs universitaires les plus réalistes, une nouvelle attitude tend à s'imposer : les avantages résultant de l'autonomie dont jouissent les universités en ce qui concerne le financement et la gestion doivent être contrebalancés par une obligation de rendre des comptes à la communauté en général. L'autonomie est à l'obligation de rendre des comptes ce que sont les droits par rapport aux responsabilités.

L'intérêt du public à l'égard de cette responsabilité externe des universités inclut et dépasse le traditionnel désir de vérifier que les fonds publics soient utilisés d'une manière appropriée. Il s'étend jusqu'au besoin de prouver que les universités remplissent bien les fonctions qui leur incombent en matière d'enseignement, de recherche et de service public, et qu'en outre elles le font aussi efficacement que possible, dans le contexte particulier qui leur est propre.

Les universités ont, à bon droit, exprimé des réserves quant à la détermination de l'étendue de leurs responsabilités par des évaluateurs ou des vérificateurs externes, peu au courant du contexte universitaire. Mais l'obligation qu'ont les universités de rendre des comptes ne peut plus être ignorée, et des procédures d'évaluation devront être imposées par les vérificateurs des gouvernements ou des législations, si les universités ne relèvent pas le défi elles-mêmes. Celles-ci doivent s'attaquer à cette tâche, non seulement pour garder ces vérificateurs à distance, mais aussi pour concurrencer avec succès, dans une période de restriction des ressources publiques, les autres demandes de nature sociale, notamment celles provenant du secteur de la santé.

L'on convient généralement que seules les université sont à même de rendre compte efficacement de la subtilité et de la complexité de leurs objectifs et de leurs activités en matière d'enseignement, de recherche et de service public. La plupart des renseignements pertinents seront d'ordre descriptif et qualitatif, et la mise au point d'un système d'évaluation universitaire approprié demandera beaucoup de temps. Mais il n'y aura pas moyen d'éviter ce processus et il ne fait aucun doute, par ailleurs, que ces renseignements ne pourront être un fidèle reflet des activités de l'université que si les universités se chargent elles-mêmes de les fournir.

La reddition de comptes dans de telles conditions laisse aux vérificateurs la possibilité de jouer leur rôle traditionnel et approprié, qui est de certifier l'exactitude des déclarations et de fournir les assurances nécessaires à ce sujet. Cette responsabilité externe est la conséquence du rapport qui existe entre les universités et les bailleurs de fonds publics. C'est aux universités qu'il incombera de prouver que les fonds reçus ont été utilisés d'une manière responsable; de leur côté, les vérificateurs auront la charge rendre cette preuve crédible.

Entre l'admission de ces principes et la production de tous les renseignements nécessaires, il y a évidemment bien du chemin.

Les participants à la discussion rapportée ici ont eu la chance de bénéficier non seulement du soutien financier de la Fondation canadienne pour la vérification intégrale (FCVI), mais aussi de la participation active aux débats d'un certain nombre de ses membres.

Étant donné l'importance de trouver un terrain d'entente, non seulement sur des principes communs et une manière générale d'envisager la question, mais également sur un processus opératoire permettant d'y voir clair à travers un véritable dédale d'indicateurs et de chiffres, la FCVI a accepté de se joindre à l'Institut de recherches politiques (IRP) pour parrainer l'atelier sur la responsabilité externe des universités et pour publier conjointement les actes de cette rencontre. Ces deux organismes tiennent à exprimer ici leur gratitude pour le soutien financier accordé dès le début par le ministère de l'Enseignement supérieur de la Colombie-Britannique, rendant ainsi possible la réalisation de ce projet, ainsi que pour la subvention du Conseil de recherche des sciences humaines (CRSH). Les éditeurs désirent également témoigner ici de leur profonde gratitude à l'égard de Heather Neufeld et Ruby Day qui, par leur dévouement infatigable et leur professionnalisme, sont parvenues à transformer l'enregistrement brut sur bandes magnétiques des travaux de cette réunion en un document d'exécution prêt pour la publication.

Aujourd'hui, toutes les décisions gouvernementales mettent de plus en plus l'accent sur les investissements sociaux que constitue l'apprentissage et reconnaissent chaque jour davantage le rôle social important que les universités sont appelées à jouer dans l'établissement d'une économie concurrentielle. Les points de vue présentés dans le présent ouvrage s'avèrent donc d'une importance particulière en vue d'un aménagement de l'enseignement post-secondaire, dans la nouvelle fédération canadienne. L'IRP et la FCVI espèrent que ce volume aidera à réaliser certains progrès dans un domaine où le progrès est crucial pour l'avenir du pays.

J.-P. Boisclair
Directeur exécutif
Fondation canadienne
  pour la vérification intégrale

Monique Jérôme-Forget
Présidente
Institut de recherches
  politiques

Janvier 1992

Introduction

James Cutt and Rodney Dobell

The role of universities in Canada has never been more important than it will be over the difficult adjustment period of the last decade of this century. The products of universities—educated and trained people, and information derived from research—will be decisive to the success and civility with which Canada weathers a period of fundamental change in its economic, social, political, and constitutional arrangements. Indeed, higher education and research are moving to the top of public policy agendas in all industrialized countries, as recognition grows that national success in an era of global competition will depend more and more on highly trained labour forces, scientific research and development, diffusion of information, and entrepreneurial innovation.

Canadian universities can best fulfil their role if they continue to enjoy substantial autonomy in decision making. But this very autonomy is under pressure. The relationships of universities in Canada—and indeed in most countries that are members of the Organization of Economic Cooperation and Development (OECD)—with funding agencies and their major constituencies over the 1970s and 1980s have been unstable and often difficult. In general, there has been a serious loss of faith in the self-regulatory model of university funding and external governance by which, essentially, universities are given resources and left with autonomy to use them as they see fit. Restrictions and conditions on funding, proposals for alternative funding models (for instance, providing a much larger proportion of funding directly to students) and increasing resort to alternative avenues of post-secondary education and research, all appear to reflect growing concerns on the part of public funding agencies, industry, and students. There is increasing agreement—certainly outside universities, and increasingly even among the more realistic in the groves of academe—that continued enjoyment of the self-regulatory model of university funding and governance must be earned by evidence of reforms in at least two respects: first, by the adoption of modes of governance and management systems, controls, and practices which provide reasonable assurance of quality and good stewardship, particularly in the core functions of teaching and research; and second, by significant improvements in the external demonstration of accountability.

Public concern for accountability includes but goes beyond the traditional concern for integrity in the use of public resources to assurance that universities are actually achieving what they claim to be pursuing in teaching, research, and public service and, furthermore, that they are doing so as efficiently as possible within their unique circumstances. Universities have quite properly expressed reservations about the determination of their accountability by external evaluators or auditors unfamiliar with these unique circumstances. But the accountability imperative must be addressed, and it will be imposed by governments or legislative auditors unless universities rise to the challenge themselves. And they must rise to that challenge not only to keep governments and legislative auditors at bay, but also to compete successfully with other demands, particularly from the health sector, on scarce public resources.

Corporate autonomy has obviously been eroded since the 1960s in Canada as universities have become essentially wards of the state. But it has also been eroded from the bottom up through the evolution of academic self-government and faculty unionization. The second and necessary step to preserve what is left of corporate autonomy therefore lies in the strengthening of modes of governance and management in universities to provide assurance to public funders that systems are in place that show due regard for quality and responsible use of public resources.

This assurance provided by strengthened governance and management on the one hand, and demonstrated accountability for actual results achieved on the other, can be seen as the price of autonomy for the university as a public institution.

Clearly universities face the 1990s profoundly and understandably concerned about the effects of general funding limits. But many seem optimistic that new federal interest in human resource development and concerns about international competitiveness will loosen the general purse strings. At the same time, some in universities appear to feel that they have succeeded in stalling or diverting approaches to reducing their autonomy or increasing their accountability, or to strengthening their systems of governance and management. There is a sense, indeed, that they have won this battle and can get back to business as usual. That impression is strongly questioned below.

The papers in this volume are the proceedings of a conference sponsored by the Institute for Research on Public Policy and the Canadian Comprehensive Auditing Foundation, with the support of the British Columbia Ministry of Advanced Education and the Social Sciences and Humanities Research Council of Canada. The conference, superbly chaired by Dr. Geraldine Kenney-Wallace, was founded on two premises. First, university concerns about the effects of general funding restraints are legitimate and well-documented, and their concerns about more specific direct controls which are not consistent with the nature and purpose of universities are equally legitimate, if not as well-substantiated.

The second premise is, however, that the current optimism of universities is misguided. Uncertainties with respect to Established Programs Financing arrangements—particularly in a period of constitutional flux in which change seems likely to be in the direction of greater decentralization of authority and responsibility—place general funding levels in serious jeopardy. With respect to specific direct controls and concerns about systems of governance and management, a skirmish or two may have been won, but the war could well still be lost. In short, the second premise is that the present situation in Canada could more accurately be described as a lull before the storm than as a return to business as usual.

Experience in the United Kingdom, Australia, and New Zealand confirms that funding governments are prepared to take fairly radical steps with respect to levels of funding, direct controls, accountability requirements, and systems of governance and management.   Canadian universities are fortunate that between the lull at the end of the 1980s and the tough years ahead lies a unique opportunity to seize the initiative with respect to both the accountability agenda and systems of governance and management.

The conference had two specific objectives.   First, speakers and discussants assessed comparative international experience over the last two decades in OECD countries, particularly Canada, the United Kingdom, New Zealand, and Australia, with respect to public policy toward universities.   Other changes in the environment of universities—such as post-secondary education and training within private and public organizations as an alternative to reliance on traditional institutions, and the contractual assembly of post-secondary educational material and services, both nationally and internationally—were reviewed.   The response of universities to these changes in public policy and the environment was examined, along with the likely future evolution of public policy, the environment of universities, and possible responses by universities in the 1990s.

Second, in the light of international experience, speakers and discussants evaluated the alternative courses of action open to university administrators and public policy makers in Canada in the 1990s.   They considered courses of action for both parties which would allow universities, on the one hand, to survive and perhaps prosper, as relatively autonomous but still largely publicly funded institutions, in an environment of increasingly severe competition for scarce public resources as well as changing expectations and technology; and public policy makers on the other hand to satisfy their legitimate concerns about how universities are governed and managed, how they use scarce public resources, and how they account for that use.

The first section of the proceedings is devoted to setting the stage, and includes three background papers which were developed and presented prior to the conference in Ottawa.   The first is a paper by Jim Cutt and Rod Dobell which reviews the relationships between universities and governments in Canada.   The second paper, by Stewart Goodings, presents the federal perspective on the debate, and the third paper, by Gary Mullins, adds a provincial point of view. These last two papers were both presented at the Canadian Society for Studies in Higher Education conference in June 1990.

Section II of the proceedings, devoted to experience in other countries, includes four papers. The first paper, comparing the role of universities as instruments of public policy with their more traditional orientation, is based on an edited transcript of remarks presented by Ronald Watts of Queen's University, which served essentially as the keynote address for the conference. The second paper, by Robert Smith of the University of New England in Australia, presents evidence of radical change in the governance of higher education in Australia and a move to a highly centralized model of university funding. In the third paper, Ken Davies of the Committee of Vice-Chancellors and Principals in the United Kingdom reviews the development of performance indicators in the United Kingdom, and in the final paper, Paul LeVasseur of OECD surveys the general development of performance indicators in OECD countries.

The third section of the proceedings includes proposals for change with respect to both accountability and systems of governance and management. A paper by Jim Cutt offers an approach to dealing with the accountability imperative by suggesting revised methods of planning, budgeting, reporting, and auditing for universities in Canada. A second paper, by David Cameron of Dalhousie University, examines the evolution of university governance and management in Canada and presents a persuasive argument for the strengthening of governing boards as a means of preserving corporate autonomy. The final paper of this section, by Cynthia Hardy of McGill University, deals with the art of university management, and argues that the reform of university management is only likely to succeed if it proceeds along pluralist and decentralized lines.

Section IV presents the perspective of four university presidents on how universities in Canada view the opportunities and problems of a changing environment. Patrick Kenniff of Concordia, Robert Farquhar of Carleton, David Strangway of the University of British Columbia, and Harry Arthurs of York University, demonstrate the willingness of chief executive officers in universities in Canada to come to terms with the new situation, but also underline emphatically the uniqueness and complexity of universities, and the importance of preserving and enhancing corporate autonomy.

In Section V, four speakers from outside the university present their perspectives on the debate and suggest the feasibility of finding common ground. Jean-Pierre Boisclair of the Canadian Comprehensive Auditing Foundation, Gary Mullins of the Ministry of Advanced Education in British Columbia, John Farrant of the Universities Funding Council in the United Kingdom, and Patrick O'Keefe of the National Audit Office, also in the United Kingdom, strongly defend university autonomy, but demonstrate the need for universities to tell their story, and to enlist auditors as allies in lending credibility to that story.

In the final section of the proceedings, Rod Dobell sums up the debate, and presents the substance of a shared vision and an agenda for action.

The following conclusions for universities in Canada seem to flow from the papers and commentary set out in this volume.

First, universities should embrace broader accountability and reformed systems of governance and management as not only in their own direct self-interest but in any case as the likely price of avoiding unproductive detailed micromanagement by "buffer monsters" or bureaucrats.

Second, they should recognize that autonomy is to accountability and good management as rights are to responsibilities. Autonomy is a right that can be sustained only in conjunction with a persuasive demonstration of accountability and good governance.

Third, with respect to accountability, only universities themselves can do the job of capturing the subtlety and complexity of their objectives and operations. A way to begin might be to describe carefully their management systems, operations, and practices—to demonstrate not only that they exist, but also that they are working satisfactorily. But universities must ultimately bite the bullet of persuasively describing and assessing results in their primary functions of teaching, research, and public service. They should make an earnest effort to measure what is important, not what is simply easy to measure.

Fourth, their story must be told directly and persuasively to funding governments if universities are to compete with other demands on scarce public funds in tough times, and to other constituencies if universities are to diversify funding sources and maintain their legitimacy with students, industry, and their communities generally. This process is as much marketing as it is accountability in any technical sense, but it is fundamental to maintaining the negotiating power and leverage of the institution in the growing clamour of many claimants for public support.

Fifth, despite all the legends, auditors need not be the enemies of creativity or autonomy; rather they are potential allies who could lend credibility to the representations of university management.

Sixth, bureaucrats in ministries and central agencies are also potential allies and advocates who can only play those roles if universities give them the necessary ammunition—that is, talk credibly and frankly with some evidence of results in the areas in which the public is holding the politicians to account.

Seventh, the single most important step in the reform of university governance is the strengthening of governing boards. A good board is the body most likely to command public confidence, while at the same time being in a position to understand the true nature and mission of the university. Strong governing boards can justify state support while respecting academic self-government.

Eighth, strengthened governing boards must resist the temptation of trying to manage the university, or to interfere in its day-to-day operations. Their role is not to manage the university. Their critical contribution is rather to see that it is well-managed and to hold the president (the CEO) to account in achieving that goal.

Finally, in the lull between the end of the post-war growth path and the tough decade ahead lies a unique opportunity to seize the initiative with respect both to accountability and to systems of governance and management. Universities in Canada should reflect on the lessons of international experience, recognize that timing is critical, and seize that opportunity. The alternative is to see a time-honoured and potentially creative mediaeval institution, crucial to our future, vanish under the weight of an unnecessary bureaucratization.

I

Government and Universities in Canada: Setting the Stage

Accountability and Autonomy in Canada's University Sector: Business as Usual or the Lull Before the Storm?

James Cutt and Rodney Dobell

Introduction: Scholars under Scrutiny

The possible entry of legislative auditors into the assessment of performance of academic institutions has recently become a matter of colourful debate (in a few restricted circles) in Canada. Possible movements of governments toward contracting for prescribed "outputs" from post-secondary institutions have generated cries of alarm. The threat of exposure of academic institutions to the chill winds of competition with commercial suppliers of education services has shaken some university quarters. Controversies over alleged underfunding of universities, transition to direct funding of students, unwarranted government intrusion in the determination of academic priorities, the threats to academic freedom inherent in government direction of academe, have all raged for some time. The questions of autonomy in academic life, independence in scholarship, discretion in research are obviously crucial, and there seems little doubt that some of the actions now under consideration could seriously weaken the independence of existing post-secondary institutions in Canada. So the issue is important.

The thesis of this note, however, is simple: greater accountability can assure continued autonomy and contribute to improved

11

funding prospects. In brief, the taxpayer deserves a better explanation than currently offered of what universities accomplish with the resources made available, and why some departures from competitive market mechanisms in the allocation and management of those resources may be useful. Institutions which live off annual allocations cannot afford the luxury of insisting on being taken on faith at all times.

Unfortunately, to develop a persuasive argument that this simple thesis is also plausible and defensible demands a rather extensive tour through some background on funding mechanisms and reporting requirements. In Canada, given federal-provincial jurisdictional issues, the story is particularly turgid. The importance of the debate warrants the effort, however, remote as the material may sometimes seem.

A Digression on Mechanisms for Control or Accountability

The university sector in Canada expanded dramatically in the 1960s and early 1970s, becoming in the course of this expansion essentially a ward of the state. In this period governments which paid for the expansion of institutions and programs generally appeared to accept the view, held by universities, that peer and professional control coupled with the control exercised by boards of governors provided a sufficient framework of indirect control. The governments took the view that government control should be limited to prior approval of university budgets in the aggregate (either for individual institutions or, where an intermediary body had been established, for the university sector as a whole) to occasional short-term earmarking of funds for new programs and to auditing of the financial statements prepared by universities. The question of value for money was raised only in terms of whether enough was being spent to meet the expanding needs asserted by universities. Funders took the "value" provided by this money as self-evident; in short, the question was not posed, either with respect to controls on decision-making autonomy by universities or on accountability for such decisions. As in the United Kingdom, however, by the late 1970s the relationship between government and the universities had changed. More difficult economic times required more careful choice in the use of scarce resources and, in the absence of persuasive evidence of the value provided by the funds allocated to universities, governments turned to a more detailed framework of direct control. This framework of control is summarized below and is detailed more fully in the annex to this paper.

Governments can employ two sets of instruments for controlling universities. The first set is directed at limiting the decision-making autonomy of universities and the second attempts to increase university accountability.

In limiting decision-making autonomy, governments may draw on a wide variety of instruments. These range from controlling the membership of boards of governors of universities to requiring, before funding, detailed information on planning and budgeting. This might even go so far as to require explicit statements about management systems, controls, and practices.

After providing the money, governments may insist on increased accountability that goes beyond straight financial accounting and legislative compliance. This could even reach the point where management is being asked to make representations on value for money; in other words, economy, efficiency, and effectiveness.

Up to now, budget (funding) levels have provided the most obvious government instrument for control of university activity, and this instrument is obviously of direct concern to both sides.

Mechanisms such as earmarking of funds or contracting for services are also important direct influences, while retrospective reporting or value-for-money audit requirements may be seen as more of a nuisance than a direct constraint on university decision making.

The point of this paper, however, is that if universities address this latter instrument in an enlightened and responsive manner, they may be able to ease the threat of more vigorous exercise of the former, and much less palatable, instrument.

The approach to the balance of this note will be to deal briefly with the two levels of government involved, the federal and provincial, and then, for each level of government, to sketch the traditional pattern of control, the evolving pattern of increased direct control, and the response of universities. The argument seeks to demonstrate the gap between what governments are moving toward and what universities appear willing to provide. The identification of the gap is intended to provide universities with an opportunity to take control of the agenda of change by developing and providing the requisite information on value for money, in considerable part by drawing on information prepared for management purposes internally, but not reported externally.

The Players

In Canada, education is constitutionally a provincial responsibility, and it is therefore at the provincial level that the foundations of the control framework, both in structure and information prescriptions and requirements, are to be found. Nevertheless, a major feature of the evolving framework of control in Canada has been the increasing frustration of the federal government, which has come to foot the larger share of the bill, with the absence of any influence on—or, indeed, any mechanism establishing accountability for use of—the funds provided under the existing fiscal arrangements. The federal role and the variety of recent recommendations for change in that role are therefore considered as a context for consideration of approaches by provincial governments.

Figure 1 shows the major players in post-secondary education financing in Canada, the flows of funds (solid lines), and the accountability relationships (dotted lines). The relationship between provincial governments and the universities is clear. Provincial governments provide operating grants (amounting to between 75 and 80 per cent of university funding) either directly or through an intermediary agency, and universities are correspondingly accountable; the actual flow of accountability information falls far short of that increasingly sought by provincial governments and legislative auditors. This gap will be a primary concern later in this note; for the moment, it is the role of the federal government which is of particular interest.

The larger part of the funds which eventually reach universities as operating and capital grants comes from the federal government in the form of transfers to the provincial governments. These transfers are made under the Established Programs Financing (EPF) Act of 1977, are unconditional in nature, and require no

Figure 1
Governments and the Universities: Accountability Relationships

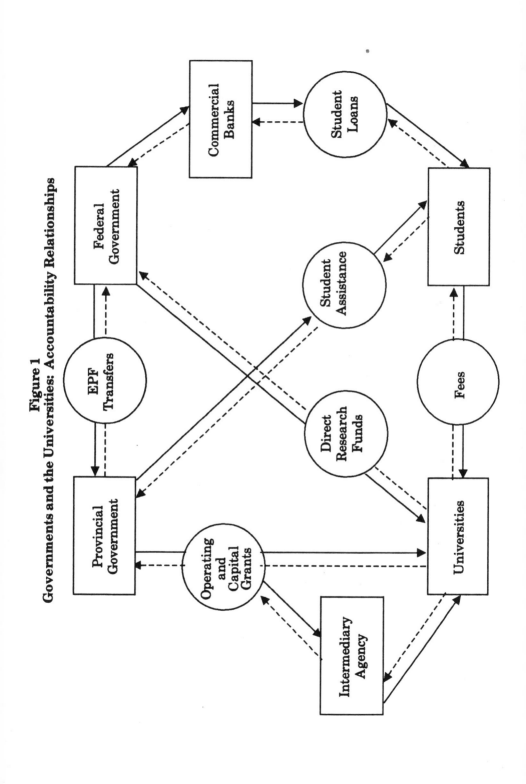

formal accountability in reporting. The federal government, through its granting agencies, also provides 60 per cent of direct research funds to faculty members in universities, and receives direct project-specific accountability reports on these grants. This granting does, however, require universities to bear the indirect or overhead costs of research, an issue to be discussed below under EPF.

The Perspective of the Federal Government

The federal government has contributed to post-secondary education in a variety of indirect ways in Canada, starting soon after Confederation. The modern era of federal support for post-secondary education dates, however, from 1951 when Ottawa, in response to a recommendation of the Massey commission, began a program of direct grants to universities to help defray operating costs. Since then, federal policy for supporting post-secondary education can be classified in three phases: direct grants to universities from 1951 to 1967; cost sharing with the provinces of all post-secondary education from 1967 to 1977; and unconditional transfers to the provinces under the EPF arrangements from 1977 to 1987.

The direct grants provided little incentive to provinces to expand their own support to post-secondary education, and were politically unpalatable to Quebec. These problems were addressed by the cost-sharing approach, under which the federal government paid 50 per cent of the eligible operating costs of post-secondary education. These payments were made to provincial governments rather than directly to universities. This system provided an incentive to provincial governments to increase expenditures on post-secondary education while maintaining their constitutional jurisdiction in the area. However, it also resulted in a loss of federal control over its own expenditures, relatively greater per capita payment to the so-called "have" provinces which expanded their post-secondary systems relatively rapidly, and a very complex auditing process for determining eligible costs.

To resolve these problems, the federal government in 1977 passed the Federal-Provincial Fiscal Arrangements and Established Programs Financing Act. Under this act, which still governs federal-provincial transfers in respect of post-secondary education, the link between federal transfer payments and post-secondary costs was removed. This act also tied increases in federal transfer payments to increases in the gross national product (GNP) and provided for equal per capita payments to each province. Actual transfers to provinces have been affected by the fact that part of the transfer is in cash and part is in "tax points," by the "six and five" program that resulted in a reduction in transfers for the years 1983 to 1985, and by the 1986 amendment to the act designed to reduce the net federal transfer by 2 per cent by 1991. Despite these changing details, the principles established in 1977 have remained, and the problems inherent in the EPF system have been the subject of much heat and a little light for the last decade.

During the second phase of the period (1967-77) of federal support for post-secondary education, both major levels of government in Canada accepted responsibility as partners in funding Canada's colleges and universities. The provinces retained their constitutional responsibility, but the federal government's support for 50 per cent of the operating costs of post-secondary education gave implicit recognition to the concept of a national interest or purpose. With EPF the nature of this political partnership changed in a fundamental way. The incentive to the provinces to contribute to post-secondary education was greatly diminished, and the change in the relationship between federal contributions to the provinces in respect of post-secondary education and actual provincial grants to the universities and colleges within their jurisdictions was well documented in the so-called Johnson Report (*Giving Greater Point and Purpose to the Federal Financing of Post-Secondary Education and Research in Canada*, a report prepared for the Secretary of State of Canada, February 15, 1985). This report argues that the federal share of the total costs of post-secondary education had risen and the provincial share had fallen to the point where, in five provinces, federal transfer payments in respect of post-secondary education actually exceeded the total amount of provincial grants to post-secondary institutions. In effect, the report implies that the partnership between the two levels of government in support of post-secondary education had been replaced in these provinces by a system of federal funding, and in the other provinces, that the 1977 balance had been seriously eroded.

The provinces, faced with tougher economic times and other pressing priorities, had responded by cutting back sharply on spending on post-secondary education, and the most immediate result of the change in the federal system for support for post-secondary education in 1977 was thus a significant decrease, relative to the growth in GNP, in the support of the core operations of universities and colleges. In the decade after 1977, enrolment in universities increased sharply and concurrently with the reduction in relative funding, and the real income per student in post-secondary institutions has therefore dropped significantly—by approximately 30 per cent—since the introduction of EPF.

It should be stressed that the provinces have not contravened any formal agreements or regulations. It is clear that the EPF Act was intended to provide them with precisely this freedom and flexibility. But provincial responses to those guaranteed, unconditional federal transfers has created a climate of frustration and mistrust and a commitment to finding ways of changing the system. The issue has been visited in a series of reports. The Parliamentary Task Force on Federal-Provincial Fiscal Arrangements in 1981 recommended the formal separation of EPF transfers for health and post-secondary education, and this division was made in 1984. No changes were suggested by the task force, however, in the block grant system of funding, and the frustration of the federal government manifested itself more clearly in later reports. The Johnson report in 1985 recommended that the growth of EPF payments should be harmonized with provincial operating grants by increasing EPF payments at the then rate of increase (geared to GNP and population) only if provinces did likewise. Johnson went on to reject other options: using the cash portion of EPF funding for universal student grants or vouchers, or for a massive increase in research funding, and the withdrawal of federal support for the core operations of universities. The 1985 Macdonald commission report was also strongly critical of the current EPF funding arrangement and went on to recommend the consideration of a range of options including replacing a portion of existing EPF cash transfers with voucher payments to students, freezing current federal cash contributions and tying future contributions to matching provincial expenditures, and using some of the funds released by freezing the federal contributions to fund university research.

The report of the Nielson Task Force education and research study team in 1986 also reviewed EPF payments critically, and considered but did not decide among various options: making future federal support conditional on agreement by the provinces to meet specified standards; the provision of federal funds to students directly through some such system as vouchers; and the recognition by the federal government that it had no role in post-secondary education and should therefore withdraw its financial support completely. In March 1987 the standing Senate committee on national finance also considered the matter carefully and recommended that the federal government terminate the post-secondary portion of EPF payments and deal with the matter by transferring adequate financial resources through tax points to provincial governments.

The general question of the federal role in funding remains uncertain. Most recently, at the National Forum on Post-Secondary Education in Saskatoon, Saskatchewan, in October 1987, there was broad agreement on the need for a continuing partnership of the federal and provincial governments in addressing post-secondary education, but also an unwillingness on the part of the federal government to increase its contributions without some role in determining how the money should be spent and some accountability for that spending.

If little agreement has emerged on the general federal role in funding other, than perhaps, the need for a change, there appears to be increasing agreement that federal funding of sponsored research should be increased to include the indirect costs of such research. The present system imposes these indirect costs on university operating budgets and, in a period of straitened budgets, has had what are generally agreed to be deleterious effects on university research. This issue has been addressed in various reports, including a strong recommendation by the standing Senate committee on national finance that the budgets of the granting councils be extended to cover these indirect costs. More ominously, however, the Macdonald commission report and the Johnson report noted that increased federal funding for sponsored research would probably have to be financed at least partly at the expense of general core funding through EPF grants.

Core funding, of course, is intended to cover all operating activities in universities, including research. The diversion of federal support from core funding grants to sponsored research would represent essentially the functional earmarking of a larger portion of federal contributions to post-secondary education in a manner not dissimilar to that practised by the University Grants Committee in its calculations of grants to universities in the United Kingdom.

Currently federal contributions are equivalent to 80 per cent of university operating grants in Canada. While federal withdrawal seems unlikely, the erosion of the level of these contributions in a variety of directions does seem likely. Given scarce federal resources, it is possible that there could be a replacement of part of the general core funding by more comprehensive grants in the area of sponsored research, including both direct and indirect costs. Some universities would, of course, applaud increases in sponsored research funding, but may have disregarded the implications for what, in effect, will become increased functional earmarking, diminished autonomy in resource allocation decision making, and sharply increased direct accountability for research funding.

The influence of the federal government has also extended to other policy instruments and targets, particularly to the recurrent theme of establishing national objectives in post-secondary education. The parliamentary task force in 1981 suggested that

> early attention should be given to the definition of purposes in post-secondary education that are of concern to all governments. In this connection, we would see priority consideration being given to the need for more highly qualified manpower in the 1980s and the confirmation of existing commitments to student mobility and equality of access to post-secondary education of Canadians (p. 130).

In 1982, the minister of finance indicated that the federal government expected to see a shift in the priorities in post-secondary objectives in favour of manpower training, failing which he would consider freezing EPF transfers for post-secondary education. The Johnson report in 1985 reiterated the importance and appropriateness of national objectives including such objectives as accessibility for all qualified students in Canada, high quality education and related research, improvement in the employment potential of students of all ages, the right to student mobility across the country, and the right of taxpayers to a full accounting of the sources of finance for post-secondary education (*Giving Greater Point and Purpose to the Federal Financing of Post-Secondary Education and Research in Canada*, pp. 33-34).

There is, of course, less difficulty with the concept of national objectives in principle than there is in practice. Agreement on the importance of a national agenda or mandate for post-secondary education appears to be growing. It emerged as perhaps the primary theme of the National Forum on Post-Secondary Education. The evolution of such a set of objectives and perhaps also an acceptable mechanism for their implementation, such as through the Council of Ministers of Education, Canada, now seems likely. More specifically, the objectives of quality (or excellence) and accessibility recur in the debate over the federal role in the last decade. The Johnson report paid particular attention to the development of world-class centres of excellence and the theme was reiterated by the recent report of the standing Senate committee on national finance. In this specific sense, excellence is taken to mean excellence in research, and the implications for federal funding appear to go beyond the specification of objectives to the concentration of funding or institutional earmarking to achieve this objective. Accessibility is another common theme. Ironically, this objective was reiterated by the Johnson report, but also criticized by Johnson as the exclusive preoccupation of university funding at the expense of excellence! The question of accessibility was, however, a major preoccupation of the national forum and it seems likely that the trade-off between excellence and accessibility will be a theme in any reform of the federal role in financing post-secondary education in Canada.

Related to accessibility is the larger question of who benefits and who loses. Only the Macdonald commission has been vulgar enough to accept fully the argument of Friedman, Weisbrod, and others that spending by the federal government on post-secondary education is counter-redistributive in nature, and to translate this concern into recommendations for higher student loans and voucher financing (although Wright commission proposals in Ontario in the early 1970s for contingent repayment schemes for student assistance went a long way in this direction). This question does not appear to be at the highest level of priority in current federal thinking about post-secondary education, but bears consideration as a complement to the larger question of accessibility. A significant escalation in the federal role with respect to objectives would be the specification of actual targets for each of these objectives. Only the Nielson task force has dared to broach the subject to this point, but it is perhaps not as silly as it sounds, particularly with respect to targets for student accessibility or training as outputs. The question should not be dismissed by provincial governments and universities; after all, the Canada Health Act sets specific conditions for the health component of EPF transfers.

The federal agenda has gone beyond looking for a seat at the table and a share in setting objectives and limiting the decision-making autonomy of universities to requiring some accountability for federal funds used in post-secondary education. There has been no suggestion to this point that the auditor general of Canada undertake an audit of federal EPF transfers, and the evolution of an increasing audit role is much more likely to occur at the provincial level. What may be more likely is some form of reporting by universities or provincial governments to the federal government on the use of post-secondary funding—in effect, accountability representations by the recipients of transfers.

The parliamentary task force in 1981 urged that federal ministers receive from provincial administrators the information necessary to account to Parliament for the federal resources allocated to post-secondary education. An amendment to the EPF legislation (Bill C-12) in 1984 was unanimously accepted by all parties in the House of Commons, and required the secretary of state to make an annual report to Parliament dealing with the following matters: first, the federal cash contributions and transfers to each province; second, provincial expenditures on post-secondary education; third, other federal programs supporting higher education; fourth, the relationship between federal transfers and programs and Canada's educational and economic goals; and finally, the results of any consultations by or on behalf of the secretary of state with the Council of Ministers of Education relating to the definition of national purposes to be served by post-secondary education and the means by which the governments of

Canada and the provinces would achieve these purposes. This report was required to be submitted to Parliament each year, beginning in 1986, and is referred to a standing committee of the House of Commons for consideration. The unanimous acceptance of the amendment requiring this report indicates concern felt at the federal level, and suggests that an approach by universities, almost certainly through provincial governments—and perhaps, indeed, through the Council of Ministers of Education—to reporting to Parliament might alleviate federal concern and remove some of the instability and uncertainty of federal funding.

In Australia, the commonwealth government and the state governments have agreed on the national purposes of post-secondary education, and have agreed on complete federal funding through an intermediary body—the Tertiary Education Commission. In Canada, constitutional constraints, and the role of Quebec in particular, preclude this solution. The fact remains, however, that the federal government pays 80 per cent of the operating costs of universities in Canada and 60 per cent of the direct research costs. The trump card held by the federal government is un-questionably the level of funding and its capacity to influence the adequacy and stability of that level. But this is a crude weapon. The evolution of the debate suggests that the federal government would prefer to ensure adequacy and stability in its general funding role in return for some form of matching provincial commitment to funding; federal participation in the establishment of national purposes for post-secondary education—particularly those relating to quality and accessibility; some form of reasonable accountability reporting perhaps through the Council of Ministers of Education; and assurances to Parliament that funds transferred to the provinces with respect to post-secondary education provide value for money.

Perspective of the Provincial Governments

The story of university independence and alleged government interference is difficult to unravel in any one province; with 10 provincial governments to consider, the tale is obviously too long for this paper. The essentials are these:

- Provincial governments have operated through a variety of intermediary granting councils or agencies—either advisory or executive, based on delegated decision-making authority—to determine the size and distribution of operating and capital grants to universities, and in some cases to decide on approval of new degree programs proposed by the universities. These grants have been in the form of block allocations—there has been no formal earmarking of operating funds, though there may have been informal leadership in government speeches about university priorities.

  Since the mid-1970s some of these intermediary agencies have been removed, either because government wants more direct control or because universities themselves have lobbied for their removal (as in the province of British Columbia).

- This general granting mode has not so far been replaced by any formal contractual mode. In no case in Canada have either competitive bids for delivery of university services or simple contracts for delivery of university services, been required by governments.

- As noted, the federal government cannot require—and provincial governments have not (so far) required—detailed information prior to making grants—except for new programs which must demonstrate "need."

- Only data on student numbers and financial costs per student have normally been required of universities in reporting on performance.

On funding levels, however, provincial governments have definitely displayed a willingness to crack the whip. It can be argued that financial constraints have resulted in part from the failure of universities to tell their story effectively, through provision of adequate planning and budgeting information, and *ex post* reporting on performance. If there is any evidence that universities are well-managed institutions pursuing goals reflecting public priorities, it is evidence well hidden. But whatever the reason, and in spite of universities perceiving financial constraints as being severe, they do not seem to have been willing to depart much from "business as usual" in response.

The result has been frustration both in provincial legislatures and among the public. From this frustration has sprung pressure to insist on greater legislative scrutiny through "value for money audits," reporting either on the simple existence of management systems in place to address accountability, or indeed on the performance indicators themselves.

One response to this frustration, and growing concerns with the structure of the post-secondary system more generally, has been to create within the Council of Ministers of Education a ministerial post-secondary education sub-committee. This committee, an outgrowth of the National Forum on Post-Secondary Education, has initiated some work to develop coordinated provincial statistical systems and data bases, with the intention of developing some coordinated assessment of quality and effectiveness.

Enthusiasm within the university community has not, to date, been overwhelming.

Conclusions

The argument of this note can be summarized in two general conclusions:

- Universities in Canada face a variety of pressures from government funders. Pressures prior to funding include information required of universities by government, information governing the use of resources prescribed as conditions on funding by governments to universities, and general constraints on funding levels. Pressures after the money has been provided relate to a broader scope of accountability including value for money, and include accountability reports by, and external audits of, universities required by governments. The set of pressures can be likened to a five-sided vise squeezing in on the autonomy and discretion of the institution.

- Universities may choose to ignore these pressures or to respond by providing incomplete or inaccurate or incomprehensible information. They may also respond cooperatively in a passive way by complying with funding and other conditions, and by providing whatever information is required, or may go further to shape the information agenda by designing and providing to funders more and better information than is actually required of them.

University response is a matter of choice. A positive approach is possible, based on the following line of argument:

1. Simply ignoring the increasing financial pressures and growing concern for accountability would exacerbate the situation and place the survival of universities in Canada as relatively autonomous institutions in serious jeopardy. The experience of British universities under the Education Reform Bill of late 1987 is instructive. Non-cooperation through inaccurate or incomplete information would have the same consequences.

2. Non-cooperation by "smothering" funders with incomprehensible and unusable data might divert the pressures in the short run but would probably exacerbate them in the long.

3. A cooperative response of a passive nature is the least that funding agencies can expect of universities, and the minimal prerequisite to any alleviation of external pressures. However, such a response leaves the agenda of information prescriptions and requirements entirely in the hands of funders. That agenda is therefore unlikely to reflect accurately the circumstances and performance of universities and, moreover, will be driven by changing political preferences and will therefore be highly unstable.

4. An active cooperative response to external pressures by universities, on the other hand, will enable them to shape the information agenda to their advantage—at the very least, having it reflect reasonably accurately their circumstances and performance—and to control its evolution. Universities will therefore enjoy a more stable environment. Further, active cooperation would likely reduce the severity and frequency of both conditions on funding and on reporting and auditing requirements. Also, by demonstrating that what is spent is well spent, cooperation might contribute to more generous funding levels.

    This last observation is based on the premise that much of the expectations gap—the gap between what external funders want and what they perceive universities to be doing—reflects the inability or unwillingness of universities to provide thorough and useful information on what they are doing. It is also likely that the information now collected internally can, suitably adjusted and wrapped, satisfy many of the external demands, but that some creative new information will also be necessary. It is also probably inevitable that universities will actually have to do some different things and report on them. But clarifying this communications gap will help to identify those necessary behaviourial changes which may not prove inconsistent with the universities' own basic purposes or interests.

5. The legitimate concerns of funders about accountability can best be addressed by the development of a reporting framework of the following kind. Universities should provide to funders information in the form of performance budgets (similar to Part III of the Estimates of the Government of Canada), and in the form of annual accountability reports which provide detailed accounts of how the terms of reference set out in the budgets have been addressed. Faced with such evidence, funders could then require of external auditors that they simply attest to the completeness and accuracy of annual reports by universities (and thus avoid the necessity of cadres of accountants attempting to develop questionable methodologies to deal with inappropriate applications in unfamiliar circumstances).

6. Universities acting together can produce a better reporting package than universities acting separately. Indeed, unless universities act together, funders have no information (from the university perspective) about the performance of the university system as a whole. Such cooperation should include the design of inter-institutional resource allocation criteria which would otherwise be determined by funders. The trick in such essential cooperative action will be to preserve the necessary and important competition among universities for students and research funds.

7. Meaningful and useful information of the sort required for budget submissions and reporting can be produced by universities. Universities are complex, multiple-product organizations, but the state-of-the-art in management systems, and in defining and measuring resource utilization and the attainment of objectives, is such that sufficient evidence can be produced to satisfy the reasonable expectations of funders. Addressing the problem seriously is also the shortest route to improving the state-of-the-art. What seems clear is that the information produced in budgets and reports is likely to be far better if universities produce it themselves than if it is designed and produced by some external agency—government ministry, central agency, or external auditor.

8. The new information produced by universities will be useful to decision makers on the funding of universities, and will make a difference to those decisions. Universities must compete for their share in the allocation of scarce resources. The more complete and persuasive the information presented, the better universities will do in the competition for scarce resources at the margin. This strong premise is based on the arguments that universities actually do much that is expected of them as a recipient of public subvention, but are generally bad at demonstrating this stewardship (4, above) and that the state-of-the-art is such that more and better information can be produced than at present (7, above).

9. The new information cannot be produced without cost, but that cost is relatively small, and is not material compared to the benefits universities will enjoy as a consequence, though these are difficult to identify and impute. If the investment resulted in improved funding levels, the case is obvious. Less obvious, but perhaps even more important would be gains, or the avoidance of losses, in decision-making autonomy, or in the opportunity to design the presentation of accountability reporting. The question of avoidance of loss is not trivial. In this, as in so much public policy, the *status quo* is not an option. Universities must move to control the agenda,

and to ease the pressures on the vise; the alternative is the progressive erosion of decision-making autonomy and a very different and much less vital university sector in Canada.

10. Part of the cost will be new institutions and new information gathering and evaluation methods and staff in universities. These new institutions, methods, and staff will have to find appropriate recognition in a university system in which to date they are relatively novel, even alien.

11. Funders must also change, tempering their expectations about information and behaviour, and providing universities with the incentives and the opportunities to plan, behave, and report in accordance with reasonable expectations.

In comparison with the experience in the United Kingdom, Australia, and the United States, Canadian universities have taken a bit of a beating on funding levels, but have emerged almost unscathed in terms of financial control (earmarking of funds, contracting of services) or accountability requirements (detailed reporting, external value-for-money audit). For universities, a window of opportunity appears to be open to shape the agenda and, perhaps, to disarm the funding weapon while meeting legitimate public concerns for greater candour and accountability. The approach would combine improved planning and budgeting submissions, fuller reporting of information and systems already in place and of new information from new internal audit systems, the whole reporting structure to be designed at two levels, first, for individual institutions and, second, the university systems in each province. Some approach to reporting to the federal government also needs to be developed, perhaps through the Council of Ministers of Education.

In sum, if there is to be a future for universities in Canada as relatively autonomous, independent institutions, it will probably lie somewhat along these lines so far as governance and accountability are concerned. It will also entail universities adjusting their activities more than they have seemed willing to do to date—but that is a different paper.

Annex A

This annex examines the evolution of the various components of the framework of control by governments over universities and argues that the development of improved management decision-making systems and controls and a more careful response to accountability reporting are needed in Canada to avert radical intervention by government of the sort visited upon universities in the United Kingdom.

Figure 2 outlines the dimensions of the question. The various instruments of control available to government are set out as the row headings; these instruments are directed at two broad categories of target—limiting the decision-making autonomy of universities, and increasing their accountability. The two broad dimensions illustrated in Figure 2 are considered in turn.

The first instrument of control relates to structures. It is assumed in all cases that governments exert indirect control through the appointment of a majority of members of boards of governors of universities. The distinction is then drawn between indirect and direct structural control. In the former, government acts through an appointed intermediary agency in its dealings with universities and, in the latter, such dealings are conducted directly by a ministry of government. Structural response by universities may involve independent or joint action in their dealings with governments.

Given structure, and thus the line of communication used by government, information requirements and prescriptions are divided into those imposed prior to and after funding, and the actual level of funding itself. Information required of universities prior to funding includes a variety of levels of detail in planning and budgeting information, and implies—or may even be extended to include an explicit statement about—management systems, controls, and practices sufficient to produce valid and reliable information of the sort required. *Ex ante* information prescriptions include various sets of general and specific conditions attached to funding, and again imply or may require explicitly that management systems, controls, and practices be in place to comply with such conditions. The aggregate level of funding itself is the bluntest and most obvious instrument of direct control. Its impact on the administration of universities will also be affected by the

Figure 2
Control Instruments and Targets

Targets of Control / Instruments of Control	Decision-making Autonomy								Accountability							
	Ends				Means				Procedural		Consequential					
	Long-Term		Short-Term		Capital		Operating		Finan-cial	Compli-ance	Economy & Efficiency		Effective-ness		Cost-Effectiveness	
	Direct	Indirect	Direct	Indirect	Direct	Indirect	Direct	Indirect			Direct	Indirect	Direct	Indirect	Direct	Indirect
1. Structure a) Intermediary b) Direct																
2. Information Requirements and Prescriptions																
(a) Ex-ante — Requirements																
(a) Ex-ante — Prescriptions																
(b) Level of Funding																
(c) Ex-post — Report Requirements																
(c) Ex-post — Audit Requirements																

time horizon over which funding commitments by government are made; indeed, the capacity of universities to respond to controls will be greatly increased if funding levels, regardless of their perceived adequacy, are predictable over, say, a three- to five-year time horizon.

After providing funding, governments may require of universities—individually and/or collectively—reports of various kinds and frequency on the use of funds and the results obtained. The degree of control exercised through such requirements for "accountability statements" or management representations will be greater, the greater the complexity and/or the frequency of report requirements. Equally, the meaningfulness of such *ex ante* controls as may have been imposed will depend on the response by universities to such controls through some form of *ex post* accountability. Governments invariably require that universities produce annually a set of financial statements to which the accuracy and completeness an independent external auditor must attest. Universities may also be subject to an additional external audit of their compliance with legislative and statutory authorities. Most important, governments or legislative auditors may choose to subject universities, individually or collectively, to a broader scope audit of varying frequency and degrees of comprehensiveness related to the utilization of resources and results obtained.

The various instruments of control are directed either at reducing autonomy in decision making by universities or at improving accountability, somehow defined, for the use of scarce public resources by universities. The generic target may be considered to be value for money. In essence, controls are directed at the ends pursued by universities, the means used to pursue these ends, the associated resources utilized, and the results achieved. Value for money can also be defined to go beyond educational and economic matters to include such matters as access to university places by students and employees.

The column headings in Figure 2 set out illustrative specific targets. The question of autonomy in decision making is divided into autonomy with respect to ends and means. Ends are divided into long-term and short-term ends, each in turn treated either directly or indirectly. This represents interest by government in long-term or planning objectives, over, say, a three- to five-year period, and/or in short-term or operational objectives over, say, one academic year, and either direct specification by government of what these objectives must be or, much milder, indirect specification of a requirement that universities have systems in place to establish such objectives. Given the inevitability of multiple objectives in universities, governments may also specify priorities among these objectives or require that universities specify them, may specify or insist that universities specify operational measures by which the attainment of objectives can be determined, and may also specify, or require the specification of, actual performance targets for the set of objectives.

It is perhaps worth pausing briefly on this question of objectives, for objectives are, in logic if not always in practice, the centrepiece of the target of government control. Public funding of universities reflects the view that broad public objectives relating to such matters as economic growth, the quality of life, and fairness or equity, can be served better than any other way through the pursuit of the objectives of research, teaching and public service in universities. In a hierarchical sense it is this "value" part which takes precedence in value for money. It is important to be efficient, that is, to be "doing the thing right" (pursuing objectives at least cost); it is clearly a prior consideration to be effective, that is, to be doing the right thing. From the perspective of public funders, doing the right thing is more than pursuing performance targets in teaching and research. It relates to broader issues of relevance, appropriateness, acceptance by constituencies or customers, and responsiveness to changing demands (Canadian Comprehensive Auditing Foundation, *Effectiveness: Reporting and Auditing in the Public Sector*; Ottawa: Canadian Comprehensive Auditing Foundation, 1987). This larger perspective of "quality" or the value ascribed by funders, reflecting public views, to the results achieved by universities (P. Bourke, *Quality Measures in Universities*; Canberra, Australia: Commonwealth Tertiary Education Commission, 1986), provides a context for the narrower and more tractable—though still difficult—perspective of the quality of teaching and research outcomes. One dimension of such quality broadly defined can be estimated in monetary terms: the productivity and corresponding income gains enjoyed by graduates or users of research. The broad concept of quality from the perspective of funders may also, as noted above, be defined to include special questions of access to universities in terms, say, of age, sex, ethnic group, and geographic location, and may go further to deal with the consequences for income and wealth distribution of public funding of universities; the question of who benefits and who pays is of central significance where direct beneficiaries assume a small portion of the costs and enjoy a large portion of the benefits. In short, the question of effectiveness is likely to be complex, multi-dimensional, difficult to conceptualize let alone measure, and to present particular difficulties of translation from the level of general public intentions, as articulated by funders, to the particular activities and outcomes of universities, and therefore also to present difficulties of monitoring and accountability.

Funders may also seek to influence the means by which universities pursue their objectives. Influence may be exerted on both capital and operating activities, again either directly by specification or indirectly by requiring that universities have management systems in place to deal with these matters. Influence on operating activities is of particular interest, and funders may actually earmark funds in various levels of detail by academic or support program, and/or by broad functions such as teaching and research. In the strongest and most direct form of intervention, funders could actually specify program design and budget breakdown. At the milder end of the spectrum, indirect intervention could take the form of a requirement by funders that universities have in place management systems and associated resource allocation criteria for dividing the operating budget among programs. The more direct and specific the detail of the intervention, the greater the reduction in the autonomy of universities in decision making.

The second set of targets defined as the column headings in Figure 2 are grouped under the head of accountability, defined in relation to ongoing and/or retrospective reporting by university management (which may build on internal audit) and external audit of university management. The concept is defined in Figure 2 to include procedural and consequential accountability. The former includes financial accountability—a requirement to provide a complete and accurate financial accounting of the use of public funds—and compliance—the requirement to comply with the various statutory and regulatory authorities associated with public funding. As for reductions in autonomy and decision making by universities, funders may insist on a direct representation or audit or may be satisfied with indirect accountability, that is, with representations or audit on the management systems, controls, and—of central importance in retrospective assessment— actual management practices which show due regard for procedural accountability. Increasing interest by funders in accountability is, of course, directed at consequential accountability which refers to the retrospective aspect of value for money. The main categories of consequential accountability are illustrated in Figure 2. The first category includes economy and efficiency: the former is defined as economy in the acquisition of resources, and is a building block of efficiency in resource utilization, formally defined as the ratio of resources used to some standard output or activity measure. The second category refers to measures of effectiveness, defined as the extent to which the objectives of publicly funded programs have been achieved; in discussing limitations on decision-making autonomy in universities, it was pointed out that effectiveness has to be seen in terms of a complex range or hierarchy of measures which reflect the perceived quality of university outcomes, and social indicators related to such questions as student access. The final category links costs with effectiveness and benefit. The former requires the matching of a measure of resource utilization with one or more measures of effectiveness; the latter obtains when the output measure matched with cost is defined in dollar terms (such as income gains attributable to university education) in which case the matching can be the basis of what is commonly referred to as rate of return analysis or, with some analytical adjustments, cost-benefit analysis. Figure 2 indicates that, as for procedural accountability, consequential accountability may be approached indirectly by representation or audit on the systems, controls, and practices with which management discharges its responsibility, or directly by representations or audit on the actual operating results attained by management. Obviously, direct representations or audit on operating results represents a higher order of accountability than indirect representations or audit, and the accountability required of management may also be considered more onerous the more complex the definition of value for money that is required— for instance, representations or audit dealing with the matching of costs and a range of effectiveness measures would be considerably more complex than representations or audit confined, say, to economy in purchasing or efficiency in the utilization of resources.

Post-Secondary Education Policy in Canada: Confessions of a Federal Bureaucrat

Stewart Goodings

My remarks are in three parts:

- First, a personal description of my three-year odyssey in the world of federal post-secondary education (PSE) policy

- Second, a review of where we are now in that world, how we got here and where we might go in the 1990s

- Third, a few reflections on what is right and wrong about post-secondary policy and some closing thoughts on why I remain an optimist about these matters

Let me start by describing what happened when a simple provincial bureaucrat changed sides and joined the federal team.

I returned to Ottawa three years ago, after working for the Government of British Columbia for nine years. It was a strange experience, going back to the federal bureaucracy. I felt sure that in my time away the whole environment would have changed—though I wasn't at all sure what to expect.

Yet I flew back east with considerable optimism. After all, I was going to work in a field in which the federal government spent a great deal of money—over six billion dollars in those days. As well, the two orders of government were about to convene a national forum on post-secondary education.

It came as a bit of a surprise, therefore, to learn that federal and provincial governments did not meet routinely to discuss important educational issues, did not prepare joint background papers, and only rarely agreed to talk about the same topics on the same day in the same room.

My initial shock was softened somewhat by the generally amicable cooperation then under way between governments to prepare for the National Forum on Post-Secondary Education in Saskatoon. This was a remarkable event, which brought together an amazingly varied group of politicians, officials, educators, academics, lobbyists, business people, students, and ordinary Canadians who, for three days, shared information, views, and dreams about the current challenges and future prospects for higher education in Canada. While not designed to generate a consensus, it did generate pretty widespread agreement on the need to raise the profile of PSE on the public agenda, on the value of more and better research on higher education, and on the critical importance of better inter-governmental collaboration.

The "spirit of Saskatoon" was infectious, but a federal election soon intervened. By the time that was over, people and priorities had changed for both orders of government. An adjustment to Established Programs Financing (EPF) was announced in the 1989 federal budget and one opportunity for a fresh start on PSE seemed to have passed. My own education was proceeding rapidly.

By this time, I had attended numerous meetings with provincial officials, and I had come to appreciate the challenges faced by our colleagues at the Council of Ministers of Education, Canada (CMEC) in trying to ensure that the interests of all the provincial governments in the field of education were represented.

I had been to meetings of the Association of Universities and Colleges of Canada (AUCC), the Canadian Association of University Teachers (CAUT), the Association of Canadian Community Colleges (ACCC) and the Canadian Federation of Students (CFS), and heard the concerns of presidents, faculty, and student leaders about the deterioration of facilities, the increasing crowding of campuses, and the shortage of research funds. A crisis seemed to be occurring, or about to occur, but we talked to the universities and colleges, they talked to the provinces, and the provinces occasionally talked to us, but we never all talked together.

Now, after three years in Ottawa (and yet another change in EPF), I often feel like a "Fed" when I'm with provincial officials, and like a "Prov" when I'm in a crowd of federal officials. In other words, I see both sides of the question, a serious handicap in a senior official, and practically fatal in the black and white world of post-secondary education policy.

What have I concluded about all this? In the final part of this talk, I'll come back to reflect a bit on what we might all do better in the field of higher education policy, and on what is unlikely to change. But first I want to talk about education support policy issues past, present and future. At this point I hardly need to caution you that these are my personal views about where we've been, and that when I talk about the future I am not announcing federal policy.

The history of federal support for post-secondary education is quite a long one, for although PSE was not mentioned directly in 1867, not too long after that the Government of Canada found itself paying for the Royal Military College at Kingston, and by 1885 it became involved in the founding of the University of Manitoba by providing a land grant. By the early twentieth century, vocational training was recognized as a national priority, and during the First World War the National Research Council was established. And the foundations of federal student aid programs were laid with loans to veterans in 1919 and the Dominion-Provincial Student Aid Programs in 1939.

In short, federal involvement in post-secondary support has a history of many decades and the main policy themes have remained the same:

- carrying out specific federal responsibilities (e.g., for native Canadians and the armed forces)

- ensuring that the workforce is adequately trained for the needs of the economy (vocational training)

- assisting access to excellent higher education by financial support to the institutions (PSE financing) and to students (student aid programs)

- supporting research, especially in universities and federal labs (granting council funding)

In the years after World War II, all of these concerns came to occupy an increasing share of federal attention and ultimately to consume an increasing share of the federal budget. They are still the main themes of federal support.

A milestone in federal commitment to PSE support was the report of the Massey-Lévesque commission in 1951, which remarked on the serious financial state of Canada's universities and called for federal action. The result was direct federal grants to universities that were in effect from 1951 to 1967.

During the same period, the government introduced the Technical and Vocational Training Act in 1959 and the Canada Student Loans Act in 1964. It also expanded support to university research and established the Canada Council. Grants to universities increased from 50 cents per capita of provincial population to $5.

Even all this was not enough to keep up with the universally accepted need for an enormous expansion of the opportunities for post-secondary education. In the fall of 1966, Prime Minister Lester B. Pearson announced new financing arrangements for both vocational training and higher education. One key feature was that support was to be not just for universities but also for the new college systems that many provinces were then creating.

The new financing arrangement provided federal support equal to 50 per cent of eligible operating expenditures for PSE in each province (a per capita option was also retained). Note that this was *not* 50-50 federal-provincial cost sharing as is often thought. The non-federal 50 per cent was made up of provincial funding, student fees, and private sources, with the exact proportions varying quite a bit from one province to another.

Let me take a moment here to comment on this cost-sharing arrangement, as many people still look longingly to the golden age when provinces were "required" to spend federal money on PSE, rather than squandering it on roads, hospitals or the elderly, as they are free to do in the EPF era. We still hear calls for EPF transfers to be made "conditional" and it seems like a reasonable proposal.

Frankly, however, I'm not sure what "conditional" really means. If it means that every dollar of the PSE portion of EPF should be spent on PSE costs, then it means very little, as any province can prove that it meets that criterion already.

If "conditional" means that the amount of federal funding should somehow be linked to PSE spending (provincial or total), then that's much like cost sharing. As such it raises all the old problems of book-keeping, definitions and charges of interference in provincial priorities that contributed to the eventual demise of the 1967 formula. That's why my first reaction when someone says EPF should be conditional is to say, "What precisely do you mean by 'conditional'?"

Back to the events of 20 years ago. I've implied that the cost-sharing arrangements were not completely satisfactory to either side. The accounting problems were something of a nightmare and the provinces objected to the "50-cent dollars" that distorted their decision making (remember that more or less the same deal applied, but with about twice the magnitude, on the health side).

By the early 1970s, both federal and provincial governments were looking for alternatives. A certain disillusionment about the economic and employment effectiveness of PSE had also begun to set in, and neither public nor governments were sure they wanted to keep feeding—at an increasing rate—the monster they had so enthusiastically created in the 1960s.

Indeed, the principal factor that caused the federal government to look for a way out was the open-endedness of cost sharing. By 1970, federal support for PSE via the fiscal arrangements was approaching $1 billion and rising at well over 20 per cent per year. The minister of finance began exploring ways to apply restraint to federal transfers for health and PSE. In 1972 the federal government limited annual increases to 15 per cent.

To skip over the details, what emerged finally in 1977 was what we have come affectionately to call EPF. The "established programs" to be financed were medicare, hospitalization and PSE, and the key concept was to link growth in the amount of funding *not* to spending on programs but simply to the growth of the Canadian economy and the population of the province. Thus, a portion of the national wealth would be made available to provinces, pretty much with no strings attached, at least on the PSE side.

What happened was not only predictable, it was predicted. Provinces were freed from the artificial inducement of cost sharing and chose to shift their resources, including EPF revenues, to suit their changing priorities. The federal government was well aware of this likely sequence of events and even encouraged it at the time of proposing EPF.

It was no coincidence that all this happened at a time when almost everyone assumed that PSE enrolments would soon level off or even decline, but demands on the health system would continue to climb rapidly. Well, they were right on the second point.

The next 10 years or so, 1977 to 1987 roughly, saw very little *real* increase in funds reaching PSE institutions but, after an initial dip, an increase of around 30 per cent in student numbers. The biggest factor in this growth of enrolments was, of course, that women finally caught up in most fields of study.

Meanwhile, many observers including some federal policy makers, politicians and officials, spent much of that period second guessing the EPF decision and yearning for the days of cost sharing. The learned journals were filled with proposals for alternative forms of financing, while writing policy documents on the subject became a federal growth industry, and federal-provincial relations in the field of PSE largely became a series of confrontations about fiscal arrangements. (It was sometimes called the era of "share wars.")

Again, it's instructive to look for a moment at the policy alternatives then on the table because they may offer some clues to the options of the 1990s. And again the same policy themes arise.

The basic proposition for these federal policy makers in the early 1980s was that a significant portion of the PSE part of EPF should be diverted to other, more direct forms of PSE financing. The proposals varied from a few hundred million to $1 billion or more out of the then total of nearly $4 billion. Not to quibble over the amount, though, the real question was just what objective should the federal government pursue with these funds.

One popular view was that the money should be given to students in the form of vouchers. The students could use these to pay the increased fees that would result when federal cuts in EPF were passed along by provinces to colleges and universities. This approach would not only make people more aware of the federal role in PSE support, but it would also increase the purchasing power and thus influence of students. This was seen as a way to make the system more effective, responsive, and efficient. (This general idea remains alive, having been put forward for example, in the Macdonald commission report.)

Another view was that funding should be channelled from EPF transfers to support the direct and indirect costs of university research. This would mean that "research" universities receiving most funding from the granting councils would benefit. (Again, the idea surfaces periodically.)

Other observers emphasized the "human resource development" aspects of support for education and training. Some proposed directing funds (in usually unspecified ways) to the most "useful" disciplines. One difficulty was determining objectively which disciplines would be most useful in a few years, when the graduates appeared on the labour market, but there was no shortage of opinions.

As far as I know, no one suggested that history should be considered among the "useful" disciplines; hence I have always had a somewhat jaundiced view of this proposal.

A particularly popular series of candidates for "useful" status was the various types of engineering. In particular it was proposed that we double the output of petroleum engineers to meet the needs of the National Energy Policy, thus illustrating the hazards of predicting specific future labour market needs.

Other proposals for increased federal direct spending included a greatly expanded federal student aid plan, increased support for vocational and other non-PSE forms of education and training, improved access for particular target groups, and pursuit of a variety of specific federal objectives. It should be noted that some of these proposals were partly implemented in 1983 and 1984 using funds made available by 6&5 restraint.

I won't lead you in detail through the federal-provincial debates of this period. Most of you remember them. But one general feature we might note is the federal interest in providing leadership to higher education and research by redirecting funds from general transfers to other, more direct kinds of support.

Since 1984, direct federal funding for PSE through research grants, student aid and other forms of support has risen over 9 per cent per year, while EPF transfers (despite restraint) have risen about 6 per cent. This, it should be noted, is in the context of general government program funding that has been held to about 3 per cent annual increases.

If the desire for greater influence through direct funding has been one pole of federal policy, however, the other has clearly been the need for fiscal restraint. Through the 1970s and 1980s we have seen a tension between these two and there is no sign of its disappearance in the 1990s. But there may be evidence that the issue can be approached in fresh ways.

To put the choice a little differently, the federal government has often sought to increase its influence in this delicate field, on the reasonable grounds that we need a concerted national approach to tackle successfully the challenges of an increasingly tough and competitive world economy, while the provinces, not unreasonably, have asserted their own constitutional responsibilities.

The late 1980s brought a serious effort to escape from this view of a federal-provincial zero-sum game. The radical idea was advanced that instead of focusing on fiscal arrangements and competing for influence on the PSE system, a more profitable approach might be to cooperate in identifying and tackling the issues themselves.

The national forum in Saskatoon was one such effort, and I've already commented on its success, at least as an opportunity to ventilate the issues and viewpoints. But I should also stress the extent to which the forum broke the federal-provincial ice. Before the forum, we couldn't even talk seriously about working jointly on the issues. Now we are gradually finding ways to view things from a pan-Canadian perspective without threatening the legitimate role of the provinces in education.

As we start the 1990s we are looking forward to the establishment within a fairly short time of a national study on human resource development, as endorsed by first ministers in November, following a proposal made by the prime minister. The study will deal with issues of education and training that just a couple of years ago would have been taboo in any federal-provincial discussion.

On the federal side, the prime minister has appointed Dr. Douglas Wright, president of the University of Waterloo, as his personal representative to work directly with the CMEC. Dr. Wright has met members of the CMEC several times to develop terms of reference and a plan of action.

The proposed study reflects a shared concern about Canada's future competitiveness. It has become conventional wisdom to agree that human resources will in the future be more critical than natural resources in determining our national well-being. The study is to look at our needs in the early part of the twenty-first century, to assess the ability of our systems of education and training to meet those needs and offer recommendations to the appropriate authorities for how to improve the responsiveness of the systems. It is to consider all levels of the human resource development system, from early childhood to lifelong learning for adults.

The aim is not to undertake new fundamental research. On the contrary, we have seen a plethora of reports and studies in recent years. The study will, we expect, seek to distil the best of the available information and views and offer a synthesis that will assist governments—and everyone who has any concern for education policy—to determine the directions we should take in the 1990s. The sooner we get this kind of broad guidance, the better.

I believe we must seize this opportunity and work closely with the CMEC to see the study launched and carried through to completion. I believe that those of us in the federal government, and those of you involved in the study of education, should do everything we can to make this work a success.

Now, I'm not so naive that I think it will come up with all the answers. What I hope it will do is to help define the questions for the 1990s, the approaches we take to developing policy.

I hope above all that the study can represent a major step in cooperation that will grow through the decade. We have enough real problems and challenges in this country. We need partnerships to tackle them. Perhaps the study will help us to shift our attention from the federal-provincial process to the real issues of education and training in this country. If so, even a small step for bureaucrats might be a great leap for Canada.

In the decade ahead, many of the broad themes of the debate over post-secondary education policy in Canada are likely to echo those of the past, but the approaches and priorities will likely differ.

For example, we will no doubt again have to address the questions of fiscal arrangements—or as our chairman, Jeffrey Holmes, put it so eloquently in a 1982 paper, "Is there Life after EPF?" This question takes on new meaning now that the AUCC has done some calculations indicating that cash transfers to Ontario and Quebec may disappear by the end of the decade.

I think we are facing a period in which those of us concerned with higher education support will need to reconsider our view of EPF. Using the transfers to increase federal leverage has been proposed by many policy makers and members of the higher education community—without notable success. Perhaps instead we might start by treating EPF simply as part of the fiscal context within which we must search for consensus about the real issues and objectives, an area in which, I think, there is great scope for agreement.

Another area of great importance for higher education is the funding of university research. While there are many broad issues involved in the overall funding of direct and indirect costs, an issue of immediate concern is the support provided by the federal government to the three granting councils. I do want to let you know that many of us in several federal departments are aware of the importance of research and development for Canada's social and economic development, and that we do understand the critical role of university research supported by the granting councils.

We work closely with the councils to help our ministers convince their colleagues of the wisdom of investing in research, even at a time of severe fiscal restraint. (That the granting councils were exempt from the recent round of budget cuts suggests significant success.)

It's not always easy to make the case convincingly, especially for support to research that seems to some people unrelated to Canada's foreseeable needs. The pay-off from curiosity-driven research is often not obvious, and we need the help of the community to show why such work is important. This is particularly true for the council my minister represents, the Social Sciences and Humanities Research Council. One of the more convincing types of argument is comparison with our competitors. If we can show that the Japanese do it, we're well on the way to convincing Canadians that it's worth doing.

On another aspect of the broad issues of federal-provincial support to PSE, we have the problems of representation. Dealing with the issues of higher education instead of the mechanisms of fiscal transfers implies that ministers and officials on both sides must be able to speak for their governments on matters of substance in this field. There needs to be on the federal side a focal point for federal higher education interests. This role has been played by the secretary of state, but discussions have tended to deal with a limited range of topics. Now, I hope, we may be moving into an era when regular federal-provincial meetings on a broader range of higher education issues might become a normal feature of the relationship.

To achieve such a breakthrough will take sensitivity, good faith and openness. The federal government can play a lead role in this field without intruding on legitimate provincial responsibilities, but only if, as Claude Ryan once said, it shows "a leadership of inspiration, encouragement and support rather than leadership based on control and supervision."

What else might one discern of the environment for our efforts in the 1990s to evolve a more concerted approach to postsecondary education?

First, don't hold your breath waiting for the Constitution to be changed to transfer jurisdiction for education from the provinces to Ottawa. Occasionally, in the briefs I read or representations I listen to from some of the interest groups, I hear a kind of yearning for a unitary state, the simplicity of some sort of central control of education. This is simply not on.

Far better for everyone to accept constitutional reality, and perhaps even to go further to recognize that, in a federal state like ours, it is actually desirable that education be under the control of governments that are closer to the people and more in tune with the cultural and social characteristics of the regions which make up the Canadian state.

Second, don't think that government fiscal restraint is a temporary phenomenon. Through the 1990s and beyond there is every reason to believe that governments will need to limit expenditures in order to tackle their debts. At the same time, demands for funding of a wide variety of programs, most obviously social programs related to the welfare of increasing numbers of older people, will continue to grow.

Some, including myself, will argue that higher education is a critical investment in the future, that it will pay off handsomely in economic and other terms. But against this will be placed the simple fact that we already spend more per capita from the public purse on education than practically any other nation.

I'm not saying we cannot or should not spend more on our universities and colleges, on research and development, on improving access for under-represented groups. I *am* saying that it is no use seeing increased funding as the quick fix. Those of us who study or advise on higher education matters will have to be a good deal more imaginative than simply to suggest that problems can be solved by spending more. To use a phrase that was popular not too many years ago, we will be expected to "spend smarter."

Finally, let me stress a theme of special importance to the Canadian Society for the Study of Higher Education (CSSHE)—the need for more and better information on higher education and related issues such as the human resource needs of the economy. The national forum in Saskatoon pointed out this need for better research and information on post-secondary education, and since then we have made some headway in improving the statistical base and encouraging research.

But more needs to be done and we in the Department of the Secretary of State are looking at ways in which modest new support might achieve substantial returns in the form of a better basis for planning and managing the higher education enterprise.

We are looking, for example, at how a Canadian focal point might be created to help coordinate and stimulate policy-relevant research and analysis on higher education. Such a centre would have as one of its priorities the comparative analysis of Canadian higher education in the international context, one of today's key issues and a problem of great complexity.

Likewise, we think that our department should be able to do more to help in the development of higher education initiatives, whether they involve dialogue among participants from all over Canada about key issues or the development of new and experimental forms of education delivery. While fully respecting the responsibility of provinces in this field, we believe that we should be able to support projects that have a significance extending potentially throughout the higher education systems of Canada.

We have already developed some ideas along these lines and we look forward to discussing them with many of you in the near future. This is, I think, potentially one of the most fruitful areas for new partnerships involving both orders of government, the higher education community and the wide range of other groups interested in the role of colleges and universities in our social and economic development.

To close, I want to suggest to you that the next two or three years could be among the most interesting and productive since the 1960s for the development of Canadian higher education. The challenges will be very different from those heady days, and the money won't flow so freely. Yet there seems now to be something of the same conjunction of views that we saw nearly 30 years ago. Higher education—indeed, all levels of education and training—are seen once again as so central to our future that we can't afford not to tackle the issues together.

Gwynne Dyer said recently that the twenty-first century has started 10 years early. He was referring to events in Eastern Europe, but in many areas of our experience, as individuals and as a nation, the sense is overwhelming that the future is coming even more quickly that we expected.

Getting ready for that future, shaping it and exploiting it, rather than being its victim, is the challenge for Canadians in an increasingly tough and competitive world. Ever the optimist, naive or not, I'm looking forward to the federal-provincial challenges of higher education in the rest of the twenty-first century.

The University/Government Interface: A Deputy Minister's Perspective

Gary Mullins

What can a deputy minister with 20 months' experience contribute to a group of individuals who have spent the better part of their professional lives engaged in the study of higher education? On questions of detail and substance, there is probably not a great deal that I can contribute. However, each of us approaches what we do from a particular perspective. I may be able to contribute to your deliberations by sharing with you, from the perspective of a deputy minister, some thoughts about the university/government interface and its importance for the education system. I believe it to be a unique perspective. I hope that I can help you understand government and the world in which I live, in the same way that I try to understand the world in which you and universities live. If we can achieve this mutual understanding, we may have an opportunity for constructive and meaningful dialogue, and we may be able to find ways of improving the university/government relationship.

In this paper, I wish to describe the role of a deputy minister and outline the current public policy environment in which governments and universities operate. I will outline how budgets for universities are established, as I believe that budgets become the focal point, and sometimes the flashpoint, in the university/government relationship. I will outline for your consideration an accountability framework that, if implemented, might lead to an honest, open dialogue, a harmonization of expectations and the strengthening of a productive partnership.

A. The Deputy Minister's Role

The perspective of a deputy minister[1] comes directly from his or her role. A deputy lives full time between a rock and a hard place. That unenviable position is also located in a fish-bowl. A deputy sits between program substance and political reality. While being a member of the professional and appointed public service and therefore closely associated with the programs of government, it is the interface between politics and programs that dominates a deputy's life. In an advisory role, a deputy is responsible for providing high quality, practical advice to his or her minister and, with the minister, to cabinet committees, Treasury Board and to full cabinet. A deputy's main value-added quality is judgment. As a recipient of ministerial and cabinet direction, a deputy is respon- sible for interpreting both general and specific policies of cabinet to a ministry and to the constituencies it serves. A deputy must ensure that a myriad of delegated managerial, administrative, financial, and program decisions are made in accordance with the general policies and values shared by cabinet.

A deputy's interface role also involves a knife-edge balancing point between stability and change. One reality of the public policy environment is that both the public and politicians expect and demand change. The very use of the term "news" in respect of the media is the simplest way of noting that "news" involves things that are new and things that change. Improvements and change are desirable and inevitable but change for change's sake must be avoided. A deputy assists government, the ministry, and constituents in overcoming institutional resistance to change. At the same time the deputy must ensure that changes occur in an orderly manner, building on strength and taking advantage of opportunities—unless a situation has deteriorated to the point where revolutionary, rather than evolutionary, change is required.

A deputy lives primarily in a strategic and tactical environ- ment. A deputy would be entirely ineffective if a minister or cabinet relied solely on that deputy's knowledge or expertise. A deputy creates an environment in which expertise from a wide variety of sources is brought to bear on an issue as that issue is analyzed, as options are developed and as recommendations are made. A deputy is an assembler of expertise from a variety of sources, both within and outside government; is coach and mentor of a process to ensure practical advice is provided and, exercising professional judgment, becomes one of the chief strategists in how a desirable outcome can be achieved.

A deputy must never lose a medium-to-long-term perspective, a perspective starting at five years and moving out several decades, with the actual definition of long term varying widely with the type of issue under consideration.

These considerations relate primarily to the deputy's role in policy development and formulation. On a day-to-day basis, a deputy is constantly involved in a variety of specific, shorter term management considerations including more detailed issues of needs identification, value for money, and a variety of "prudence" and "probity" considerations required when living in a public policy fish-bowl.

These considerations are shared by all deputies of education and higher education in Canada and by all deputies with significant policy responsibilities. Each deputy lives in his own unique space characterized as being between the political and the substantive, between the short term and the long term, between the strategic and the operational and between the desirable and the affordable.

In the deputy's world, a *win* at somebody's expense—i.e., a *win-lose* situation—is untenable. Our role is to assist our ministers in creating only situations in which good public policy, acceptable to government, is viewed by that minister's constituencies as good public policy acceptable to them. Creating *win-win* situations, particularly in the short term, is almost always difficult, but is *always* the goal.

B. Public Policy Environment: Higher Education

No two provinces organize their cabinets or their departments in a similar manner. The following "environmental scan" is largely comparable to the environment in which each of my provincial counterparts lives. There are, however, some differences. I am the only deputy of higher education in Canada who also has responsibility for science and technology policy and labour market policy. The presentation of my own environmental scan will reflect those additional responsibilities and therefore may differ from that which others might present, but only in that my scan may be a little broader. For the purpose of a later discussion of the university/government relationship, the broader perspective of my responsibilities is probably advantageous to our discussion.

The first and most important feature of the human resource development and social policy environment in which we live is the pattern of unemployment in Canada. The Economic Council of Canada has studied long-term secular trends in unemployment and the results are, in a word, "scary." During the boom years in each of the past three decades, there has been an increase in the underlying rate of unemployment. Each decade has had its booms and its busts. During the boom years of the 1960s, the underlying rate of unemployment was 4 per cent. During the boom years of the 1970s, the underlying rate was 6 per cent and during the boom years of the 1980s the underlying rate of unemployment hovered around 8 per cent. The social and income costs of such an accelerating pattern have been very negative for unemployed individuals and families. The financial impacts on governments and taxpayers have been equally negative, with increased "safety net" social costs being accompanied by reduced tax revenue. The impact of the pattern of dramatically increased social program costs and reduced tax revenue of the 1980s is that universities learned the lesson that "as goes the economy, so goes the pattern of funding available for those universities." Canadians individually see their own personal prospects fluctuating with a rise and fall in the economy. The same expectation holds true for our institutions of higher learning.

The second major impact of the 1980s, this time the late 1980s, was the emergence of persistent structural unemployment. Even with unemployment above 8 per cent, many job vacancies were hard or impossible to fill because of a serious mismatch between the capabilities of the unemployed and the opportunities available. As a result, a national consensus has emerged that the most significant mechanism for strengthening the prospects for individuals and for our economy is "human resource development."

By human resource development I mean increases in individual levels of education and marketable skills across the full spectrum of our society and at all age levels. In the economic sense, human resource development involves a targeting of education and training efforts to individuals capable of moving into the more difficult-to-fill positions.

Without getting into the details, the consensus around human resource development permeates the work of opinion leaders, including the Royal Commission on the Economic Union and Development Prospects for Canada (Macdonald, 1985) and the more recent report, *Adjusting to Win: Report of the Advisory Council on Adjustment* (de Grandpré, 1989), the work of the Economic Council of Canada, particularly its 25th anniversary report entitled *Back to the Basics* (1989) and its more recent report entitled *Good Jobs - Bad Jobs* (1990). The Canadian Manufacturers' Association report, *The Aggressive Economy: Daring to Compete* (1989), recognizes the pivotal role of universities in the human resource development equation as well as the need for a variety of technical and technology-related skills training and retraining.

National Task Force on Human Resource Development

The most significant human resource development issue on the federal/provincial agenda today is the national Task Force on Human Resource Development to be established by Canada's first ministers. When the prime minister and the premiers assembled on November 9 and 10, 1989, for their annual conference on the economy, they came prepared to discuss Canadian competitiveness. Most focused on human resource development and all recognized that Canada's public per capita expenditures on education and training is among the highest in the world,[2] yet most feared that we may not have a competitive economy by the year 2000. They committed to establish the Task Force on Human Resource Development, and their communique outlined the following guidelines:

- to assess Canada's human resource development needs
- report on the human resource requirements of the twenty first century, knowledge-based economy

- identify the results of the current systems, from pre-school to university and skills, technical and vocational training

- develop recommendations that will address the changes required

- examine ways of allocating resources more effectively with a focus on results

Since then, the Council of Ministers of Education and the representative of the prime minister, Dr. Douglas Wright, president of the University of Waterloo, have developed draft terms of reference for a task force which is expected to be appointed shortly.

In my judgment, a number of elements will come together through this study. First, there is a strongly held view, particularly in the federal government, that there is as much public financial support for education and training in Canada as is required and the challenge for the 1990s is how to get better results for those expenditures. Second, there is a very broad consensus that education and training are the cornerstones of our competitive economy.[3] Third, there is a clear recognition of unmet "needs" in the economy and society, and a clear government bias that those needs should be met directly, rather than serendipitously. When related, the separate concepts of value for money, education providing benefits to society as a whole, and policy and program targeting lead me to one inescapable conclusion—the national exercise is principally about accountability for results.

I will return to the issue of accountability for results. Accountability and budgets are becoming two sides of the same coin, so before discussing accountability, it is helpful to discuss the public budget building process.

C. Budgeting in Government: Questions of Perception

I believe the biggest frustration in the university/government relationship to be the budget issue. It need not be so. Frustration is mutual and, in my judgment, about equal on both sides. What are the bridges of dialogue and understanding that need to be built to overcome the mutual frustration? What form will those bridges of understanding take? In order to understand the budgeting process, it is necessary to understand ministers and their role in the process. The key to understanding a minister is to understand the public. A minister will be much better informed than members of the public, but two critical points must be made.

First, before his or her election a minister is a member of the public. Only in dictatorships is being a minister considered a life-long career. In our democracy, members of legislative assemblies (MLAs) are elected from the public at large and the process of cabinet building is neither predictable nor scientific. It is a political art. There are no expressed criteria by which a premier selects and appoints a minister of advanced education or a minister of finance—the two most important portfolios affecting advanced education, in addition to the premier himself. The only *a priori* assumption we can make about ministers is that they are knowledgeable members of the public with higher than average levels of personal ambition and much higher than average concern and caring for the betterment of the society which they have been elected to serve.

Second, if a minister is to be successful, he or she must be able to understand the public mind and relate to, and communicate with, the public in a manner it can understand. In making its decisions, a cabinet must focus on the acceptability of those decisions to the public it serves. When the background of ministers and their need to communicate with the public are taken together, it should come as no surprise that the marketing challenge facing all public policy advocates and stakeholders starts with the public's needs and expectations.

Although ministers accept that universities have a dual mandate of teaching and research, there is no question that undergraduate teaching ranks as the highest priority. That should not be surprising—after all, parents and students are both citizens and voters. There is a general attitude in our society that a university degree is highly desirable, if not prized, and that acquiring a degree is one of the most visible social and economic escalators. In British Columbia, where universities and colleges are not the "two solitudes" they are in many provinces, a better education is synonymous with our public college, institute and university system. In the minds of our young people, "getting ahead," "getting an advanced education," and "getting a good job" are almost synonymous.

With that background, how do ministers decide and on what do they base their decisions?

Budgeting: The Process

The process of budget building is time consuming, technical, and subjective. A minister and a ministry establish a strategic direction containing one or more themes around which a number of specific proposals are advanced. The review by the minister, his deputy, and executive committee is both comprehensive and serious. There are a dozen or more iterations. Several oral and written presentations are made to one or more groups of officials and ministers. Members of the government caucus are involved in some jurisdictions, but not in all. The focus of presentations is on outputs. For any proposal the question, "What is the benefit to society?" must be answered directly or indirectly—and the more directly the better.

Treasury Board ministers, and their advisers who review budget proposals, have the unenviable task of choosing from a plethora of proposals, most with significant merit and with aggregate fiscal demand far exceeding budgeted revenue. Theirs is an almost superhuman task with both substantive and political aspects and subjective and objective components. But essentially, ministers are choosing between differing proposals, with widely varying costs, differing levels of discretion and with different kinds of stated benefits. There are proposals with clear, quantifiable outputs and benefits, and others where the goal is attractive, if not compelling, but where the specific outputs or benefits are just not quantifiable.

The key is for government to state priorities and for funds to be allocated in accordance with those priorities. And in selecting proposals to include in the budget, it must be remembered that budgeting is both an art and a science. When push comes to shove, the final decisions are inevitably subjective, and made usually by the minister of finance and the premier. How else can one characterize the choice between three hypothetical $8-million items, such as a half per cent further increase in welfare rates, additional environmental inspection and enforcement measures, and a package of largely unspecified means of improving the quality of our universities? In spite of the process being subjective, the more carefully crafted and demonstrably beneficial the proposal, the more likely it is to be supported through the budget chain, from the managers, through the deputy, the minister, Treasury Board and premier, and then ultimately funded.

Setting Budgets for Universities

But what is the environment of budget making when it comes to universities? Before I answer that question, I should share with you an exchange with Dr. Strangway, president of the University of British Columbia, during our second meeting, within two months of my appointment as deputy minister. I asked Dr. Strangway: "How would you like your funds from government, with strings attached or without strings attached?" His reply, not surprisingly, was: "Without strings attached." But when I asked the follow-up question, "Would it make any difference if there was more money with strings attached?" his reply was, predictably, "Yes, it just might make a difference."

Those who know me well, know that I am basically not a "strings attached" sort of person. But Dr. Strangway and I were both familiar with the reality I mentioned a few moments ago: the biggest frustration in the university/government relationship surrounds the budget issue and tying some mutually agreeable strings might help to minimize that frustration.

Governments see universities hiding behind the University Act, treating that act as a university's "charter of rights and freedoms," with most notions of acute independence based on reference to the concepts of academic freedom and university autonomy. What is the unintended negative but real consequence of that focus on independence? In my judgment, it is the inability of universities and the government to communicate effectively so that the desirable social outcomes of university funding alternatives can be presented convincingly in the budget-setting process. Good communication, I believe, is extremely important between universities, a ministry's executive and a minister. The consensus and the momentum it creates should carry through the full budget-decision making process.

Accountability and Budget

In my opinion, universities are the only instruments of public policy in British Columbia which rely predominantly on government funding, but receive only limited policy direction from government and almost no direct government control. The direct provincial operating grant of $239 million to a single university, the University of British Columbia, is larger than the individual budgets of 13 separate government ministries, each with separate ministers, deputy ministers, important program mandates and appropriate staffs. The total of provincial grants provided to our three universities of $425 million exceeds the *combined* operating budgets of nine separate ministries. For example, public opinion polls consistently show environmental issues as being of greatest concern to British Columbians, yet the budget for the Environment ministry is an amount equal to only 10.4 per cent of the budget for my ministry and only 27 per cent of the total operating grants to our three universities.

Are these relative priorities correct? Are universities that important? In my judgment, the answer is an overwhelming YES! Universities are, and should remain, important instruments of public policy. Public monies are, after all, spent for a purpose and there are valid purposes for which universities are provided with public funds. But can a case be made that universities should be largely exempt from public accountability? I think not. When ministers allocate monies for a purpose, do they not have the right in a democracy to be assured that monies allocated for a specific purpose are in fact spent for that purpose? That, I think, is the essence of both democracy and accountability.

Let me give you an example. In developing university budgets for the past fiscal year, universities made the case, supported by my own staff's analysis, that the restraint program during British Columbia's long and difficult recession of the early-to-mid-1980s, cut deeply into each university's equipment replacement budget. Some kind of base budget adjustment to correct this was proposed but initially rejected in the budget-setting process because universities received "block funding" and ministers could not be assured that money allocated for that purpose would be spent accordingly. To follow up on the spirit of my earlier conversation on "budget strings," I asked the universities if they would agree to control a separate equipment-replacement budget composed of the amount of their actual expenditures in the previous fiscal year and a sizeable additional amount that could be provided expressly for that purpose. Two universities agreed, but one was initially hesitant. When I sent a message to the reluctant university in the simple form, "No ticket—no laundry," I received an immediate, affirmative reply.

What had we done in this instance? We had created a *win-win* situation. We met a real need in each of the universities and we provided the government with the confidence that money allocated for a purpose would be spent for that purpose. The reaction within the universities was even more positive. A long-standing source of real frustration had been eliminated, faculty could order equipment for which there was a compelling need and faculty had the confidence of a continuing budget.

Does the above approach get into the question of accountability? Yes, but only in a small way. Clearly, on some issues of base funding such as equipment replacement, agreeing to tie a budget has unquestioned merit for both parties. Agreement between the university and the government serves all parties well. Similarly, if incremental funding for enrolment growth is provided over-and-above base budget funding, then instruments reflecting the agreed basis for budget growth serve both parties well.

In the case of our current fiscal year, two British Columbia universities wished to expand undergraduate enrolments, whereas one did not. Our ability to create agreements around differing percentage increases to university budgets on the basis of agreed undergraduate enrolment levels enhances understanding and reduces frustration levels. It is also of great assistance to presidents in explaining to boards, administrations and faculty the differences between the budget increase of one university in comparison with others.

These examples of budget agreements deal only with administrative or financial matters. The much larger challenge involves the substance of what the university does. This larger challenge is the one which I believe the national Task Force on Human Resource Development will tackle. If addressed openly, honestly and cooperatively by all parties, it is also the challenge that will lead to the greatest mutual satisfaction. It is the issue that is central to our discussions at this conference.

D.   The Challenge of Accountability

There are two fundamental accountability issues that must be considered in the university/government context. First, there is the need to determine the strategic issues of *what* should be done— a focus on the desirable outputs of universities. It is a statement of the individual, social and economic benefits that will relate to budgeted expenditure levels. Second, there is the need to determine operational issues of how the agreed outputs of a university are to be achieved. The question of *how* is directly related to its companion, *how well*. In my judgment, totally different approaches are needed for each of the *what* and *how* issues of accountability issues.

The Strategic Issue: Accountability for Outputs

The two main outputs of a university are its graduates and its contribution to the advancement of knowledge. I say "advancement of knowledge" rather than "research" because research is an activity, but "advancement of knowledge" is a result. Accountability for results will focus on what a university is expected to produce and should include identifiable, quantitative and qualitative measures of those outputs.

We can expect the Task Force on Human Resource Development to outline the human resource development needs of a competitive economy and articulate the role that universities should play in meeting those needs. Given both constitutional and administrative realities, it will be up to each province to determine how each of the agreed task force recommendations will be implemented and to determine how each province will establish its own accountability framework. I believe the resulting exercise will provide each university with the most attractive opportunity in the last quarter of this century to articulate and communicate its vision, its mission, its contribution and its needs.

There are several components to human resource development issues, but I will focus only on two, namely the mix of programs and their content. Within each there are several dimensions, for example, needs of the individual, of our society, and of our economy, plus other considerations such as academic quality, acceptance of graduates to graduate programs, etc. I will focus largely on the human resource development needs of a competitive economy as that is the likely main focus of the task force and because student expectations are in large—but not exclusive—measure wrapped around the concept of a university education providing an excellent launching pad for a challenging and rewarding career.

In looking at the needs of the economy there are several observations being made by opinion leaders within a variety of forums on the mix of programs. These observations are each worthy of considerable investigation and are illustrative of the issue of program mix. These opinion leaders advise that there appears to be excess demand over supply of both the active number of graduates as well as the existing university capacity in general science, engineering, nursing, other science-based disciplines, education and commerce. By comparison appropriate or possibly excess capacity exists in the arts and humanities.[4] Within the entire post-secondary system, there also appears to be an imbalance in student demand between a variety of higher order career programs, such as technologists and general academic programs. I understand that in Ontario, for example, there is current excess capacity in the college system, whereas in British Columbia, waiting lists for some career, technical and vocational programs is evidence of demand in excess of capacity. In both British Columbia and Ontario, there is probable employer demand in excess of current program capacity in many areas.

If we accept that providing a university education to a generation of Canadians represents a significant national investment, it is not too difficult to accept some targeting of that investment. Joint university/government targeting of the mix of programs within the university component of our human resource development system is preferable to unilateral targeting by either one or the other and is preferable to no targeting at all.

A related strategic issue is the content of undergraduate degree programs. The extent of undergraduate concentration in a single discipline has increased over the last few decades, in large measure reflecting graduate admission requirements. As only a small minority seek a master's degree or doctorate in their undergraduate concentration, it is uncertain that current graduation requirements are optimal for the terminal B.A. or B.Sc. student, or for the student seeking a degree in law, medicine, education, business or another professional field. If individual, societal and economic needs have any relevance, a focus on undergraduate degree content is clearly appropriate. Developing degree requirements more attuned to actual needs may have the desirable outcomes of increasing participation rates, success rates, a more educated citizenry, and a more competitive economy. As universities are instruments of public policy, surely a joint search for the objectives to be achieved, and an honest university response to those objectives, is a fully supportable goal.

There are other strategic human resource development output considerations, including desirable participation rates and patterns, and an identification of the abilities and competencies expected of a university graduate, regardless of the actual degree awarded. These could be topics themselves for future sessions.

The second core activity of universities is research and its main output, the development of knowledge. I will not try to add to the volumes of written material on what is an appropriate balance between research and teaching. But a few comments about research intensity, teaching loads, and priority setting are clearly in order as research is a cornerstone activity in our universities and a major cost within them.

In his article, "Higher Education: A Changing Scene," Dr. Fraser Mustard observes that there are only enough resources to support a limited number of research-intensive universities, that there is a need to balance conflicting requirements and that institutions will become more differentiated. He observes that ". . . the choices that are made will determine the characteristics of the university" (page 14). He concludes, "It will be the responsibility of each university to make the difficult trade-offs among faculties, facilities, research intensiveness, breadth and quality of its education programs. In Canada, we need to develop funding arrangements that will make it possible for some of these universities to make these choices and to differentiate themselves." I agree.

The development of priority setting and funding arrangements which support excellence and the needs of society and the economy should be joint university/government planning activities. They are too important to be left to one or the other. Let me give an example of a recent strategic initiative.

In 1986, the Government of British Columbia established the Fund for Excellence in Education Program. Essentially, a competition was established and targeted funding was allocated to universities on the basis of that competition. Some observed that this targeted funding was at the expense of proper base budget funding and others that funds should not be tied. Nevertheless, universities swallowed their pride, accepted the conditions, took the money and didn't "look a gift horse in the mouth." The result was a selective significant strengthening of research capabilities. In the words of Dr. Bob Miller, vice-president of research at the University of British Columbia, "the Fund for Excellence in Education Program provided the underpinnings of outstanding strength that was recognized in the awarding of leadership to UBC of three networks under the federal government's Networks of Centres of Excellence program." The benefits of that joint targeting were significant.

There will be differences between the capabilities and reputations of universities, of faculties and departments within universities and of faculty members within departments. In other words, there will be significant differentiation between universities, departments, and faculty. There are very significant opportunities for each institution to identify its unique research mandates and to develop true excellence in those mandates.

The discussion of strategic considerations related to human resource development and the advancement of knowledge focused on what ought to be achieved. I believe the interests of both university and society will be best served by cooperative, open dialogue and by achieving consensus on outputs. This joint process regarding outputs is remarkably different from the companion process of accountability for how the results should be achieved.

The Management Issue: Accountability for Performance

Universities should also be accountable for how well they perform as organizations. In the case of results, I outlined a process involving dialogue and agreement, and those agreements may end up in some form of "contract." In the case of how those results should be achieved, I have an entirely different accountability model in mind. This model reflects the complexities of universities, the need to tackle, head-on, the tendency of outside groups including bureaucracies to want to meddle in the affairs of others, and the legitimacy of the concept of academic freedom.

What management issues within a university are meaningful within the context of an accountability framework and how can they be satisfactorily handled? There are many and they are complex. There are clear exceptions to every observation, but I find that university boards, administrations and faculty are careful guardians and husbanders of administrative and support budgets. Significant and honest efforts are applied to stretching every dollar as far as possible and searching out opportunities for leveraging funds from a variety of other sources.

The area where the public perceives that universities are not as vigorous in managing their resources is in the area of its truly productive resource, its faculty. Most would agree with me that faculties are composed largely of outstanding individuals committed to their university and their discipline. The challenge is how to address the issue. This is an area where the concept of academic freedom legitimately prohibits the direct involvement of those outside a university. There is no argument from me whatever with that point. I suggest the quantitative and qualitative dimensions of the challenge be handled in two very different ways.

First, a mutual set of expectations must be articulated on average faculty workload as measured by undergraduate contact hours. The numerical capacity of a university to educate its students is a function of average contact hours and average class size. Second, it will be the responsibility of a university to manage itself so that averages are met, within an environment of differing research intensities as between disciplines and as acceptable class sizes vary between disciplines and course level. Finally, universities must articulate the management processes they have put in place to ensure a productive faculty—the very strength on which a university's reputation is based.

The details of how a university organizes itself and responds to agreements it has reached on outputs is an internal issue, that is, it is internal to a university. In California, for example, the state education plan provides a framework for determining what is to be achieved. The actual *how* itself is determined by each university. In a Canadian context, I can foresee the development of an agreed process. The parties would agree to a management process, but universities alone would be responsible for implementation. The needs of government would be met solely by confirmation that a university had competently followed the agreed process.

In summary, a plan would outline mutual expectations and the universities would be funded on a formula basis consistent with those agreed expectations. The university would be responsible for managing within the framework, subject only to an audit that the university has complied with the framework conditions.

In my judgment, it is reasonable in a publicly funded system for joint priority setting and budgeting, including agreement on a variety of management indicators that would be applied by a university. Management indicators would include ratios such as average undergraduate and graduate student/faculty ratios and average contact hours/faculty. Performance indicators would include a variety of peer review or process indicators, including a university's success in securing research grants, awards, contracts, technology-transfer rates, spin-off companies, and other forms of external, non-governmental recognition.

What are the alternatives? The alternatives are not very attractive. Universities, as now, are obliged to rely on government generosity, but universities as supplicants make their case on a much less attractive basis than their competitors. Under current circumstances, a government dictates the agenda and a university responds to it. How much more attractive would be a true partnership in the planning process.

Accountability and Budgets

As discussed earlier, the main frustration between governments and universities is expressed through budget concerns and takes two main forms. Universities most frequently express their frustration through some form of statistical comparison, such as "our current funding per student in constant dollars is only X per cent of what it was in 1977 or some other year." The year chosen may be the most generous one in that university's financial history and may well have reflected a year which combined unusual financial generosity and lower than anticipated enrolments.

While the statistic may be correct, and whining of that nature may be illustrative, it is seldom helpful. In short, universities advise that they face different cost drivers than other kinds of private activity or publicly funded activities and that funding has not kept pace with these cost pressures.

Government observations take a similar and not much more helpful form. A government may observe that in constant dollar terms, student fees are the same today as they were in the early 1960s, but today only cover 15-20 per cent of costs compared to 30 per cent 25 or 30 years earlier. The real per student grants have therefore almost doubled over that period of 25 to 30 years. What more can a university ask for? While such bragging may also be correct, and illustrative, it too is seldom helpful. In short, governments observe that universities have failed to change the way in which they operate, as business and other publicly funded activities have been obliged to adapt, and that their only response to the "productivity challenge" has been to keep increasing undergraduate class sizes.

If we can replace a very general and subjective budgeting process with one based on joint agreement to strategic goals and output objectives, within an agreed operational framework, we will have elevated the quality of debate on higher education to a level where the needs of all participants, particularly the needs of society, can be more effectively met.

E. Summary and Conclusions

A deputy's perspective of the university/government relationship reflects his or her unique location between program substance and political reality. Universities are instruments of public policy, and because of the clear human resource development needs of our economy and society, governments view higher education spending as a long-term investment rather than as spending for current consumption. Unlike other social and economic spending, the sense of output—that is, what benefits are being derived from differing expenditure levels—has been difficult to describe and even more difficult to quantify. The result has been a mutual set of concerns focused largely on the financial relationships between universities and governments.

In my judgment, the tension characterizing the university/ government relationship reflects the structure rather than the substance of that relationship. Universities demand a level of autonomy that effectively prohibits constructive dialogue. Governments are exposed to public pressure for a responsive, high quality education system meeting the needs of individuals, society and the economy. In the absence of agreement, governments do not have confidence that programs to meet these needs will be delivered if they are funded and may be reluctant to approve additional funding for otherwise desirable goals because of that lack of confidence.

A central characteristic of the current system is that universities unintentionally abdicate the right to be fully involved in policy development and in articulation of visions, missions, and programs. These issues are too important for universities to ignore. The concept of academic freedom has fully protected universities from political interference right across Canada. The separate but related concept of university autonomy has unintentionally restrained the ability of universities to maximize their contributions to the societies they serve.

The solution to the challenge facing the 1990s and the response of governments and universities to the ultimate findings of the national Task Force on Human Resource Development (and other challenges that will be posed) is to establish a variety of joint university/government accountability or framework agreements. Each would deal with strategic outputs recognizing the need of universities for both academic freedom and a level of autonomy on the *how* questions. The process would recognize the unprecedented challenges facing society and governments in the area of human resource development that are so critical to individual, economic and national well-being.

The nature of those agreements through which public accountability will be expressed will have several important realities, the most important of which is a clear definition of roles. Universities and governments will agree on strategic outputs, the *what's* of universities' achievements. Both parties will agree to an operating framework within which the strategic outputs and budgets can be articulated. The universities themselves will be responsible for operating within that framework, subject only to verification that the agreed process has been followed. Once outputs and policies are jointly defined, government's role will be as contract administrator, providing funding on an agreed basis and receiving confirmation that the agreed process had been followed. Agreement will remove the arbitrariness perceived by the universities. Governments will gain the confidence of spending on the basis of funding allocation and of the ability of universities to meet needs jointly identified.

The above conclusions provide several challenges. The most important is the challenge of jointly identifying and targeting needs of individuals, society, and the economy. For universities and governments, the challenge will be one of developing the tools to participate openly and effectively in a new area of cooperative activity. Universities have been leaders in developing analytical tools and of measuring what was previously thought to be unmeasurable and will face the challenge of developing and applying such measures and tools to their own activities. Governments, as the largest "corporate" organizations in their respective provinces, have excellent track records in managing complex and diverse programs and have the challenge of developing a *modus operandi* for bringing together the substantive and the political into a framework acceptable to their university partners, a group whose professional cynicism is an essential ingredient for their professional success.

These issues are too important for us to ignore. The clear need to succeed becomes its own imperative.

Notes

1. For clarity, a deputy minister is referred to simply as "deputy" to avoid confusion with the very different role of "minister."

2. Based on international data, in 1985 Canada spent US $936 per capita on public education, the second highest among all OECD nations (United States - $966; Japan - $533; Germany - $464). Source: International Competitiveness Report—1989 World Economic Forum.

3. In a recent survey undertaken by the Canadian Labour Market and Productivity Centre (CLMPC), business and labour attributed a higher importance to human resource development issues than to other factors such as lower interest rates, federal deficit reduction or increased spending on research and development. Source: Business

and Labour Leaders Speak Out on Training and Education. CLMPC National Survey, January 1990.

4. In the last 10 years, while applications to university arts courses have doubled, applications to Canadian engineering schools have increased by less than 4 per cent. In computer sciences, enrolment has dropped by 36 per cent in the last five years. The Canadian Engineering Manpower Board predicts a shortage of 30,000 engineers in Canada by the year 2000 as demand increased by 48 per cent. In the United States the shortfall is expected to be in excess of 500,000. Source: Learning to Compete: Redefining the Business-Education Relationship. Speech given by Gedas Sakus, president, Northern Telecom, Conference Board of Canada "Reach for Success" Conference—Toronto, April 18, 1990.

II

Experience in Other Countries

Universities and Public Policy

Ron Watts

I propose to talk about four issues in broad conceptual and comparative terms to set the ground for our more detailed discussions later on. To identify these as the context for the discussion, I want to say something first about how we regard the relationship of universities to public policy; second, to look at ways of organizing and managing universities within society; third, to look at strategies for public policy relating to universities; and fourth, to look at instruments for public accountability. In each of these, I will use a broadly comparative approach, ranging over the United States, Britain, Australia, New Zealand, Europe, Japan, and, of course, Canada.

Such comparisons are valuable, but obviously we need to keep in mind their limitations as well. We want to look for both what is in common and what is different. These help to point out for us possible alternatives for consideration within Canada, but they should also point out to us, or help us to recognize, the limits to our ability to import other arrangements into Canada, because of variations from country to country in political, social and cultural circumstances.

Let me turn first to the role of universities. My topic refers to "universities as instruments of public policy." This phrasing immediately raised in my mind the question whether universities are in fact simply instruments of public policy and caused me to wonder about the assumptions that underlie such a characterization of the role of universities within society. It is important to examine these assumptions before we talk about the appropriate scope, strategies, and instruments for public policy and public accountability. In doing this, I propose to look at three different views of the role of universities within society, thus setting the context for any discussion about public policy relating to universities. These three views I have labelled the instrumentalist view, the autonomist view, and the mutually interdependent view. Let me just say a few words about each of these.

I developed those three views more fully in a paper that I gave to the Royal Society some years ago, but I want to recapitulate briefly because I think it is important in setting the context for our discussion.

The *instrumental view* is often advanced by those in government and the business community, and, of course, it has also been advanced by a growing number of academics who see it as the rationale for greater governmental and corporate support for research and educational programs within the university. The conventional wisdom advocated by those who hold the instrumental view runs something like this. Our society is undergoing a change from an industrial economy to a knowledge-based economy. A knowledge-intensive economy is one in which the greatest proportion of new jobs created are in the knowledge processing and handling sector rather than materials processing, and hence productivity and prosperity in society will increasingly depend on how well we use the brain of technology rather than the brawn of industrial workers and industrial machines. Education and research, therefore, become the key economic resources in our society. Universities are thus the key instrumentality by which society achieves economic competitiveness and prosperity.

According to this view, our current economic problems in Canada can be attributed to our grievous neglect of investment in human capital, which is the key to productivity growth; studies are cited which indicate that the most important factor in Japanese productivity, for instance, is the high quality of that country's educational system. It follows then that unless our universities accept the challenge to create new generations of workers and managers who understand and use the new technologies, Canada's efforts to achieve economic recovery and international competitiveness will fail. Moreover, the problem is seen as urgent, given the rapidly increasing rate of technological change. We no longer have time for this nation and its senior educational institutions to engage in a leisurely debate on how we should respond to the new order.

Many such statements have been made in Canada by corporate leaders or governmental policy makers, but it is worth noting, if one reads, for instance, the OECD publication of a couple of years ago entitled *Universities Under Scrutiny*, that such statements and propositions are common throughout the OECD countries in terms of the role that universities should play within society.

The implication of this instrumental view of the role of universities is that they should be geared up directly to this urgent task, although how that should be done usually involves one of two approaches. That perhaps most common within the universities harks back to the golden age of the 1960s and argues that all that is required is more adequate public and corporate funding support of research and educational programs within the universities. That which is most common outside the universities is the view that given constrained public and corporate resources, what is needed is a rethinking and rationalization of university priorities concerning educational programs and research, all directed at creating greater effectiveness and efficiency. Coupled with that is the view that insofar as universities themselves fail to meet this challenge, governments will need to intrude or intervene to direct universities either by regulation or by strong funding incentives.

I should note here that universities looked at as an instrumental value for society need not be directed simply at national economic development. There's a second dimension which relates universities to the importance of transforming society from a closed society to an open society. Here universities are seen as instrumental in enabling society to become more open by serving as a channel of mobility for members of society. That is, through the development of individual capacities and their certification, universities provide the opportunity for upward mobility within society. So there's a public interest in universities, not simply as instruments of national economic development but also as instruments ensuring the transformation of society from an elite society to a mass society, one in which there's an opportunity for people to move out of the circumstances in which they were born. Perhaps this view, in application, is strongest in North America where the accessibility rates are highest, compared with those in some of the other countries we are looking at, but it is an increasing pressure elsewhere.

(In this connection we often think of ourselves as achieving less accessibility to universities than the United States, although our figures tend to be higher than those of any other of the advanced or developed countries. But I came across an interesting statistic when I was chairing the New Zealand universities review committee, whose function was to try to assess the New Zealand universities in the international context. I discovered that, although we may be somewhat behind the Americans in terms of accessibility, in terms of productivity, we do somewhat better. That is, if one looks at graduates produced per 100,000 of population, the figures—according to estimates of the United Nations Educational, Scientific and Cultural Organization (UNESCO)—run like this: New Zealand, 272; United Kingdom, 280; Australia, 430; Japan, 432; United States, 621. The Canadian figure is almost equal to that, at 616. So while we are concerned, legitimately, about accessibility in Canada, we should also note that there are different ways of measuring the concept. Presence in university is one; completion of university programs is another, and we do somewhat better on that latter scale, I would point out, than we might think in comparison to the American performance against which we tend to measure our results. But that's just an aside.)

I have suggested, then, that there are two important motives underlying the instrumentalist view of universities within society. An alternative and antithetical view of the role of universities within society is that which might be described as *autonomist*. I take this term from Max Beloff, one of the founding lights of the private University of Buckingham in the United Kingdom. He argues that it is only by standing apart from the immediate concerns of society that universities can realize their full potential as centres of learning. In his words, to take the King's shilling, or to become the tool of the corporate world by focusing educational programs or research upon areas of more direct or immediate economic relevance, is seen as misunderstanding and even prostituting the true function of higher education. This view emphasizes that universities, as centres of learning and discovery, are concerned primarily with the preservation and creation of knowledge for its own sake and not simply as means of economic or social development.

Furthermore, there is the danger that if universities come to see themselves as the servant of immediate social and economic needs, this will undermine their vital role to act as both the critical conscience of society and the institution through which the values of society itself are transformed through critical evaluation. Those who hold this view emphasize that the function of the university as a whole is not just to enable economic development or social mobility, but rests in the civilizing mandate of transforming societal values themselves.

For those who hold this fundamental conception of the university, there is a very real concern about the "steering" effect upon students in their choice of programs, or researchers in their choice of focus, exerted by the needs and requirements of the economy as perceived by governments and the corporate sector. In the contemporary world, they would point to the beleaguered position of the humanities; to the pressures from corporate personnel offices favouring graduates from professional programs with job-related skills; to the pressures from research councils to do research to fit identified national needs; and to the growing predominance within universities of contract research with its focus on more immediate requirements and results. This anxiety is fuelled by such statements as those of a government spokesman that I saw a few years ago in *The Financial Post* in which the individual declared: "You must understand, we don't want to fund actual research in universities. We are more interested in funding the transfer of knowledge from university to industry where it will produce immediate benefits in terms of products."

I would suggest that perhaps a better view than either of the two that I have outlined so far is a third, which I will call the *mutually interdependent* view. In this third view I think there is a possibility of reconciling the apparently antithetical elements of the instrumentalist view and the autonomous view. I think we have to begin by emphasizing the role of the university as intrinsic, rather than instrumental. The role of the university then is not merely one of serving the needs of society, but the broader one of discovery. Lord Ashby put this point well by contrasting higher education and further education.

I think a discussion paper prepared for the AUCC by an ad hoc committee chaired by Jeffrey Holmes nearly a decade ago put it well when it identified the fundamental function of universities in the following terms: "They are committed in the long term to extending and communicating man's understanding of matter, energy and materials on the cosmic scale of galaxies, on the human scale of nuclear reactors and oil refineries, and on the molecular scale of chemistry, physics and biology. Of the nature of life, the processes of development, disease and death in cells, in organs, in animals, plants and man, in communities, peoples and nations. Of the roots and forms of political ideologies and power. Of why economies flourish and flounder. Of the behaviour of man in families, cities, organizations. Of man's sustaining imagination as expressed in literature, drama, philosophy and religion, and about the shape of society as it has been and might become." In this view then, the university is concerned with questions at the frontiers of human understanding and experience, not just with the immediate needs of society.

But having emphasized this intrinsic role and value of the university as an institution, we must recognize at the same time, however, that it cannot live apart from society, for there is a natural congruence in the goals of universities and the effort of society to achieve those goals. Knowledge has always been important for society, and therefore universities have to recognize the contribution that they make to society. Furthermore, universities in turn cannot fulfil their own intrinsic function of discovery and pushing forward the frontiers of knowledge without the resources and culture of society to nourish them. As John Gardiner put it, "Universities don't spring up in the desert, or in primitive societies. Great universities are the products of great cultural traditions and vital civilizations, and can flourish only in societies that have the will to nourish the tradition and the vitality to support it."

Thus the point I am trying to make in conclusion about this first conceptual set of issues is that neither universities nor society can be isolated from or independent of each other, for each is dependent on the other; but also that it is important not to look on universities merely as instruments of public policy. To see universities merely as instruments of public policy is to underrate them; to see them as institutions isolated from society is equally to underrate them.

Having said that, let me go on to the second, third and fourth set of issues that I wanted to address. If universities are dependent upon society, and society dependent upon universities, that has important implications for the way in which one reconciles accountability for the massive use of public funds with society's need to leave universities free to undertake their intrinsic functions.

My next point is that if universities are not merely instruments of public policy, but certainly must be affected by public policy, what are the ways of organizing and managing universities within society? Here, following the writings of Burton Clark and Martin Trowe in their comparative studies of higher education, I want to point to four ways of organizing and managing universities within society. One is through the power of professional guilds organized as departments or faculties or academic senates or learned societies as these act through committees, chairmen, deans, rectors, vice-chancellors, or presidents, applying academic norms and values as defined by professors and the former professors who hold higher administrative offices.

The second is through political decisions, through the outcome of the play of power and interest in some political arena— that is, in legislatures, a cabinet committee, a governor's or cabinet minister's office, or, in the United States, a presidential office.

The third is through bureaucratic regulation, essentially through the management of the higher education system or its institutions by a ministry or the civil service.

The fourth is through the operation of markets where events are not willed or planned by central agencies or by political decisions, but emerge as the outcome of the myriad decisions of many actors competing for various goods, for money or power, for students or teachers or graduates. These markets themselves, of course, are usually constrained and regulated, formally or informally, in part by the rules of the larger society, in part by the norms of academic life.

Now the point I want to make is that each national system has organized itself and made its decisions through some combination of all four of these modes of governance. But what differs among them is the relative weight and importance of these four different ways of governing higher education. That is, the particular blend and emphasis and weight given to professional guilds, political decisions, bureaucratic regulations or market mechanisms have varied greatly between national systems. For example, in the United Kingdom, Australia, and New Zealand the enormous growth in the costs of higher education has led to a rapid growth in the role of the state in university finance and organization. And so over the last 30 or 40 years we have seen a rapidly changing balance, a balance which began with perhaps the predominance of the traditional roles of the academic guilds, a context in which boards of governors or trustees as we know them in North America were either non-existent or played an extremely weak role; a movement from that toward a situation in which buffer bodies exercised an important role; and now a movement with a heavier emphasis upon bureaucratic regulation, backed by political decisions. Certainly in the United Kingdom, Australia, and New Zealand, by comparison with North America, there has been a relatively weak reliance on market mechanisms as a factor in the governance of universities.

Thus the United Kingdom, Australia, and New Zealand have moved closer to the traditional European pattern of giving heavy weight to bureaucratic predominance. The continental European tradition was to emphasize the academic profession, but to incorporate the academic profession within the civil service. Thus in Europe the strongest elements of the four that I have referred to have been the roles of the professional guilds and increasingly of the bureaucracy.

These patterns, I think, are to be contrasted with those in the United States and Japan. In the United States, the market has played a much stronger role in the governance of universities, in part through the parallel operation of private and public institutions, and through the emphasis on tuition fees as an important element in funding universities, representing the payment for private benefits which individuals receive from universities as opposed to the public benefits which society receives. There has also been in the United States a stronger political, rather than bureaucratic, element in the management of universities; at least in the public systems, the role of state legislatures in going through university budgets line by line represents an element of political decision making, as opposed to bureaucratic. Japan, like the United States, has parallel public and private institutions. And there too, therefore, the market system has had a greater weight than in the United Kingdom, Australia or New Zealand tradition. But rather than the political, the bureaucratic role has had a stronger element, particularly in relation to the imperial and national universities, which have predominated in the more expensive areas of science, engineering and so on.

Now in this array which I have just sketched briefly in an introductory way, Canada falls somewhere between the United States, on the one hand, and the United Kingdom, Australia, and New Zealand group, on the other. There is certainly a much greater emphasis on market mechanisms than exists in the United Kingdom, Australia or New Zealand, and therefore a lesser direct governmental or bureaucratic role than has occurred, at least in the last decade, in those countries. But by comparison with the American model, I think, we have seen more bureaucratic regulation and less reliance upon political decision making, and this relates in part to the form of government we have; and that leads me to the second aspect of this issue of forms of managing universities within society.

It's important to recognize that the form of governmental system itself affects the character of public policy as it relates to universities. There is a danger, if we look at it all from the point of view of the universities, of simply asking how universities affect public policy; we need also to look at how the form of government affects public policy. And here I make two important points. First of all, within a parliamentary system such as that in Britain, and Canada belongs in that tradition, where the cabinet is fused with the legislature and where as a result the executive tends to dominate the legislature, the bureaucratic element tends to be stronger in the regulation of public policy. In the United States or Switzerland, where you have the separation of powers, where the executive and legislature are more separated, and balance and check each other, there is a larger role for legislators, as occurs, for instance, in the role of Congress in the United States, or in individual state legislatures. Hence, lobbying in the legislature becomes even more important than lobbying with the executive branch. While lobbying in the legislature may occur in Canada, most of us would recognize (and certainly this is particularly so in Britain) that the important place to change opinions or affect policy is in working with senior bureaucrats, cabinet ministers, and so on. In the United States, the important place to influence policy making is particularly with representatives of the legislature. So the key arenas for public accountability depend on the form of government.

An even more important variation in the form of government is the difference between unitary and federal systems. Federal systems involve a dispersal of public policy-making power. Even though normally education as a subject is allocated to the states or provinces as an area of jurisdiction in federations, almost invariably in all federations the federal governments have become involved in policy making in relation to universities, in terms of the need for funding support, for research, for ensuring mobility of citizens, and so on. Now the multiple sources of public policy making in a federal system may appear messy and untidy, but I always like to quote on that subject a noted authority on federalism, one of my predecessors at Queen's, J.A. Corry, who always argued that a neat and tidy mind was a crippling disability in attempting to understand any federal system. And indeed the virtue of a federal system is its messiness, its ability to disperse decision making into multiple centres. One of the outcomes of this is that it is typical of most federal systems that there has been less intrusion upon universities by bureaucracies and governments in the general sense because of this dispersal of public policy making. Whether that's a virtue or a vice, I leave for you to discuss. But the point is, it is a characteristic of federal systems.

While noting this about federal systems, we also have to note that there are variations among federations, between centralized federations and decentralized federations. I noticed that in the papers distributed to you is a paper by Bob Smith, who had some experience in Canada as a president pro tem at UBC, is currently a vice-chancellor in Australia, but has also played a role in public policy making there. In that paper he makes the distinction between hard federalism and soft federalism related largely to the Australian situation. There, even though the universities, with the exception of Australian National University (ANU), are in effect state universities, the federal government has virtually taken over the funding, and indeed regulation, of those universities, through the degree of centralization that has occurred within that federal system. So the degree of centralization within the federal system will have an impact on the relative roles that different governments play.

So also will the degree to which federalism is collaborative or competitive. Our federation operates with a good deal of competition between levels of government; some others like Germany and Switzerland emphasize legislative policy making at the national level with administrative responsibility at the state level, and have developed mechanisms for collaboration between governments which are quite different from those that we know in Canada. It is therefore not surprising that you would get in the German scene, for instance, national framework legislation relating to universities, which is then applied with appropriate variations, state by state, by the state governments. This sort of arrangement is certainly not known in Canada.

Thus I emphasize the point that the federal, as opposed to the unitary, system influences the patterns of policy making affecting universities, but so do variations within federal systems themselves.

Let me make just one other point on that issue of the role of federal governments. It is worth noting the various options that face federal governments in terms of public policy relating to universities, particularly in matters of funding. In Australia, Canada and the United States, we get three sharply different variations. In Australia, the federal government funds the institutions directly. In Canada, we fund the institutions via the provinces. In the United States, the federal government funds the universities indirectly via the students, via its student aid program. These three different patterns in the role of federal governments themselves have obvious impacts on accountability relationships and patterns of policy making.

I'll try to condense and collapse what I wanted to say about strategies for public policy. Having recognized that in each system the ways of organizing and managing universities within society have varied, with different emphasis on the elements of professional guilds, political decisions, bureaucratic regulation, and market operation, in part related to different forms of governmental organization, I think we need to look at the strategies which governments use in applying public policy to universities. And here I would simply draw to your attention the four strategies that David Cameron identified in his theme paper for the

Saskatoon forum in 1987. That is, complete and direct government control, coordination by governments, governments establishing a framework for competition, and simple privatization.

Again, it is worth emphasizing that most systems have not relied solely on one of these, but that the weight given to each has varied. In generalized terms, I think it would be said that complete and direct government control has been strongest in the European countries, especially where academics have been regarded as part of the public service. Thus you have in countries like Germany, for instance, the imposition of internal patterns of organization with universities, that is, a laying down of framework legislation decreeing exactly how universities should be organized internally. Of course, the net effect of that sort of role for government has been to make the internal organization of universities a partisan political matter. The result is that when individuals run for the position of rector (or president, depending on which title is used) in many German universities, they run on the party ticket. And one party runs a candidate for rector or president as opposed to another party. This seems, at least to me in the Canadian scene, a very different picture from the way our universities are organized internally. But that shows what happens when you get direct government control of internal organization of universities; it politicizes the internal operation of universities.

In the United Kingdom, Australia, and New Zealand, we have had a strong movement away from the use of so-called buffer bodies, or intermediary agencies, which for a period were used in all three systems, toward more direct governmental bureaucratic intervention and regulation. That process is still under way and perhaps we will have an opportunity to discuss it in more detail. In the United States there are, not surprisingly, variations from state to state in the degree to which, in the public systems, the states emphasize coordination. In a number of American states— California for example, with its multi-campus system forming the federated University of California—there is a high degree of coordination; in others there is much less. Some states have attempted to establish frameworks for competition. But the impact in all of them of the parallel private system has been to provide a strong competitive element, a measuring stick by which to assess the public systems in terms of quality, performance, and so on.

In Japan, the element of coordination within public universities has generally been strong, particularly in the imperial, national and provincial universities, but there too, like the United States, the variety of public systems and the parallel private system have also introduced a strong element of reliance on the private sector and on market forces.

Finally, we come to instruments for public accountability. I was going to say something about the application of these in different countries, but since a good deal of the subsequent discussion will be focusing on these, I think I will simply list them and, if the discussion gives the opportunity, draw out what I was going to say about them. Of the instruments that have been employed for public accountability, I would identify here eight that we need to consider, at least in terms of identification. The first is the development of performance indicators, particularly efforts in this respect in the United Kingdom, the OECD countries, and in some American states. These were intended to replace input measures by some sort of measure of output or of value added. The efforts were begun with some optimism, at least in the United Kingdom, but I think many of these efforts have found that there are real problems in trying to measure quantitatively the unmeasurable. The United Kingdom Green Paper, written some time after the first efforts of the Jarratt committee, declared that often in this area higher education is simply not amenable to measurement with any pretension of objectivity, but it went on to argue that it is important that the existence of indicators should at least always be kept in mind. So I think there's an ambivalence there, and at least a recognition that performance indicators are not the sole answer.

The second is the use of funding, block funding or earmarked funding. There are two aspects here. One way of exercising control is by the level of funding, the second is by earmarking. The most clear example of this, I suppose, is in the United States with the line-by-line budgeting that occurs in some states. A broader form of earmarking is the use of envelopes for particular areas or their use as a supplement to block funding, as the Bovey commission recommended and as some recent developments in Ontario have carried forward. In passing, let me note that I always find it amusing that my academic colleagues invariably object to earmarked funding for universities, and then complain that because federal funding to the provinces is not earmarked, the provinces don't perform their responsibilities to higher education. I think we need a little consistency here on the degree to which grants should be unconditional. What's sauce for the goose is sauce for the gander.

A third area is the issue of the degree to which the notion of user-pay for private benefits should be introduced. There are great variations among systems in terms of the proportion of tuition fees in total funding. It's often assumed that low or non-existent tuition fees are important to accessibility. I found to my surprise that virtually non-existent tuition fees and open access in the New Zealand universities have produced about half the accessibility that we have achieved in Canada with higher tuition fees. So fees by themselves are not the sole issue; indeed the Labour government of New Zealand of that time was increasingly concerned that low tuition fees were in fact regressive, that they were subsidizing the middle class for benefits that the working class were not obtaining. There is a real issue of attempting to distinguish—and it is very difficult to distinguish—public benefits from higher education and private benefits. When we talk about the private benefits we are not just thinking of education for individuals, but also of the benefits which industry receives from the products of higher education, in terms of both graduates and research, and the degree to which industry has a responsibility, given the benefits it derives from higher education, to contributing toward payment for it.

A fourth issue is the degree to which funding should be via student aid or direct to institutions. One variant of the student aid proposal, of course, is the voucher proposal which the Macdonald commission recommended for Canada. I found when I was in New Zealand, that the National Party, which just came to power this week (1990), and particularly its then spokesman on education, now, I think the finance minister, Ruth Richardson, was very keen on the voucher system. I understand that the National Party may have moderated its views. I am not up to date on what it has been saying in the last week or two, but it is important to note that I found a very strong advocacy of that position, at least when I was in New Zealand a couple of years ago, on the part of the party that has now come to power in New Zealand.

So, one variant is the voucher proposal. Another is simply forms of student aid. It is worth noting that in 1972, when Congress decided to increase federal support for higher education substantially, most of the higher education community in the United States pressed for block grants to institutions based on a formula. That is the Australian pattern, with the federal government making block grants to institutions based on a formula on the advice of some sort of commission. Clark Kerr of the Carnegie Foundation almost alone opposed this and urged a greatly expanded program of student aid and support through a combination of means tests, grants, and loans. And, in fact, that is what Congress decided to do. Thus, in the United States, there has been a greater emphasis upon institutional competition in the market with government, particularly the federal government, giving assistance to institutions via the student, with, incidentally, this process making possible the continued existence of private institutions where the students get assistance from the federal government.

The fifth is buffer bodies. I will skip what I was going to say on that topic, except to note that in the United Kingdom, Australia, and New Zealand, and some Canadian provinces, they have had an important history, although in all those places, there has been a movement away from them toward more direct bureaucratic control. We need to rethink the role of these buffer bodies. My impression, at least in reviewing what has happened in countries like the United Kingdom, Australia, and New Zealand, is that the replacement of buffer bodies by more direct governmental regulation has not really improved the situation at all.

A sixth is the role of boards of governors and trustees. These are strongest in North America, or in the Japanese private institutions. They are virtually non-existent on the continent of Europe, and they have tended to be weak in countries like the United Kingdom, Australia, or New Zealand; indeed that has been an important factor in the shift toward government intrusiveness. But it is also worth noting that the effectiveness of boards of governors, or of trustees, as a way of ensuring public accountability of universities, depends very much on the sorts of people who are appointed to such boards, particularly their government representatives. I recall, when I was a member of the Council of Ontario Universities, our dismay when we found that the then

Conservative government in the 1970s was shifting from a pattern of seeking the advice of universities about who might be valuable members of boards of governors, to simply turning the selection process over to the party headquarters to decide what members of the party deserved rewards for their services to the party by being put on boards of governors. That certainly was not a way of ensuring accountability of universities at a time when the government had the opportunity to put public citizens in an important role where they could have some valuable bearing on university policy.

The seventh is encouraging university-industry links; that has been a common trend in most of the OECD countries. And of course it has been typified by such public policy initiatives in Canada as Centres of Excellence Programs, research parks, and so on.

The eighth is encouraging university-society links. I think this has been underestimated in terms of importance. Martin Trowe makes this point very strongly in contrasting the United Kingdom with the United States. One of the reasons why the United Kingdom universities have been so susceptible to more direct governmental intrusion is that they have always seen themselves as serving the national government rather than their local communities or their local societies. In the United States, on the other hand, the universities have cultivated their social and local roots through emphasizing the role of alumni, local communities, and so on, to ensure that they have a sympathetic local community supporting them. You can just see this if you drive across the United States. When I drove across to California some years ago, I was fascinated to observe how every community at the outskirts has its sign proudly proclaiming its local community colleges or universities, or whatever. I thought that would be a good idea for Queen's, but found that such advertising would be illegal in Canada, or at least in Ontario, which illustrates how much we might differ from our American neighbours in this notion that universities should put their roots into society as a counterbalance to being simply run by governmental bureaucracies.

I want to say in conclusion that to look on universities, their research and educational programs merely as instruments of public policy is to distort their intrinsic function. Nevertheless, as I have argued, universities depend on society to perform their intrinsic function, and society needs universities for its national development, economic development, social development and mobility internally. In such a situation, if universities are to survive and preserve their integrity as institutions intrinsically devoted to the creation of knowledge, they will have to undertake imaginative and innovative changes themselves. They will have to respond and recognize their importance to society as contributors to economic and social development. In this sense, I welcome the theme of this conference, which is to challenge universities to look at ways in which they can be more responsive to society, rather than waiting for governments as agents of society to impose change on them. I hope we can pursue some of these ideas in our further discussion.

Synthesis of Commentary and Discussion on Watts Paper

Glen Jones (Higher Education Group, Ontario Institute for Studies of Education) opened the discussion on Professor Watts' paper with observations on the changing quality of accountability and autonomy. His major observations were as follows:

i) Responding to pressures for greater restraint in public expenditures, and for greater efficiency in the utilization of public funds, governments in many western nations have re-evaluated, and in some cases reduced, funding for higher education. They have also adopted new or revised strategies for the regulation of higher education, and these regulatory changes indicate a number of common trends:

   a) One of these trends is a movement towards managerialism, through which governments try to stimulate and strengthen the capacity of universities to manage strategically their own affairs. Institutions are being asked to define their missions and long-term objectives, and then to develop strategic plans to meet these objectives.

   b) A second major trend has been the change in the role and timing of evaluation in higher education policy. There is an increasing interest in strategic evaluation, and in evaluating the outputs of the higher education system in addition to, or instead of, system inputs.

   c) The third trend is the emergence of conditional contracting, that is, the negotiation of specific terms of agreement covering the relationship between universities and governments, or in some cases between universities and the private sector, in clearly defined policy areas.

ii) These basic trends have had a direct impact on both the accountability and autonomy of universities. The impact has varied in different higher education systems with different traditions, but a substantive change in the quality of the notions of accountability and autonomy can be observed. In the case of accountability, there has been a considerable change in what governments are asking universities to be accountable for; the quality of accountability now implies accountability for the quality of the products of the higher education system. There also appears to be a change in the quality of institutional autonomy in many western higher education systems. There is some evidence that governments are willing to increase the level of institutional autonomy but only in the sense that universities should have the flexibility to determine the best course of action within government-established parameters. There have been changes in this direction in the Netherlands, Finland, and what used to be West Germany.

iii) While Canadian universities would appear to enjoy the highest level of institutional autonomy of all publicly funded universities, there is evidence that many of the changes occurring elsewhere are also occurring in Canadian higher education, although there appears to be a subtle difference in the way government strategies are employed. The Canadian approach might be termed "managerialism at the margins," or the adoption of new strategies, including managerialism, conditional contracting, and a change in the role and timing of evaluation, in specific policy areas. In general, within the entire slate of higher education policies, governments in Canada appear to be adopting new strategies to regulate the margins. Policies concerning research and technology are an excellent example of these new strategies, and examples in other policy areas include the development of new provincial government funding categories or envelopes. Purse strings are attached to allocations, such as funds earmarked for equipment replacement in British Columbia, and the wide range of funding envelopes which have appeared in Ontario in the last decade.

iv) These changes in the approaches adopted by Canadian governments likewise are having an impact on the quality of accountability and institutional autonomy within Canadian higher education. New targeted funding mechanisms establish parameters within which institutions must operate if they are to access new funds. Policies encouraging specific types of university-industry linkages, and identifying strategic areas for research, represent a moderate form of remote government control. Accountability mechanisms, especially for research support, are changing and beginning to involve the evaluation of outputs. There are also indications that at least some provincial governments are interested in obtaining evaluative data on the quality of academic programs and the quality of graduates.

The discussion following Jones's commentary focused primarily on the three models presented by Professor Watts—the instrumentalist, the autonomist, and the mutually interdependent—and on how to find, within a mutually interdependent model, a suitable balance between the desires of universities for autonomy and the desires of government to use universities as instruments of public policy and to seek appropriate accountability for such an instrumental role. In response to a question on how pressures by governments and employers to pursue highly specialized education could be reconciled with the desires of universities to provide a general education, Professor Watts noted that society could best be served in any event by a balance between the two pressures which provided specialized education which was firmly grounded in a general education base and which could therefore be adapted and developed to changing circumstances.

In response to a question on whether universities, individually or collectively, should seek a particular position on the spectrum of interdependence, Professor Watts noted, and there was broad agreement with his view in the subsequent discussion, that universities could not unilaterally position themselves but must negotiate with governments and other funding agencies to find an acceptable compromise. He also expressed his support for a pluralist response, that is, a response by individual institutions in the light of their own objectives and circumstances, as the approach most consistent with the tradition of the competition of ideas, and most likely to produce a variety of flexible compromise positions.

Professor Watts went on to argue that finding an appropriate place on the spectrum of interdependence required a recognition by both universities and governments of the need for a balance between autonomy and public accountability. He argued that universities must be accountable for the resources provided by governments, but that at the same time they could only do what they were supposed to do well if they enjoyed a considerable measure of autonomy. In short, if governments chose to exercise too much bureaucratic control in the name of public account-ability, they might destroy what they were trying to create by making universities less able to provide teaching, research, and public service of high quality. He illustrated his position by citing developments in Germany in which governments decided to take the running of universities out of the hands of the old senior professors and to democratize the internal operation of universities by requiring that senior administrators be elected through a complex voting procedure which assigned proportional voting rights to various sectors in the community. The consequence, he argued, was the politicization of the process, the replacement of the competition of ideas by partisan political rivalry, and the weaken-ing of the autonomy of universities in Germany to pursue their primary functions. The point was made in the discussion that autonomy was really the critical question, since only autonomous universities could best serve the instrumental needs of society. Professor Watts agreed that autonomous universities could serve society best, but went on to emphasize that universities had to reconcile this autonomy with the legitimate claims of public funders for accountability in how public resources were used. There was broad agreement that appropriate accountability could be seen as the price of continued autonomy.

There was some discussion, reflecting the findings of the Jarratt committee in the United Kingdom, about whether uni-versities should consider modifying their modes of governance and management systems to provide responsiveness to the changing needs of funding governments and society in general. Professor Watts pursued this argument by noting that universities were interdependent with and accountable to society in general, not simply to funding governments. He pointed out that universities served and were interdependent with other elements in society— industries, communities, etc.—and that governance and manage-ment systems in universities should be responsive to these various other elements in society; he argued that one of the strengths of American universities had been to recognize the need for building a variety of bridges to society at large.

An interesting research question which arose, but was not resolved, at the conclusion of the discussion of the need for balance between autonomy and control, was whether alternative positions on the spectrum of interdependence actually had any impact on the day-to-day operations of the laboratories and classrooms of universities and therefore on the nature and quality of teaching and research outputs.

The discussion of Professor Watts' paper concluded with a brief examination of the question of voucher funding. Professor Watts was asked why funding individual students through vouchers rather than universities by operating grants had not been more widely adopted. Professor Watts agreed that the idea had enormous appeal, and had received wide support in the academic literature, in various commissions on higher education, and in the statements of politicians, particularly of the radical conservative variety. He pointed out, however, that application had been limited to a few small, local examples in the United States, mainly at the secondary education level, and argued that this limited implementation reflected the scale of the change from present funding arrangements, and the concerns of politicians that such radical change might have unforeseen consequences of a politically damaging nature. Vouchers might also, he added, be costly to administer. However, he noted that, while the federal government in the United States had not adopted a voucher system, it had gone part way by increasing the proportion of total post-secondary educational funding going in the form of means-tested grants and loans to students. There was general agreement in the discussion that a voucher system created difficulties of uncertainty and insecurity. There would be difficulty in predicting what a post-voucher world would look like in terms of student mobility and student access, and considerable uncertainty about the future of marginal institutions that might have problems in attracting students. Not least, university planning would become more difficult in such an insecure environment, and it was pointed out that the cost of operating universities went beyond operating costs to the underlying capital costs; the argument was made that the voucher hypothesis was predicated on the false assumption that if the customers moved, the cost centre could be moved as well. It was added that long-term commitments had to be made on the operating side as well as the capital side. It was conceded at the end of the discussion that a modified voucher or student aid system might nevertheless be used to check on student demand and the responsiveness of institutions to that demand.

Higher Education in the Public Policy Agenda: Hard Federalism and Soft Federalism

Robert H.T. Smith

Abstract

Higher education in Australia is very much on the public policy agenda. It is seen as an essential component of the restructuring and reform agenda that is part of the coordinated policy thrust toward positioning Australia for the twenty-first century. The policy environment has changed dramatically and involves new program advisory and delivery arrangements, the creation of a unified national system of higher education institutions, the identification of system and institutional management and governance as a priority area, new funding and administrative arrangements for research, and adoption of a user-contribution approach to funding higher education. All of this reflects an increased concern for accountability, and a deliberate move from soft federalism to hard federalism.

The title of this keynote address—Higher Education in the Public Policy Agenda—is rather predictable, given that it is a major theme for this conference. Your program chair, John Dennison, suggested that I might address the issue from the perspective of the federal structure as developed in Australia. He also suggested that you may be particularly interested in my "analysis of the unique reconstruction of higher education" which has been under way in Australia since 1987. My subtitle, Hard Federalism and Soft Federalism, is intended to reflect two views that I hold, one about Australian developments in higher education, the other on points of similarity and difference between our two countries. With respect to the former, I would argue that what we have seen in the last few years in Australia is a deliberate move from soft federalism to hard federalism, in which the central government has asserted a far more interventionist role than in the past.

That this has occurred in a country in which the vast majority of higher education institutions operate under state statutes is just one of many policy dialectics in Australia of the late 1980s (Smith, 1986, 139-140). It is also significant that it has occurred in a country whose constitution enshrined from the beginning sweeping powers for the federal government with respect to fiscal transfers. I refer here to Section 96 of the Constitution, which states:

> During a period of ten years after the establishment of the Commonwealth and thereafter until the Parliament otherwise provides, the Parliament may grant financial assistance to any state on such terms and conditions as the Parliament thinks fit (Hamilton, 1989, 277).

The phrase, hard federalism and soft federalism, also reflects my view that while our two countries have federal structures in which education is clearly a matter for provincial or state discretion, they are very different in the extent to which the federal government plays a role in the development and implementation of higher education policy.

In Australia, at least, there is no question about whether higher education is on the public policy agenda—it is. But having been peripheral to public policy for so long (Johnson, 1990, 66), the major debate now is about whether the policy settings are correct. Questions are continually raised about whether it is appropriate for the federal government to articulate such things as participation targets, priority areas for undergraduate and graduate enrolments, priority areas for research funding, the overall number of institutions (reflecting a desire to decrease the number of autonomous small institutions), appropriate features of industrial awards, and many other matters. I cannot claim to be sufficiently well-informed to present a detailed comparative analysis of the Canadian and Australian situations. [Indeed, it would be presumptuous of me to try, given Hamilton's authoritative essay (1989, 261-78)]. While I will attempt to identify some of the major points of similarity and contrast, much of this will of necessity be implicit.

******

Let me commence by setting the problem in context. Australia now finds itself in a situation almost unique in its 200-year history. On the one hand, there are strong mining and agricultural sectors which have consistently provided export income. Thus, for almost a century the country has depended on highly efficient agricultural and mineral extractive industries and on receptive commodity markets. However, in recent years, the market situation for Australian exports from the agricultural and mining sectors has been altered by improvements in the efficiency of these industries elsewhere in the world. On the other hand, the manufacturing sector is persistently in deficit so that there is a severe trade imbalance. The reasons for the problems in the manufacturing sector are well known: protected from foreign competition, encouraged to focus on the small home market, and to import rather than to develop technology, Australian manufacturing could scarcely have been expected to evolve differently. Yet Australia cannot afford to ignore the rapid technological developments and increasing productivity in the European countries and in the Asia-Pacific region, both of which have become—and will continue to be—extraordinarily competitive. That Australia is already at a disadvantage in this fiercely competitive environment is confirmed by the following observation in a recent report:

> The technological base of Australian industry has changed little since the 1950s, while our industrial contemporaries (Japan, Singapore, Sweden and others) have undergone revolutionary change. Over 60% of the export earnings of Japan, France, Sweden and Italy are the direct result of developments of intellectual skills, compared with less than 5% from Australia (DITAC, 1986, 91).

The nexus between the technology base, export earnings, and intellectual skills (or the knowledge base) is crucial for a modern nation, especially for one with Australia's unique set of problems. The creative exploitation of this nexus presents a formidable challenge, involving as it does education and training, retraining, research, improved technology transfer, the development of scientific and technological skills, and an improved international outlook including an understanding of Asian, Pacific, and European cultures and economies. Nowhere is the challenge—and opportunity—greater than in the higher education institutions, because it is in them that much of the research and development capacity of Australia is to be found. And research and development is the activity through which the nexus may be exploited most effectively. As the prime minister put it during the recent election campaign: Australia has been the lucky country; it now needs to become the clever country.

Given that this is the context, it should be no surprise that change and adjustment were the imperatives of the 1980s and continue to be the imperatives of the 1990s. They flow from the massive program of restructuring involving deregulation and microeconomic reform embarked upon by the federal government since 1983: restructuring of the public service; of the financial markets; of social security arrangements; of industry; of communications, shipping and transport; of industrial awards; and, yes, of education. The general rationale for this agenda is a conviction that there is an urgent need to position Australia to survive and thrive in the twenty-first century. As with all grand agendas, it is not without its critics, detractors and activist opponents—but this is as it should be in a democratic society. This is especially so in the arena of higher education where the arrival of Green (Dawkins, 1987a) and White Papers (Dawkins, 1988b) in December 1987 and July 1988 respectively precipitated a relentless process of internal review and public debate. The papers set the agenda, thus placing the initiative firmly in the hands of the federal government.

Perhaps the best beginning point for a discussion of the challenge for higher education is with some brief reflections on the context within which all of this occurred. Several initiatives to do with change, accountability and management in higher education institutions had been gathering momentum during the 1980s. One of these related to staffing issues, which the Commonwealth Tertiary Education Commission (CTEC) had flagged regularly in its triennial reports. Thus, the CTEC reports for 1982-84 (CTEC, 1982), 1985-87 (CTEC, 1985), and 1988-90 (CTEC, 1987) included references to such academic staffing matters as inflexibility, salary loadings, assessment and promotion procedures, mobility and probation. Some of these, as well as many others, were consolidated in CTEC's late 1986 *Review of Efficiency and Effectiveness in Higher Education*, which included recommendations for change across an extraordinarily broad front. Nevertheless, its effectiveness as an agent of change was limited—just why, I don't know. Perhaps it was related to the ownership of the report; perhaps because of government impressions of higher education and frustration with apparently high levels of unmet demand; and perhaps because of what some saw as the attitude of terrified conservatism in which higher education problems were approached in Australia.

The major statement on higher education delivered in the House of Representatives on September 22, 1987, by the minister for employment, education and training, J.S. Dawkins, can be seen as a decisive response to the kinds of issues and concerns raised by CTEC and others during the 1980s. A key statement in that speech read as follows:

> To the extent that further additions to resources will be necessary, the funding base for higher education will need to be considerably broadened. The implementation of these and other measures will require changes in at least three important areas:
>
> - changes in *attitudes*, to reflect national imperatives and to ensure that the education system is more flexible and capable of responding quickly and positively to national needs
>
> - changes in *processes*, in the way of doing things, to enhance our ability to produce quality graduates with necessarily limited resources
>
> - changes in *structures*, to remove impediments to change and barriers that dampen innovative approaches (Dawkins, 1987b; emphasis added)

That statement also foreshadowed the Green and White Paper process and the designation of 1988 as a pause in the customary triennial funding arrangements. In addition, it was the fore-runner of a policy environment for higher education which was dramatically different in at least five respects from that which had obtained from 1974 to 1988.

The five relate to: program advice and program arrangements; the unified national system of higher education institutions; system and institutional governance and management; research funding management and priorities; and the Higher Education Contribution Scheme.

First, there has been a change in the nature and composition of the federal portfolio with which higher education institutions interact. The Department of Education became the Department of Employment, Education and Training, thus signalling a policy commitment to a coordinated, integrated view of efforts in these areas. In addition, there was a separation of program delivery—now the responsibility of the Department of Employment, Education and Training—from program and other policy advice—now the responsibility of the National Board of Employment, Education and Training and its subsidiary councils as well as the department.

The establishment of the national board followed a review of portfolio advisory structures after the reorganization of the Australian public service in mid-1987, following Labour's return in the July election. The board is a statutory body and is the principal advisory body to the minister. The board incorporates a number of functions of earlier advisory bodies including the Commonwealth Schools Commission, the Commonwealth Tertiary Education Commission (CTEC), the Australian Council for Employment and Training, and the Australian Research Grants Scheme. The board has four subsidiary councils:

- The Schools Council
- The Higher Education Council
- The Employment and Skills Formation Council and
- The Australian Research Council

Membership of the board and its councils is drawn from business, unions, education and training providers, and a variety of interested groups across the country; it is thus a corporatist body. It is meant to be the *National* Board of Employment, Education and Training, not the federal or the commonwealth board. The board, which both responds to references from the minister and provides advice on policy issues on its own motion, coordinates the independent and expert advice of its councils. Its reports to the minister, whether in response to his reference or on its own motion, are tabled in Parliament. The board is intended to provide an integrated approach to employment, education, training and research, ensuring that policy issues are considered in the context of the government's broad social, economic and resource policies.

It is at this point that a major implication of the changed policy environment should be identified. The mandate of the former CTEC (the Commonwealth Tertiary Education Commission) could be taken as follows: it shall report independently and may advise the minister. In contrast, the mandate of the successor body, the National Board of Employment, Education and Training (NBEET), is that it shall respond to the minister's formal references and it may pursue matters on its own motion, provided that this latter activity does not compromise its ability to respond to the minister's references. More than anything else, this has become the symbol of the change from soft federalism to hard federalism.

The second feature of the policy environment that represents radical change has been the introduction of the unified national system of higher education institutions. Possibly the most controversial characteristic of the new policy environment, this requires that all higher education institutions with at least 2,000 EFTSU (equivalent full-time student units), regardless of designation as universities, colleges of advanced education, or institutes of technology, are now required to join the unified national system. Size is a critical consideration, and the government has declared its intention to

> ... retain the 5,000 EFTSU and 8,000 EFTSU benchmarks as a guide to determining the appropriate range of an institution's teaching activities and in assessing the extent to which it should be funded for research across its educational profile (Dawkins, 1988a, 45).

To quote again from the government's White Paper:

> Under the new system, there will be fewer and larger institutions than at present, and there will be more effective coordination between them on issues such as

course provision, disciplinary specialization and credit transfer (Dawkins, 1988a, 27).

And later:

Diversity and quality are paramount; the unified system will not be a uniform system (Dawkins, 1988a, 28).

It is well to pause and contemplate the implications of this policy initiative, under which the binary system—first created in the mid-1960s—has been dismantled. Universities, colleges, and institutes are required to declare themselves formally part of the unified national system of higher education institutions. That is, institutions must opt in; they cannot simply regard themselves as part of the system and retain the choice to opt out. By opting in, institutions do two things: first, they make a formal commitment to pursue certain goals and objectives related to equity, credit transfer, management, staffing, a common academic year, and institutional consolidation. Thereby, they ensure explicitly their eligibility for federal funding—an eligibility heretofore implicit and, indeed, even taken for granted. Second, by opting in to the unified national system, higher education institutions symbolically reject the binary system, under which institutions received different levels of funding according to their designation as universities on the one hand and colleges, including institutes, on the other. Membership of the unified national system ensures that

Institutions will enjoy ... guaranteed triennial funding based on agreed priorities and institutional performance against those priorities, rather than on an arbitrary system of institutional classification (Dawkins, 1988a, 27).

Under the binary system, institutional title conferred resources and mandate: universities received a higher level of funding per EFTSU than colleges and institutes and had an implicit, if not explicit, mandate for research, especially but not exclusively for basic research. Thus, institutional status conferred by title came to be associated with resources, and on perceived variations between groups of institutions called universities on the one hand, and groups of institutions called colleges and institutes on the other. There was precious little consideration of within-group variation which, although sometimes denied, undoubtedly existed, as is confirmed in the following statement from the CTEC's *Review of Efficiency and Effectiveness in Higher Education*:

> The original universities in each of the state capitals developed a normal range of disciplines covering the humanities, social sciences, sciences and professional courses such as medicine, law, engineering and in some cases veterinary science. All but one of the universities established in outer metropolitan and regional areas during the 1960s and 1970s have offered a much more limited range of disciplines (CTEC, 1986).

Elsewhere I have suggested that the status argument in the context of the binary system generated a great deal of heat precisely because it offended the pervasive egalitarianism that informs much of the higher education debate in Australia (Smith, 1987, 98).

The intention of policy and procedure under the White Paper is to allocate resources on the basis of agreed educational profiles (which include institutional bids for funded expansion in national priority areas; in 1991, these are computer science, engineering, accounting, mathematics and science teacher education, Asian languages, and environmental studies); and also on the success or otherwise of institutions in meeting objectives specified in those profiles. Such a performance-based process under which institutions—*all* institutions—will be funded for what they do and how well they do it, should be welcomed by the vast majority of those in the higher education community. Indeed, this principle could well cast in a different light institutional title or designation, whether college, institute, or university, especially with respect to resource allocation.

Let me pause again to re-emphasize this second example of a move from soft federalism to hard federalism. Before the 1987 restructuring, an implicit assumption was made by public institutions—all public institutions—about their eligibility for, indeed, right to, public funding. The introduction of the unified national system has required institutions to opt in to the system, and to address explicitly several policy issues as part of their case for federal funding. May I note that I have not developed the theme of institutional consolidations which also flows from the adoption of the unified national system (Dawkins, 1988a, 41-48; Ramsey, 1989). That the number of higher education institutions will have been reduced from 65 to about 35 by 1991 through amalgamations is little short of astonishing, especially as the legislative responsibility for the vast majority of them rests with the states and territories. The process was of course assisted by the federal government's allocation of $260 million for capital projects to facilitate amalgamations (Ramsey, 1989, Chapter 5).

The third component of the policy environment to have undergone major change relates to the declaration of system and institutional management and governance as a priority area. There was a clear view in the Green and White papers about the efficient and effective use of resources, and especially the need for more expert attention to management.

The concern with management finds expression at two levels: at the state and territory level, there have been established joint planning committees involving processes for consultation between federal and state or territory governments with respect to the articulation of state and federal priorities; and the governance of institutions, involving the role of councils, boards of governors and senates; of chief executive officers (whether vice-chancellors of universities, or directors or principals of colleges of advanced education or institutes of technology); and of internal, predominantly academic bodies such as academic senates, academic boards or professorial boards (Dawkins, 1987a, 50-53; Dawkins, 1988a, 102-104).

The federal concern with institutional governance, tempered as it is by the fact that, except in the case of the Australian National University, and the Canberra College of Advanced Education (now the University of Canberra), all operate under acts of the state or territory parliaments, is shared in the wider community. Thus, there is considerable confusion about what it is that governing bodies are supposed to do. The corporate sector, unions, and the community at large have expectations, as have politicians and public servants—and yes, members of the academic community as well. This is compounded by the fact that institutional governing bodies vary substantially in size and in composition.

If we focus on university governing bodies in Australia, we find that they are relatively large, some numbering in excess of 40 (the Australian National University Council comprises 44 members). Several of the revised University Acts in New South Wales provide for a governing body with fewer than 20 members, but in most Australian universities they have more than 20 members. They are thus considerably larger than boards of directors of corporations with budgets of comparable size and, as will be seen, they are quite different in composition as well. They usually include members *nominated* by government; *elected* by (i) a graduate body such as convocation; (ii) staff, academic and non-academic; (iii) students; (iv) one or other or both Houses of Parliament; *co-opted/elected* by council/senate/board of governors itself; and *ex officio* (e.g., vice-chancellor, president of student body, heads of selected government departments, etc). Some include observers, individuals from particular interest groups who may participate in discussions but normally who have no vote. Governing bodies typically include a majority of "external" members, that is, persons other than students or staff members (academic and general).

In Australian public universities, the "supreme" level of authority normally is vested in the council, senate, or board of governors. Such bodies act on reports and recommendations from a number of sources: the chief executive (normally the vice-chancellor); from the senior academic body to which faculties, schools and departments report; from bodies such as convocation; and from bodies specifically established by the council, senate, or board of governors (normally but not always through the vice-chancellor, who is the chief executive officer in fact, if not in name). They are the ultimate locus of authority and responsibility for academic, financial, legal and property matters, and they appoint (and have the power to dismiss) the chief executive.

The confusion arises through different views of the role of individual members. While membership can be a source of prestige to the incumbent and of patronage to those who nominate or elect, the governing body ought to be seen by the university community and by the polity and society as being composed of trustees for the institution, whose main role is advocacy rather than regulation. A different view of the governing body is that it consists of delegates, persons with a responsibility to represent a particular point of view and with an obligation to report back to the constituency. Clearly, these roles are mutually exclusive;

equally clearly neither one alone adequately characterizes the functioning of any governing body today.

A recent example of the delegate role is provided by some reactions to the composition of the board of governors of the recently established Charles Sturt University in New South Wales. The minister for education appointed two deans of schools to the board, only one of whom had been included in the list of nominations provided by the academic staff union. The union president said the two deans would have " 'management-orientated responsibilities' and the teaching staff would lose out . . . ." Of one of the deans, the president said ". . . he is appointed to the board as a dean, not as a *representative* of the 300 academic staff here . . . it is critical that we have a voice on the board during the period when the terms and conditions under which we are employed are established" (Bye, 1989; emphasis added). This characterization of the board as comprising union as distinct from management representatives focuses on board members as representatives of constituencies rather than as trustees for the institution. If I may digress briefly, academic unions in Australia have successfully claimed a role in academic policy making as well as in the familiar area of conditions of appointment and compensation. In my view, this confuses what I see as the dual identity of the academic staff member: the identity as an academic member of a department or school and faculty; and the identity as an employee. It is the former identity that ought to inform participation on governing bodies.

Many have seen this declaration of institutional management and governance as a priority area as the embodiment of an activist, interventionist stance by the federal government—or, to use my term, a move from soft federalism to hard federalism.

The fourth feature of the new policy environment relates to research funding, national research priorities, and a determination to increase the research resources allocated competitively against performance and capacity criteria, at both the individual and institutional level (Dawkins, 1988a, 89-94). This concern with research management was foreshadowed well before the publication of the White Paper in 1988. Indeed, it was very much a part of the interactions between the former CTEC and institutions, and it featured prominently in the *Review of Efficiency and Effectiveness in Higher Education* (1986). The federal government has identified effective research management as a central element in the achievement of its objective to maximize the productivity and quality of Australia's research effort. It is worth going into some detail about research because this is the area which has attracted the most sustained criticism from the research and higher education community.

Since the adoption of the White Paper, there has been: a challenge to the view that teaching and research are inextricably linked; an emergence of new systems of funding; a sharper sense of the real importance of research; and a growing appreciation that for relatively small countries like Australia, concentration and selectivity are essential in any national research policy. The key development to date has been the establishment of the Australian Research Council (ARC) as one of the four subsidiary councils of the National Board of Employment, Education and Training. This structure is contrary to the recommendation of the Australian Science and Technology Council (ASTEC, 1987), that the ARC be a statutory body; however, the ARC does report directly to the minister on allocations under the various research granting programs it administers. Only in policy and research priority matters does it report through the national board.

Aitkin (1989) has argued that the post-1986 changes are grounded on a drive to achieve concentration and selectivity in research. This in turn can be seen as a number of dialectics: from "process" to "product"; from "equality" to "excellence"; from "playing safe" to "risk taking"; from "amateur" to "professional"; from "collegial" to "managerial"; from "reaction" to "planning."

The national board approved a committee structure recommended by and for the ARC, which established committees on planning and review, institutional grants, research training and careers, and research grants. The predecessor body, the Australian Research Grants Committee (ARGC) effectively had only one of these, the research grants committee, which allocated funds on the basis of excellence, as judged by peer review (Aitkin, 1990). The ARC structure is partly a response to the increased range and variety of granting programs for which it is responsible. It also reflects a conviction that planning and review activities, for example, must be accorded a high priority along with the process of assessing research grant proposals in the national research environment of the 1980s and 1990s.

A related development in 1988 was the appointment by the minister of a committee to review higher education research policy (Smith, 1989). The committee's terms of reference were quite broad and addressed funding issues, personnel issues, higher education-industry interface issues, general process issues, and ARC-related process issues.

The government response to the committee's report included the allocation of additional infrastructure funds to stabilize at $45 million in 1992 along with the maintenance of the redirection of funds from the aggregate operating grant pool of pre-1987 universities as previously announced by the minister (Dawkins, 1988a, 83; Dawkins, 1988b, 28). The committee had argued that the redirection ($65 million in total) should be matched dollar for dollar by the new fund, especially as all of the new infrastructure funds might not find their way back to pre-1987 universities.

Two sets of recommendations on personnel issues should be noted. The first involved an increase in the number and level of stipend for Commonwealth Postgraduate Awards, and was adopted by the government, thus meeting at least some of the concerns that have been expressed about the need to attract able young scholars to research careers. The second contemplated the establishment of a system of national career fellowships. While the government declined to accept the recommendation as presented, it sought advice from the national board and the ARC on this matter. Recently, the minister announced the establishment of a modified career structure for researchers which provides potentially an 18-year path from the post-doctoral level to the senior fellowship level for full-time researchers.

The government noted the committee's statement on national research priorities to guide the ARC in formulating its advice to the minister on the allocation of research funds. That statement is consistent with the objectives of selectivity and concentration, and with the preservation and support of a substantial capacity for fundamental research within and across disciplines and fields of study. In developing a statement on priorities in research funding, the ARC takes the view that all programs funded through it should be seen as serving seven broad aspects of the public interest:

- the well-being and harmony of Australian society

- the understanding and advancement of human culture and values
- the advancement of Australia's geopolitical interests
- understanding and managing the environment
- furthering the contribution of research and education to society
- enhancing the nature and potential of the primary industries
- developing the science and technology underlying industrial development

The council's view is that three questions must be addressed if a given national need or problem is to be reflected in an ARC research priority area:

- does the need have a significantly long time scale?
- does the national need possess an obvious and important research and development or research training dimension?
- does that research and development dimension fit the council's essential role?

The council consults widely and openly through invited submissions as part of the process of developing priorities, before presenting them to the national board for adoption. In this activity, it is far more proactive than its predecessor—the Australian Research Grant Scheme—which is consistent with the move from soft to hard federalism.

The final feature of the new policy environment to which I would draw attention is the reintroduction of the principle of user-contribution or partial user-pay, through the Higher Education Contribution Scheme—otherwise known as HECS. Until the decision to abolish tuition fees was taken in the euphoria of the early 1970s Whitlam era the funding of higher education was a state responsibility, albeit with a steadily increasing federal contribution. From 1974 until 1989, no tuition fees were levied, and the entire funding responsibility for higher education institutions was assumed by the federal government.

The Green Paper argued the need for a massive expansion of places and of graduates, and canvassed the sources of funds that would enable the achievement of this objective (Dawkins, 1987a, Chapters 3, 10 and 11). Significantly, the final section of the

Green Paper entitled "Other Funding Sources," foreshadowed the establishment of a cabinet-endorsed committee—chaired by Neville Wran, a former Labour premier of New South Wales State—whose terms of reference included a charge to "develop options and make recommendations for possible schemes of funding which could involve contributions from higher education students, graduates, their parents and employers" (Dawkins, 1987, 87). Four months later the report of the Committee on Higher Education Funding was released (Wran, 1988). The report's acceptance by the Labour Party was, if tentative and reluctant, certainly more widespread than its acceptance by students and also by some of the academic unions. The federal government moved on to introduce legislation to establish the HECS effective January 1, 1989. It provides that each student enrolled in an award course in a higher education institution incurs a future "tax" liability; when the student's post-study earnings reach the level of average weekly earnings, the accumulated liability is recovered over a period of years. While its authority to do this flowed unambiguously from Section 96 of the Constitution, its determination to proceed against the wishes of a considerable body of public opinion—including significantly, many in the Labour Party itself, is further evidence of the emergence of hard federalism.

In summary, the new Australian policy environment for higher education involves changed advisory and program delivery arrangements; the establishment of a unified national system of higher education institutions in which all publicly funded institutions must seek membership; the declaration and pursuit of system and institutional governance and management as a priority area; a dramatically different set of structures and processes for research support; and finally, the reintroduction of the principle of user-contribution and partial user-pay, explicitly to establish a source of funds for a greatly expanded level of participation in higher education.

*****

Reflection on these features of the new policy environment suggests that a quickened concern with accountability is the source of the new dynamic. How then should higher education institutions deal with this new situation? In these concluding remarks let me share with you my answer to this urgent question.

The overriding challenge for any higher education institution in this new policy environment is to articulate its mission with clarity of purpose and to pursue it with vigour and commitment. I would argue that the mission of all higher education institutions is to foster creativity and responsiveness to change; to do this well, they must sustain and nurture a high quality learning and research environment. This statement of mission can and should be modified by the role statements of individual institutions, in which they declare their unique characteristics based upon their strengths and comparative advantages. On the basis of the role statement, the institution seeks to secure and preserve a niche in the higher education landscape. The associated deployment of resources reflects choices made by the institution. And as higher education institutions in Australia are supported overwhelmingly by the public purse, accountability has become of increasing importance in much of the recent policy debate.

This was expressed in relatively simple terms in a recently published survey of community attitudes to universities in Australia:

> The community does not really know whether universities are efficiently administered or not. Not surprisingly, this lack of knowledge is particularly evident among those groups with little or no contact with the system. Some suspect that there may be inefficiencies (as there are in large organizations) and feel that universities should be accountable for their spending because they are funded by the taxpayers. However, accountability is not seen to conflict with independence (ANOP, 1989, 28).

Walter Kamba, vice-chancellor of the University of Zimbabwe, made a very perceptive remark about public universities and public accountability during the Association of Commonwealth Universities Congress in Perth early in 1988:

> Some State control is inescapable; some institutional autonomy is indispensable; the challenge before us is to bring the legitimate consensus of the university and the

legitimate concern of the community into a rough and workable balance."

The achievement of this "rough and workable balance" should be the major preoccupation for higher education institutions everywhere, especially as the changed economic and political circumstances of the 1990s will inevitably require that we do more with less yet with no compromise in quality.

References

Aitkin, D., 1989. "Research and the Research Council," Octagon Lecture, The University of Western Australia, August 9, 1989.

Aitkin, D., 1990. "How Research Came to Dominate Higher Education and What Ought to be Done About it," Sir Christopher Ball Lecture Series, Leeds Polytechnic, May 3, 1990.

ANOP. *Community Attitudes to Universities in Australia: A Qualitative Research Report* (North Sydney: July 1989).

ASTEC, 1987. *Improving the Research Performance of Australia's Universities and Other Higher Education Institutions—A Report to the Prime Minister* (Canberra: ASTEC).

Bye, Clarissa. "Riverina Staff Threaten Action," *The Australian*, 26 July, 1989, 18.

CTEC, 1982. *Report for 1982-84 Triennium* (Canberra: AGPS).

CTEC, 1985. *Report for 1985-87 Triennium* (Canberra: AGPS).

CTEC, 1987. *Report for 1988-90 Triennium* (Canberra: AGPS).

CTEC, 1986. *Review of Efficiency and Effectiveness in Higher Education—Report of the Committee of Enquiry* (Canberra: AGPS).

Dawkins, J.S., 1987a. *Higher Education: A Policy Discussion Paper* (Canberra: AGPS).

Dawkins, J.S., 1987b. "Higher Education in Australia: Ministerial Statement," *Hansard—House of Representatives* (Canberra: AGPS), 460-466.

Dawkins, J.S., 1988a. *Higher Education: A Policy Statement* (Canberra: AGPS).

Dawkins, J.S., 1988b. *Higher Education Funding for the 1988-91 Triennium* (Canberra: AGPS).

DITAC (Department of Industry, Trade and Commerce), 1986. *Selecting Technologies for the Future* (Canberra: AGPS).

Hamilton, W.B., 1989. "Educational Policies and Federalism: Australia and Canada, 1920-1980," Chapter 11, 261-78 in Bruce W. Hodgins et al., editors, *Federalism in Canada and Australia* (Peterborough: The Frost Centre for Canadian Heritage and Development Studies at Trent University).

Johnson, R., 1990. "Past, Future and Open Learning," Chapter 6, 65-78 in Ingrid Moses, editor, *Higher Education in the Late Twentieth Century: Reflections on a Changing System* (Kensington, NSW: HERDSA).

Kamba, Walter, 1988. "Accountability of a National University System." Paper delivered to the meeting of Executive Heads of Commonwealth Universities, Perth, Western Australia, February, 1988.

Ramsey, G., 1989. *Report of the Task Force on Amalgamations in Higher Education* (Canberra: AGPS).

Smith, R.H.T., 1986. "Tertiary Education in Times of Change: A North American Model," *Journal of Tertiary Education Administration* 8(2), 139-49.

Smith, R.H.T., 1987. "The Binary System and Alternative Structures: Two North American Models," 85-99 in Edwin Kerr et al., editors *W(h)ither Binary? A Seminar on the Organization of Higher Education for the 21st Century* (Perth: WAPSEC).

Smith, R.H.T., 1989. *Report of the Committee to Review Higher Education Research Policy* (Canberra: AGPS).

Wran, N., 1988. *Report of the Committee on Higher Education Funding* (Canberra: AGPS).

I wish to acknowledge with gratitude the ready assistance of Charlotte Passmore and Gayle Smith in the Office of the Vice President (Academic) and Provost at UBC in the typing and final preparation of this paper at short notice.

Monitoring Performance in U.K. Universities

Ken Davies

Monitoring performance is a universal activity. Performance indicators pervade all societies. It was Molière's *Citizen turned Gentleman* who said that for more than 40 years he had been talking prose without knowing it. So it is with performance indicators—we've been using them all our lives but not calling them by that name. The terminology, but only the terminology, is new.

Indeed, performance indicators have been present from the beginning, or even before the beginning. God must have had his own performance indicators before creation. After each day of creating light and darkness, earth and water and so on he noted what he had done and "saw that it was good." The first recorded assessment of performance! (self-assessment of course, but only God can do that—mortals have to be assessed by somebody else).

I will be arguing that monitoring performance, including the use of appropriate performance indicators, should be regarded as an integral part of good management practice in any organization. Performance indicators are of equal, if not greater, value for internal use than they are for use by external agencies. It is not enough to be seen by others, or even to see ourselves as others see us; we need to see ourselves as we really are and performance indicators can help in this.

A formal start to performance measurement was made in the U.K. universities as long ago as the 1960s, i.e., long before the government took an interest. Studies were made and reports published on the use of teaching space and residential accommodation. Then in the 1969-70 academic year a major inquiry was conducted into the use of academic staff time—a study which has not been repeated, at least on a national scale, but whose results are still used as a factor in the allocation of resources. It was then up to each institution to compare and contrast their own situation as they saw the need. The information was, incidentally, supplied in an anonymous form.

The Political Imperative

Over the more recent years there has been a strong political imperative for U.K. universities to develop indicators relevant to their work. To a large extent, of course, this has meant defining and standardizing the sort of management information already in use in many institutions. Much of the pressure has been a result of government initiatives stemming from its "market place" philosophy of public sector activities, incorporating the concepts of value for money, accountability, efficiency, effectiveness. The civil service and the National Health Service have not escaped their own efficiency studies leading to the development of performance indicators. The report of the Steering Committee for Efficiency Studies in Universities, chaired by Sir Alex Jarratt and published in 1985, recommended:

> A range of performance indicators should be developed, covering both inputs and outputs and designed for use both within individual universities and for making comparisons between institutions.

The report saw the lack of a systematic use of indicators for resource allocation purposes as well as for management use as a major omission and therefore called for reliable and consistent performance indicators to be developed urgently both for individual universities and for the system as a whole. Then the University Grants Committee (UGC) in a letter to universities in the same year said:

Universities would increasingly be expected to be able to demonstrate that they are using their resources effectively and efficiently. To this end, it will be necessary for the UGC and the universities to develop and use appropriate indicators of performance for teaching, research and for provision of academic services.

A Green Paper, also published in 1985, stressed:

"The need to develop and use measurements of performance." These were considered to be "important for the internal management of institutions and for the development of a policy for the allocation of resources more generally."

The Committee of Vice-Chancellors and Principals (CVCP) took up the theme or the challenge on behalf of the universities in a statement on "The Future of the Universities" published in January 1986. The committee accepted that:

"the very great support ... [which universities] now receive from taxation, and the key role which they have come to play in national development imposes duties and obligations upon them" and we drew attention to "The development of reliable and consistent performance indicators as a key management information tool."

In May 1986 the then secretary of state, Sir Keith Joseph, made a statement in which he spelled out government's attitude to university funding and management in the context of that year's public expenditure survey. He spoke in the following terms:

"If we are to continue to improve the quality and effectiveness of our universities we must provide positive incentives to individual institutions for better management and better teaching and research."

He made it clear that additional financial provision would only be made if there were evidence of real progress in these areas. There was to be a direct *quid pro quo* between the provision of funding and the evidence of what the government regarded as "better management."

A higher profile was therefore needed for the kind of performance monitoring activities which already existed in universities, but had not been given much prominence.

The political imperative continues to be strong. There is a clear need to publish so as not to be damned.

Actions Taken by U.K. Universities and the University Grants Committee/ Universities Funding Council (UGC/UFC)

1. *Performance Indicators*

In 1985, the CVCP and the UGC set up a joint committee on performance indicators with terms of reference taken from the recommendation of the Jarratt committee which I quoted earlier.

> A range of performance indicators should be developed, covering both inputs and outputs and designed for use both within individual universities and for making comparisons between institutions.

The committee's first task was to examine the benefits of performance indicators and to survey what was already happening in universities. I would like to dwell for just a very short time on their conclusions concerning the use of indicators and how they might be developed.

The production of a set of common indicators is intended to bring a measure of consistency, reliability and above all credibility to performance monitoring. Professor John Sizer, in writing on the qualities of performance indicators, has said that they should be "relevant, verifiable, free from bias, quantifiable, economically feasible, and institutionally acceptable."

Even at the best of times—and we are far from those—universities' resources are relatively scarce and it is necessary not only to account for their use, but to be able to identify the strengths and weaknesses in the interests of effectiveness and efficiency, so that the inevitable exercise of choice can be well-informed. Performance indicators can assist in this task.

But it is *judgment* that counts in the end and must continue to do so. This is most important. It was stressed in the performance indicators committee's first report which stated categorically:

> The use of performance indicators is an *aid* to judgment and not a substitute for it.

In other words they are a means to strengthen peer review.

It was noted by the committee that, while performance indicators could be used to provide significant questions, they could not necessarily provide meaningful answers. The Jarratt report itself said that "inter-university comparisons should be treated with care but may at least lead to asking important questions."

If this is not constantly borne in mind both within and without universities there could be a real danger of performance indicators being slavishly followed, or being expected to be followed, at all costs. This would not only distort performance of the job in hand but also create a disincentive for innovation and change, both of which can and do require risky academic decisions. Performance indicators must therefore be evaluative rather than prescriptive, and their formulation and use should be undertaken in a positive way which encourages rather than inhibits those within the system. For them to become threatening would be totally counter-productive, and by threatening I mean endangering an attitude of mind that is so concerned about the possibility of adverse reports that it leads to excessive caution in order to avoid mistakes and evidence of apparent waste.

The committee divided performance indicators into three categories:

- *Input* indicators, which are concerned with the resources, human and financial, employed by universities

- *Process* (or operating) indicators, which relate to the use of resources by universities, to the management effort applied to the inputs and to the operation of the organization

- *Output* indicators, which relate to what has been achieved, i.e., the products of the university

Arguably output indicators are the most significant and the only true *performance* indicators but they are also the most difficult to define and develop for universities because of the intangible nature of the output. One of the criticisms of the committee's first statement was that it concentrated too heavily on input and quantitative measures as opposed to output and qualitative results. The reason for this approach was that the data for input measures, such as numbers of staff and students, were either already available or could be readily collected, and it was necessary to start somewhere.

At a later stage it was argued that input and process indicators were really only management statistics and so the annual volume which is now produced—and I have here the fourth edition which came out last month—is called "University Management Statistics and Performance Indicators in the U.K." I have available for you a copy of the contents page so that you can get some idea of our present range of data which is presented by the named university. We now have statistics over a five-year period. This is important as comparisons of departmental performance over time are much more useful than the single snapshot.

What, then, is the difference between a management statistic and a performance indicator? We see a performance indicator as something which compares accomplishment with intention—it provides evidence of achievement. Thus "successful leavers as a percentage of those ending their studies" is a performance indicator; but "computer services expenditure as a percentage of a total general expenditure" is a management statistic.

Management statistics and performance indicators are to do with the use of resources. They can also be classified, therefore, according to the generally accepted aims in the use of resources. These are:

Effectiveness: that is, how far the output achieves predetermined objectives. (It is possible to measure service performed as an indicator of effectiveness, e.g., student success rate, the example already given)

Efficiency: that is, output divided by the resources consumed, e.g., cost per graduate. (A *ratio*, not just a matter of cutting inputs)

Economy: that is, how actual input costs compare with planned or expected costs, e.g., the actual cost per graduate compared with planned cost per graduate

The dangers of misuse abound and for this reason the volume which we publish has "health warnings" in a general foreword with important notes and caveats attached to every table.

But I must stress again that a collection of performance indicators cannot in itself constitute a policy—it can only assist in policy formation if looked at in the context of objectives and priorities. We all know that universities are complex organizations with multiple objectives and functions so no one is pretending that it is a simple matter. Again it is essential that differences from the norm or average mean "better" or "worse," when all they really mean is "different." Indeed a particular academic department will surely *aim* to achieve differentiation in pursuing its own area of study.

Performance indicators can be likened to caricatures, which the dictionary defines as "a grotesque or ludicrously exaggerated representation." Nevertheless, a caricature has *some* truth in it and a collection of caricatures complement each other in building up a picture which is somewhat nearer to the truth than any one of them taken individually.

Some concerns have, of course, been expressed about the publication. Among those are the following:

- the difficulty of ensuring that like is compared with like, within, and more particularly between institutions, underlining a view that the same performance indicators cannot necessarily be used for both types of comparison

- the need to give due weight to local or regional factors, be they geographical, structural or economic

- the fear that concentration on the quantitative and the measurable may create "the illusion of certainty where certainty is impossible," and, as a corollary to this "there is a real fear that indicators that began as pure measures providing quantifiable information will become identified as averages and norms, and thence as standards to be achieved"

All this serves to reinforce the view that there is as much skill in the interpretation of data as in its presentation.

I will mention the development we now are planning in the area of performance indicators and management statistics in later sections of this paper.

The title of this paper is "Monitoring Performance in Universities." This embraces more than the use of performance indicators in the narrow sense and so I would like to describe other ways in which the performance of U.K. universities is monitored.

2. *Monitoring Financial Performance*

If universities are to be financially accountable and valid comparisons are to be made between their published accounts by those who have an interest to do so, a legitimate interest in their financial position, they need to have a uniform method of presenting their accounts. The CVCP published last year a *Statement of Recommended Accounting Practice* which had been "franked" by the U.K. Accounting Standards Committee. With effect from 1989-90 all universities have conformed to this common method of accounting practice.

U.K. universities are subject to five levels of audit:

1. The *National Audit Office* has the right of access to universities' accounts, and is empowered to conduct value for money studies (but they are excluded from commenting on academic matters).

2. Each university appoints *external auditors* to report on annual financial statements.

3. Each university is expected to set up its own *internal audit* as a service to management.

4. The *Universities Funding Council* (UFC) is required to ensure that universities have a sound system of internal financial and management controls and proper arrangements for internal and external audit.

5. The *Department of Education and Science* internal audit service may accompany the UFC auditors on visits to universities to check their methods—but not to undertake the actual examination of universities' accounts.

I would advise you to do whatever you can to ensure that you do not get into such involved and potentially overlapping systems— we are still arguing about the way in which the arrangements should operate!

Another important development proposed by the joint CVCP/UFC working group on performance indicators is a set of indicators on the financial health of institutions. These are currently with universities for comment. Let me give you three examples of the indicators under consideration:

- relating to sources of income; percentage ratio of overseas student fees increase to total income excluding depreciation

- relating to long-term strength and solvency; percentage ratio of long-term liabilities to total general funds

- relating to short-term liquidity and solvency; days of total income represented by debtors

Another development is a requirement of the UFC for financial forecasts by universities each year. The information asked for is the financial out-turn in the previous year, and a forecast relating to the current year and the next four years. Conclusions are drawn relating to the system as a whole and to individual institutions in order to note any university which appears to be in particular danger. A university seen to be potentially at risk is asked what steps it intends taking to rectify the situation, e.g., reducing staff numbers, increasing student numbers, expanding commercial research and other activities.

3. Monitoring Research Performance

The UFC has now completed two selectivity exercises, one in 1986 and one in 1989. The purpose was to assess the research qualities of all departments (cost centres) in all universities on a five-point rating scale using "informed peer review." Judgments were "output-led" and a considerable emphasis was placed on data about publications. The results of these exercises—which it is estimated incurred a total cost of £4 million and 36,000 man-days of staff time—is reflected in the grants given to institutions.

The UFC also reports each year to the secretary of state on the way in which universities themselves implement selectivity between academic departments in the use of their general funds for the support of research. In its latest annual report on the matter which was prepared in December 1989 the UFC looked at the facilities employed in universities for a management overview of the use of such resources, at research policy machinery (especially at departmental level) and the use of selectivity within departments. A few institutions (not named publicly) were judged to have made insufficient progress in this area.

The CVCP-UFC joint committee on performance indicators is working on the development of research indicators. Universities were asked to comment on the report which made proposals for the development of data bases that could be used for quantitative assessment of research. The work has been concerned so far exclusively with publications. Citation indices have been discussed but the level of criticism has been high.

4.   Monitoring Academic Standards

U.K. universities, as autonomous institutions, i.e., independent bodies existing for the most part under royal charters, are themselves responsible for the quality of the teaching and research and the standards of their degrees. The CVCP is confident that their academic standards are equal to the highest in the world but we accept that the procedures used for maintaining and monitoring the standards should be more public. Recognizing this, the CVCP set up a group in 1983 which was given the task of studying universities' methods and procedures for maintaining and monitoring academic quality and standards.

Reports have been published on recommended methods and procedures and on the work of external examiners. The latest development was the establishment on October 1, 1990, of an academic audit unit. The unit has been set up to run a program of academic audit covering all U.K. universities. Working its way round the universities, it will probably adopt the following procedure:

- briefing will be requested from the institution on the methodology used to safeguard academic standards
- visit by an audit team composed of academics seconded from other institutions
- a draft report from other institutions will be sent to the institution for comment
- final report to the vice-chancellor
- consideration by institution and encouragement for it to publish the report

- follow-up action

Particular mention will be made of the use of internal performance indicators and other management statistics used to inform judgments.

Briefing will be provided by the institutions on its systems for the safeguarding of academic standards.

Visits to institutions will be arranged by teams of auditors seconded from universities. The auditors will submit a draft report to the institution itself on the quality assurance mechanisms which they find in use. A final report will be sent to the vice-chancellor. Individual institutions will be encouraged to make their report publicly available and there will, of course, be follow-up action as necessary.

The unit was scheduled to be fully operational by Easter 1991, when a tested methodology based on the experience of completing three of four full audits was expected to be in place.

5. *Monitoring Teaching Quality*

The CVCP/UFC joint group on performance indicators has been under some pressure to take this matter forward but recognizes that there are considerable difficulties in the production of quantitative indicators, although some of the data already published could be of help. A form of extended peer review of teaching quality at departmental level has been suggested. There are difficulties in defining teaching quality and the initial focus might well be on the management of the teaching function. This is not a task for the academic audit unit. Research has been done on this matter and papers written and we are currently reviewing the literature—the real work lies ahead of us!

6. *Monitoring Staff Performance*

All performance monitoring consists directly or indirectly of monitoring staff performance. Without people there would be no performance to monitor.

In 1987 a requirement to introduce staff appraisal was associated with a pay settlement for academic and related staff (i.e., senior administrators and researchers). The CVCP prepared guidance on staff appraisal schemes which are now operating in all universities on a regular basis. Their objective is to improve the management efficiency of institutions by improving staff performance, to help individuals develop their careers, and to identify changes in the organization that would help performance.

Although not directly related to the staff appraisal exercises, for the past two years a part of each pay settlement has been set aside to reward exceptional performance. It is clear that such discretionary payments will continue to increase in scale. But this, of course, is only to introduce something which is already well established on this side of the Atlantic.

Conclusion

I have tried to outline the principal ways in which performance is formally monitored in British universities. Our universities have always been accountable but now they are more open to inspection than ever before.

Let me remind you of the action which has been taken in the United Kingdom. This has been in relation to:

- performance indicators
- financial performance
- research performance
- academic standards
- teaching quality
- staff performance

When I spoke of the political imperative in the United Kingdom I gave in relation to performance indicators two purposes of performance monitoring:

- to assist in the better management of institutions
- to assist resource allocation

I know that you are concerned about the second of these two purposes. You are right to be worried. There is a movement in the United Kingdom to separate off parts of the civil service into self-contained agencies. But, of course, they will not and cannot be self-funded, they will still depend upon central government for their resources. So performance will be monitored and measured—

no doubt even closer than before—and modern techniques make this much easier than it once was. The new managers will be subject to periodical reappointment or disappointment, and so on.

The U.K. universities were supposed to be set free, or at any rate more free, under the 1988 Education Reform Act. But the controls—or euphemistically performance indicators—are tighter than ever. I spoke of the danger of such measures distorting performance and acting as a disincentive for innovation and change. These can be developments which, to quote the cover of the program for this conference, "are not consistent with the nature and purpose of universities." We have always accepted the need for accountability; but accountability should not, indeed must not, equate with outside control. He who pays the piper may well seek to call the tune, but he must not be allowed to determine how the instrument shall be played.

There is a real danger, that much scrutiny is bad for a university's health. But the catch is that *we* need the money, *you* need the money, and this is the price that we have to pay for it. The only advice I can give is that if studies of efficiency have to be undertaken, or performance indicators introduced, volunteer to do it yourselves rather than let a government department or other external body do the work!

I came across a neat phrase the other day: "paralysis by analysis"—too much self-examination and especially examination by others at the expense of real work. We are very conscious that there is a real danger of this. We fully recognize the hazard well and are doing all we can to avoid it.

But perhaps, as I said at the outset, none of this is *really* new. Like Molière's gentleman, every one of us has been using the prose of performance indicators without knowing it.

The Development of Indicators in OECD Countries

Paul Le Vasseur

Many presentations about higher education begin with an overview of developments during the last few decades. But I think that, with only a few exceptions, the pattern of growth in higher education during the 1950s and the 1960s which was followed by a levelling off and the subsequent financial constraints imposed on higher education systems in the 1970s and 1980s is a common pattern across the OECD countries. So rather than dwell on the historical development of higher education systems, I thought it would be interesting to go back a bit and to look briefly at the historical development of performance indicators, which is the topic of this session, as reflected in the work of OECD's program on institutional management in higher education during these some 20 years.

The first study that the program commissioned when it was set up in 1969 was a survey of costs and resource use which was carried out by Professor Keith Legg, who was director of Manchester Polytechnic and then moved to Hong Kong where he was director of Hong Kong Polytechnic. The purpose of this study was to arrive at norms which could be used to determine resource requirements to meet the various growth rates in different OECD countries at that time. I found it interesting to look back on that study. Although averages were being sought from the different universities, such things as average costs, space utilization norms, class size, student-teacher ratios, the question as to whether the differences observed reflected efficiencies or inefficiencies in the systems really did not arise. And, therefore, there was no real concept of productivity in this study. Later, Jean Bénard, who is a French professor, undertook a study which was a systematic approach of cost analysis in eight French universities, one Swiss university, and two Belgian universities. The results of this study were presented at the first Institutional Management in Higher Education (IMHE) general conference in 1973. Here again, costs were analyzed but completely independently of performance considerations, and the desire was simply to know more about the cost components of different activities in the university. At this same general conference, however, the members chose as one of the priority areas for future research among our member institutions, means and methods of evaluating institutional performance. By the time we came to our next second general conference in 1975, Derek Birch, John Calvert, John Dockerill and Professor John Sizer presented the results of their work on the identification of performance indices for teaching activities. Also at that time, a German pilot study had been launched on performance indicators in which a number of universities compared the cost differences between the same faculties in their universities as an indication of the relative efficiencies of those faculties.

So by this time, from 1973 to 1975, work had definitely begun in what could be properly termed performance indicators; and, in fact, performance indicators continued to be discussed, both at IMHE general conferences as well as at several workshops which were devoted specifically to this topic.

I would now like to move up to more recent times. In 1984 it was decided that the time had come to launch an international survey, and IMHE was asked to do this. The purpose of this survey was to find out more about the development and use of performance indicators at that time. The survey focused on institutions because it was felt that performance assessment was essentially an institutional responsibility, and institutions were discussing the use of performance indicators as part of their decision making for purposes of allocating resources internally, and, more generally, for institutional self-evaluation and improvement. At that time, performance indicators were not really a high priority of governments in Europe. Even in the United Kingdom, they only began being spoken about widely as a result of their inclusion in a government Green Paper about one year after this survey was launched.

The situation is quite different today, and I'll come back to that. But I think it would be useful to review the results of this particular survey. We developed a rather detailed mail questionnaire to carry out the survey. A total of 70 institutions, mostly universities, responded to this survey. These institutions were in 15 different countries. Over 700 citations of performance indicators in use were recorded in the replies we received, and the results of the survey were published and reported on in the July 1987 issue of the IMHE journal. I would like to summarize them now.

For purposes of the survey, the performance indicators were defined as "numerical values which provide a measurement for assessing the quantitative and qualitative performance of a system, and which can be derived in different ways." Four categories of indicators were distinguished, and a few examples of indicators within each of these categories were given to help respondents answer the questionnaire. The first category was for internal performance indicators, and these were indicators based on information available within the institution. Examples of these would be success rates, graduate rates, and average length of study. The next category was for operating indicators, which described aspects of the internal functioning of the system; examples were student-staff ratios, unit costs, and class size. The next category was for external performance indicators, which were based on information available outside the institution; examples of these might be the acceptability of graduates in employment, and reputation as judged by external observers. And finally, we had indicators that were related specifically to research and were used to assess research activities in institutions. These would be, for example, citation indices, the share of contract research, and the number of dissertations accepted.

I would like now to summarize the main conclusions of this particular survey. The first thing noted was that indicators were being used to a widely varying degree in the different countries that were covered. Second, we also found that the concept of a performance indicator needed to be defined more precisely; that all too frequently there was confusion about the meaning of a

performance indicator. Third, indicators were used primarily for
the allocation of human and financial resources within an
institution, but also, to some extent, for student planning and for
decisions about courses to be taught. We found that indicators
were often used informally in decision making to prove or to
disprove an opinion or a point of view. Next, institutions were
found to provide a rather vast array of raw data, as well as
indicators, to their supervisory authorities, but they were somewhat sceptical about the usefulness of all this information. Finally
there was, however, some measure of agreement about what
indicators were the most important in relations with outside
bodies.

In a recent contribution on "Accountability in Higher
Education" in Philip Altbach's forthcoming *International Encyclo-
pedia of Comparative Higher Education*, Klaus Hüfner of Germany
said the following about this survey, and I quote: "In sum, it can be
said that the IMHE survey contributed to the transparency of the
problematique of the use of performance indicators in order to
increase accountability in higher education. In some countries, for
example, Australia, Germany, the Netherlands, and the United
Kingdom, the IMHE survey contributed per se to the political
discussion about performance indicators in higher education."
Hüfner then illustrated this point by describing developments in
the United Kingdom, which we have heard about from Ken
Davies.

At a meeting in Paris in December 1986 to discuss the results
of this survey, along with other developments in performance
indicators in the OECD countries, it was generally agreed that
progress in this field was not so rapid as to warrant continued work
at the international level. Rather, it was suggested that more time
be allowed for work to advance on a national level before undertaking further international studies of this kind. This conclusion,
however, probably underestimated the rapid growth of interest by
governments in performance indicators, and by 1989 our directing
group was asking the secretariat to take up this topic once again.
They felt that there really was a need for somebody to monitor
developments internationally because more and more governments were beginning to show an interest in developing performance indicators as an aid to decision making for central

administrations. The IMHE program, therefore, set up a new study project on performance indicators, which is continuing.

The first meeting of this project group was held at Danbury Park Management Centre in the United Kingdom in January, 1990, and a second meeting in November, 1990. Twelve countries participated in that project: Australia, Austria, Canada, Denmark, Finland, France, Germany, Greece, the Netherlands, Norway, Sweden, and the United Kingdom.

Now although institutions in most of these countries had replied to our survey five years earlier, the difference now was really that interest had shifted to the governmental level. And I would like to examine some of the trends that brought about this shift.

First, in recent years, governments have come to feel a need for better information about higher education institutions. And this has led, in a number of countries, to the establishment of common data bases among universities.

Second, in many countries, governments have given greater autonomy, as we have heard, to institutions, sometimes through the introduction of a policy of contractualization. This means that government financing will be provided on the basis of targets, which will be set by the institutions themselves, and institutions will be free to decide on the day-to-day decisions to be made to achieve these targets. As we heard earlier from Professor Watts, in terms of continental (European) universities at least, this is somewhat of a radical departure in giving freedom to institutions to decide how they spend their money. The results will be evaluated by governments on an *ex post* basis. And of course it is this that drives the need for some sort of indicators agreed upon by the institutions and the governments as a means of this evaluation.

Third, a number of governments are asking institutions as part of changes in the methods of financing these institutions to submit medium-term plans, roughly from three to five years. Once again, this involves target setting by the institutions, which are also expected to put in place measures for introducing quality control and activity auditing.

Next, there is a general desire on the part of central authorities for more competition among institutions of higher education. In some countries, new national evaluation bodies have been set up. For example, in France there is the Comité nationale d'évaluation; there is a new inspectorate in the Dutch ministry of education and science which did not exist two years ago. Finally, in a number of countries, actual study groups on performance indicators have been set up at the national level. The task of these groups is to suggest performance indicators that could be used by governments for purposes of decision making and resource allocation.

All these trends, of course, have combined to put pressure on the different governments in the OECD countries to develop performance indicators for the higher education sector. The country statements submitted to our January meeting have been edited by Professor Herb Kells. He edited these in the form of a compendium which describes the current developments in 11 of these 12 OECD countries. Obviously, there is not time to summarize developments country by country. But some general observations can be made from the composite picture which emerges from the country statements in this compendium.

First, there has been a substantial development in this area over the last two years in most European countries. This development clearly reflects the importance of national and cultural settings. By that I mean the way in which performance indicators are dealt with in different countries will vary from country to country, and will be a function of the national setting in that country and certain related cultural aspects. The political agenda of governments figure very strongly in this work, particularly in terms of the balance between the forces of public accountability, institutional autonomy, and the so-called market in higher education.

There is a wide variation among consumers of performance indicators information in terms of their needs and the use to which they put indicators in different countries. Institutions are rather concerned about the emerging relationship between performance indicators and funding mechanisms, and, in fact, by the political dynamics to which it gives rise within institutions and between institutions and governments. There is a growing interest in well-defined goals for institutions and for systems of higher education, as a means of stimulating institutional change through institutional self-regulation.

Next, government requests for three- to five-year institutional development plans require more sophisticated monitoring processes than at present. There is also a widespread concern as to the adequacy of management information systems to sustain performance indicators. Making progress on this is a major priority and will be a shared activity between funding agencies and the institutions themselves. Although there is some satisfaction with progress on indicators related to research, much work apparently remains to be done in the areas of teaching, finance, and in public service indicators.

And finally, there is a great concern about the publication of indicators for comparing institutions and for ranking institutions. Clearly, various parties use such comparisons for their own purposes and it is felt that a lot more has to be known before one can use these in a neutral fashion. The debate about performance indicators, of course, is only beginning in Europe, as it is here. And clearly it is destined to continue for some time. During the last meeting of the American Education Research Association (AERA), which was held in Boston last April, several sessions focused on the development of educational indicators. Alan Gibson, who is with the Department of Education and Science in the United Kingdom, was asked to review these sessions for the OECD. One of the things he noted was the optimism of the central policy officials who see education indicators as a positive and constructive force for raising standards, for enabling progress to be monitored and measures for improvement to be targeted. He contrasted this with the scientific community's warnings about the difficulties involved in introducing education indicators and the limitations on their trustworthiness. He questioned whether the scientists were setting unrealistic, research-laden standards of validity and reliability which might be inappropriate to the levels of confidence needed for simple broad strategic planning and monitoring. On the other hand, they may be right to demand contextual and descriptive data which are complex enough to enable practical remediation and prescription. Maybe the debate over indicators simply reflects a change as to what is to be considered to be quality in education. The prime criterion of educational success may be shifting from that of emancipator of individual talent to that of generator of economic prosperity, along the lines of the instrumentalist view we heard from Professor Watts. The wide interest in performance indicators may simply be a signal that human capital formation has finally eclipsed personal enrichment as the principal motivator of educational activity in each country. These, of course, are some questions of a more fundamental kind which you may wish to ponder during the next two days. It is, of course, difficult to anticipate the final outcome of the national debates. But I think it can be said already that the introduction of performance indicators is a major decision of educational policy which will have important implications for the future goals and for the future organization of national higher education systems.

Synthesis of Commentary and Discussion following Davies and LeVasseur Papers

The discussion on the Davies and LeVasseur papers began with a commentary by Dr. Guy Steed of the Science Council of Canada. Following is a summary of his comments.

These are exciting times for higher education in Western Europe and North America—too exciting and perilous for some, perhaps, with higher education reeling in a state of ferment and seen by many as ripe for bold experimentation. During the 1980s we were witness to the combination of decaying infrastructures, rising enrolments, growing pressures for drastic budget reductions, and the evolution of strong disillusionment in some countries with higher education performance. Universities were increasingly perceived in many cases as not measuring up, as not generating the desired quality, nor providing value for money. One approach to dealing with this problem of accountability is the development of performance indicators.

In the OECD countries, an evaluative ethic has emerged with strong emphasis on the development and use of performance indicators, and these indicators have been used quite extensively in the United Kingdom and the Netherlands. The use of performance indicators in the United Kingdom, as Ken Davies pointed out, has contributed in recent years to important shifts in the method of allocating resources among British universities and to preferred management systems and controls. In the Netherlands, state bureaucracies are in charge of helping to establish priorities and conditions on research funding, and setting framework conditions for state-controlled competition, without infringing on a system with a long-standing and highly-valued tradition of academic freedom and institutional autonomy. As outlined in the most recent OECD publication on performance indicators, the Netherlands government is moving toward bilateral consultations, using in-depth discussion with each higher education institution about its mission and performance as a means of stimulating institutions to anticipate future challenges, make their mission explicit, and make strategic choices.

Performance indicators have thus become relatively central to the relationships between governments and universities in such countries as the United Kingdom and the Netherlands, and the question arises whether the seemingly innocent objective of monitoring performance may generate circumstances leading to more government intervention, as some fear, or whether performance indicators are simply a matter of great advantage for internal managerial use? Is the very concept of performance indicators too strongly marred by an association with dominance and control? Or indeed is the realistic alternative even more dominance and control?

I do not intend to focus my remarks on the specific strengths or weaknesses of particular performance indicators, but rather to make four general points.

First, the development of performance indicators certainly has been long, but it is, in fact, still really in its infancy. And those for research are far more advanced than those for teaching and assessing how much students learn. This is unfortunate, not only because of the interdependence of research and teaching, but because of the importance of demonstrating good teaching as part of public accountability.

Second, performance indicators involving input, process, output, and outcome measures have been developed in an attempt to assess and justify the use of resources and institutional performance in terms of economy, efficiency, and effectiveness. Useful as these measures are, they have to this point looked only at the past, not to what is being aimed at, and they need to be linked to mission and to future opportunity. There are also dangers in viewing and interpreting any of them in isolation, particularly since many of the performance goals that they reflect may themselves be in conflict. This conflict may be between the short run and the long run, and within institutions the pressures for efficiency in the short run need to be balanced against actions that will contribute to organizational effectiveness in the long run.

My third point concerns the use of performance indicators at higher levels of aggregation and for institutional planning. It is difficult to make sense of performance measures in the aggregate for an institution, particularly measures of long-term effectiveness. Assessing such effectiveness assumes the availability of comparable data at least between institutions and over time, to show trends. It also presumes some reasonably explicit generation of institutional missions and system goals and strategy. In this regard, some British universities have made quite original efforts when confronted with the clear need for strategic planning. They have used performance indicators to establish their strengths and weaknesses in the relative performance of departments to help in the process of selective reallocation of resources away from perceived weaknesses toward areas of strength or promise. An example is the use of a policy directional matrix by the University of Strathclyde. This involved a matrix using eight internal and three external performance indicators, and some of these external performance indicators came from the Scottish Development Authority and were defined in terms of regional goals. This information was central to preparation of the university's rolling five-year plan.

My final comment is that recent European experience in refining the development and use of performance indicators may prove increasingly helpful for North Americans to learn from, although we must obviously remain mindful of differences in approaches to management, degrees of university autonomy, and public policy objectives. It seems clear to many prominent American and Canadian academic leaders that our universities, particularly the major research universities, are facing a fundamental transformation as they move into the next century. They face a strong external driving force for assessment and institutional accountability. Debate about the quality of higher education in North America has intensified, with growing concern expressed about value for money as well as the usual balancing of quality as a policy goal against equality of access and equity variously defined. With education primarily a provincial responsibility, it is likely that provincial governments in Canada will find the developments in performance indicators of greatest interest in their attempt to achieve declared goals and objectives. But then, of course, which provincial governments in Canada have actually declared reasonably explicit goals? Consumers and taxpayers will no doubt continue their pressure on institutions of higher education to provide increased access, to substantiate that they are delivering what they promise, and to try to erase any significant gap between the rhetoric and the reality of higher education performance. So management and faculty in these institutions are likely to find it to their advantage collectively to support development and application of any meaningful performance indicators, especially results-oriented outcome performance measures which are being increasingly extensively used in the United States to justify access to scarce resources. Indeed, if ever the managers of higher education needed to monitor performance and track progress as a matter of routine, then now is the time, when budgets are tight and difficult choices must be made. But then in the current environment, what do you do with poor performers? The European experience with performance indicators should help us to identify what is useful, get rid of what is unnecessary and irrelevant, and try to ensure that such indicators are used sensibly and wisely, essentially to sustain a constructive dialogue in the way that the Dutch, for instance, have done, as a means to better informing decisions and aiding judgments. I confess to some doubts about the case, as argued in the U.K. chapter of the most recent OECD document, that performance indicators are best interpreted and employed by the managers who can influence their outcomes. There is a question here of guarding the guardians, I think. What is beyond doubt is that uncritical or superficial use of performance indicators could radically change incentives and damage the quality of universities in Canada.

Several themes emerged in the ensuing discussion.

First, there was general agreement that performance indicators were an aid to, not a substitute for, judgment and decision making, that they were more helpful in posing questions than in providing answers. There was also agreement that they would be more helpful to both government and universities if they were viewed constructively and positively as a means of improvement in university management rather than in a threatening or negative way as a means of identifying deficiencies. Common ground emerged among all participants in the workshop that performance indicators should be developed internally by universities to the greatest extent feasible, and that governments and universities should seek to avoid multiple layers of external auditing.

Second, there was considerable discussion on whether the increasing interest in performance indicators was related to, or represented in some sense a substitute for, the role of market forces in signalling university performance. It was noted that some of the performance indicators used, for instance, in the United Kingdom and the OECD volume, directly reflected the responsiveness of universities to market forces—contract research income was the most obvious example, but changing enrolment patterns could also be seen in this light. Performance indicators were seen then essentially as supplementing the signals provided by the market, but also as providing information that the market would not reflect on such matters as the preservation of knowledge and skills, and specific information on the efficiency of university management. The question arose whether performance indicators had had the effect of steering students or faculty toward universities considered to be relatively good. The response from Ken Davies and Paul LeVasseur was that there was no indication to this point that students had been heavily influenced by such information, but that some such effects at the margin were both likely and desirable in the longer run. It was pointed out that the Government of the Netherlands had shown an interest in putting performance indicator information in the hands of students with a view to influencing their choice of programs and institutions, and some debate ensued on whether this represented appropriate use or abuse of performance indicator information. The general sense of the meeting was that such external uses of performance indicator information were almost inevitable in the longer run, and that universities should respond by endeavouring to ensure that the performance indicators in question were valid and reliable measures of performance in teaching, research, and public service.

Third, there was lengthy discussion on the use to which performance indicator information could and should be put. It was generally agreed that such information would serve university management, but that the focus of the debate was on external accountability, and therefore on the use of performance indicators as a vehicle for a dialogue between governments and universities. There was agreement that universities should not wait for the script of this dialogue to be given to them, but should themselves play the major part in designing the performance indicator information which was to sustain the dialogue. Indeed, the view was expressed that universities should recognize the inevitability of such information being used in the dialogue with governments on funding, and should pay more attention to the design of indicators that would interest and even persuade government and serve universities in general in their competitive bid for a share of total public funding and, perhaps, set one university against another in their bids for a share of funding. It was pointed out that universities should recognize that their cause would best be served by providing governments with consistent information using common definitions across universities to provide information that was a valid and reliable reflection of the university sector as a whole, and provided valid and reliable comparative information on the performance of individual institutions within that sector.

It was noted that indicators designed for dialogue between government and universities are often interpreted to mean that governments value some types of behaviour, and therefore provide incentives to institutions seeking to persuade government funders to make these indicators look as favourable as possible. It was agreed that the incentive effects were very important, and therefore that universities not only should take responsibility for designing indicators, but should also ensure that these indicators were consistent with what universities were actually trying to achieve.

An important use of performance indicators in the financial management area which emerged from the experience in the United Kingdom was the identification of institutions in which financial management was seriously deficient. A particularly serious case in the United Kingdom was identified, and there was agreement that university autonomy had to be consistent with demonstrated competence at least in basic financial management and probably across a wider set of measures of performance. There seemed no disagreement with the view that government funders were entitled to interfere in the affairs of universities if evidence emerged of financial incompetence.

There was some discussion of the question that too much should not be made of institutional autonomy, but rather of the necessary autonomy for individual scholars. There was agreement that university administrators playing their proper role as servants of scholars for whom they were responsible could best preserve the autonomy of scholars to pursue research of their choosing and be social critics if necessary, by the careful design of performance indicators and by participation in a constructive dialogue with government on the use of these indicators.

Finally, discussion of the question of individual and institutional autonomy led to some discussion of what lessons Canadian universities and governments should take from experience in the United Kingdom and in other OECD countries. Paul LeVasseur emphasized the important differences between the experience of universities in the United Kingdom and those in continental Europe. The increasing emphasis on performance indicators has coincided with a perceived reduction in the autonomy of institutions in the United Kingdom, but with a considerable increase in the autonomy and delegated authority of institutions in most continental European countries. There was a sense that the increasingly decentralized continental European model offered an interesting analogy for Canada, and some sense that the Council of Ministers of Education in Canada might play a coordinating role among provinces not unlike that played by the OECD in Europe.

III

Universities in Canada:
Pressures and Responses

University Response in Canada: A Proposed Approach

James Cutt

Economists always make forecasts like members of a rowing crew—rushing into the future looking backwards—but let me nevertheless begin with a couple of punts on the future with which there will probably be little disagreement.

First, the 1990s are going to be an extremely difficult, unstable, and testing period for Canada, constitutionally, politically, and economically. Perhaps the only safe bet is that, however one defines nation, some national government or other will begin to take drastic measures to come to terms with the deficit that reflects our fiscal profligacy over the last two decades.

Second, the role of universities has never been more important than it will be in this difficult period. The educated and trained people (human capital) and information derived from research (intellectual capital) produced by universities in cooperation with its various constituencies—governments, industry, students—will be decisive to the success and the civility with which Canada deals with the period of change.

In short, I am predicting tough times ahead, critically scarce resources, and a vital role for universities.

Are universities ready for the challenge? Well, the circumstances are not at first blush auspicious.

First, universities face the challenge with their resources, and perhaps their will and enthusiasm, stretched thin by two decades of funding which by any standards has not kept pace with the demand for their services by students and other constituents.

Second, universities in Canada as elsewhere face a serious loss of faith in the self-regulatory model of university funding and external governance by which, essentially, universities are given resources and autonomy to use them as they see fit. The pressures on universities have taken many forms. General and specific restrictions and conditions on funding, proposals for alternative funding models which, for instance, would provide all or a larger proportion of funding directly to students, and increasing resort to alternative avenues of post-secondary education and research, appear to reflect concerns by public funding agencies, industry, and students, that are related to both perception and fact. On the one hand, universities are perceived rightly or wrongly to have performed inadequately, in some sense, because of the limited information that they provide externally about their plans and results; this is a question of incomplete accountability, or perhaps marketing, broadly defined, to constituencies. On the other hand, concerns reflect, first, the general reluctance of universities to introduce modes of governance, and management systems, controls, and practices, particularly in the core functions of teaching and research, which provide reasonable assurance of quality and good husbandry, second, the generally categorical rejection by the university sector of proposals for alternative funding models and third, the relatively arthritic competitive response of the university sector to alternative innovative models of teaching and research.

Third, as they look back over two decades, universities in Canada can establish fairly quickly that things to this point could have been much worse. Tough as funding restraints have been, Canadian universities have experienced less severe general funding restraints than universities in the United Kingdom, Australia, and New Zealand, and, more important, unlike universities in these other countries, have experienced relatively little additional financial limitations on autonomy (earmarking of funds, contracting of services) or accountability requirements (detailed reporting, external broad-scope audit). But how have Canadian universities reacted to the relatively mild additional financial controls and accountability requirements visited on them? The general answer, I think it must be said, is that the response has been one of reluctant acquiescence at best, and certainly one that has been reactive to external initiatives. There has been little evidence of any willingness to lead the debate and shape the agenda of change.

So the last two decades have been a period of scarce resources, loss of external confidence, general funding limitations, some additional pressures in the form of increased controls and accountability requirements, but little evidence that universities are willing to respond positively to these new pressures. In the light of these two difficult decades, what mood seems to be abroad in Canadian universities at the beginning of the 1990s? Well, the mood seems to suggest both short memories and short-sightedness. Reflecting a couple of years of slightly easier times, a new mood of optimism is abroad. There appears to be a relatively widely held view among Canadian university administrators that the new federal interest in human resource development and concerns about international competitiveness will loosen the general purse strings and, further, that universities have succeeded in stalling or diverting approaches to reducing their autonomy or increasing their accountability, that, indeed, they have won this battle, and can get back to business as usual.

So that brings us to the 1990s. Is this new mood of optimism justified? The first point in the balance of my argument is that it is not. The argument is that uncertainties with respect to Established Programs Financing arrangements place general funding levels in serious jeopardy; and, that, with respect to specific direct controls, and deflecting experience elsewhere, Canadian universities may have won a skirmish or two, but could well lose the war. In short, the present situation can more accurately be described as a lull before the storm than as a return to business as usual.

In the absence of new, more positive initiatives by universities, there could be a storm with the following characteristics: first, the enforcement by government or its agents (such as legislative auditors) of reduced autonomy and increased accountability; and second, the development of a variety of alternative approaches to the traditional post-secondary model in Canada. These alternative approaches, which are obviously not mutually exclusive, include the following: first, alternative modes of public financing such as vouchers to students, or increased subsidies, direct and indirect, to existing or new private post-secondary institutions; second, radical reductions in financing through traditional channels, reflecting, say, the withdrawal of the federal government from financing post-secondary education; third, the growth of market-oriented alternatives in the private post-secondary institutional sector, involving innovation, entrepreneurship, and the development of alternative education services; fourth, post-secondary education and training within private and public organizations as an alternative to reliance on traditional institutions; and fifth, the contractual assembly of post-secondary educational materials and services, both nationally and internationally.

But a lull before the storm is also a window of opportunity. What initiatives by universities might make some of these changes less likely or less serious?

Universities should look, I would argue, at changes in two areas: first, changes in accountability—information provided externally about what they plan to do and have done; and second, changes in systems of governance and management.

First, with respect to accountability, the argument is that an active, cooperative response to external concerns about information will enable universities to shape the information agenda to their advantage—at the very least, having it reflect reasonably accurately their circumstances and performance—and to control its evolution. Further, active cooperation would be likely to reduce the severity and frequency of both prospective conditions on funding and retrospective reporting and auditing requirements, and might even—by demonstrating in a very competitive public sector that what is spent is well spent—contribute to more generous relative funding levels for universities. This last observation is based on the premise that much of the expectations gap— the gap between what external funders want and what they perceive universities to be doing—reflects the inability or unwillingness of universities to provide thorough and useful information on what they are actually doing. It is also very likely that the information presently collected internally can, suitably adjusted and wrapped, satisfy many of the external demands, but that some creative new information will also be necessary.

What form should this active, cooperative response take? The legitimate concerns of funders on accountability can be met by the development by universities, in consultation with funding agencies and possibly also external auditors, of a framework of strategic planning and budgeting which tells funders what they intend to do, and a matching framework, first, of internal monitoring to serve management and, second, of external reporting which tells funders what has been achieved. There are obviously many alternative configurations for the matching budgets and annual reports. What is critical is that they be prepared by university management. They are thus, respectively, statements of management intentions, and management representations on achievements. The role of the external auditor with respect to management representations on achievements—and conceivably also on statements of management intentions—is to attest to and therefore lend credibility and support to these statements. The monograph which I produced at the Institute for Research on Public Policy and which has been handed out at this conference suggests a framework of reporting which is a variation on the theme of the 12 attributes proposed by the Canadian Comprehensive Auditing Foundation.

This argument is based on the premise that meaningful and useful information of the sort required for prospective budget submissions and retrospective reporting can be produced by universities. There has been major progress in Europe on the development of approaches to evaluation and performance indicators for universities, particularly in the area of efficiency in resource utilization; so there is not much doubt that progress can be made here. But can management representations be made about the central purposes of universities—about activities and achievements in the difficult and complex areas of teaching, research, and public service? Indeed they can. But the performance indicators will be primarily descriptive and qualitative, they will take time to develop thoroughly, and the task can only be done by senior university managers who understand the subtlety and complexity of the objectives and operations of universities. It is really a classic case for the management representations approach to accountability. It amounts in essence to telling the story, and then looking to auditors to give that story credibility. It is certainly also true that the information produced will be a far better representation of the university story if universities produce it themselves, than if it is produced by external agencies of one sort or another.

Second, with respect to the other suggested dimension of change, the argument runs that in the light of experience abroad, universities should consider changes to modes of governance, and to management systems, controls and practices, which would serve their internal accountability requirements and at the same time provide reasonable assurance to funders of quality and good husbandry, promote a more innovative response to competitive models of teaching and research, and provide a more rational framework for response to proposals for alternative funding models.

There is one important observation, perhaps qualification, that should be made with respect to reforms in these two areas of accountability and governance. In both areas the necessary improvements in the use of inputs—efficiency and resource utilization—should not be purchased at the expense of the quality of outputs—effectiveness in teaching, research, and public service. The maintenance and improvement of quality should drive the whole exercise if universities are to make the contribution they must make to the difficult 1990s. Quality can also, of course, be affected by other policies imposed on or elected by universities with respect, say, to student access or so-called equity in hiring, and universities would do well to implement these policies with a careful eye on quality. The enemy is often internal.

To conclude, universities are too important for Canada in the 1990s, and too vulnerable in their present condition, to be funded, governed, and managed in the traditional manner. Universities are accepting and should accept constraints on traditional autonomy, but an acceptable framework of constrained autonomy—one which retains the essence of the self-regulatory model—can be negotiated provided universities address the accountability issue and the question of changes to modes of governance and management systems. The ball is in the court of Canadian universities. There is enough international evidence around to suggest some alternative courses of action. The question is whether universities have the vision and will to adopt them. They will be both more comfortable and more successful if they do.

Synthesis of Commentary and Discussion following the Cutt Paper

The discussion on the Cutt paper began with a commentary by Dr. Christopher Hodgkinson of the Faculty of Education at the University of Victoria. Following is a summary of his comments.

I generally subscribe to the thesis of the Cutt paper that Canadian universities take seriously the question of external accountability in order to preserve the autonomy they need to do their job well. I would, however, like to mention four major concerns, and then give a concrete illustration from the marketplace of how quality gets subverted by quantity.

My first major concern is that there is something peculiar about universities, something which has to do with their intrinsic nature that requires them from time to time to bite the hands that feed them. One of the greatest functions of the university is to criticize the political and social culture of the day; indeed in the long run, in the very long run, this may be the most important purpose of the institution. Michael McCrum, the vice-chancellor of Cambridge, has described this as the primary source of stress between universities and government. But there is an overarching mastership and servantship relationship here, and in the last analysis both government and the academy are servants of the people. This delicate, but profound, master-servant relationship and its implications for institutional ownership should not be obscured by the over-simplistic paymaster model. There is a very complex symbiosis here which could be damaged by too forceful demands for the spelling out and cashing out of value for money, or the superimposition of ever more quantitative managerial controls. The ownership in this case, the people, perhaps ought to be prepared to accept as part of the freight a certain measure of inefficiency, ineffectiveness, and at times, perhaps outright chicanery.

My second concern relates to Jim Cutt's specific proposal for a rather elaborate accountability reporting matrix. My concern is with the problem of homogenetic fallacy. The author may not recognize that a dollar's worth of principle value might not be the same either in degree or in kind as a dollar's worth of cost-benefit analysis, or a dollar's worth of sentiment. The cells in his complex matrices may indeed provide information not now provided, although the means of quantifying the qualitative are not spelled out. But will that information ultimately darken rather than enlighten understanding? Worse still, could it become merely fallacious pseudo-information?

Third, I would like to pursue this matter of quantifiability. While the demand for quantification is as fitting for the accountant or the econometrician as is the bracketing of emotion for the logician or the engineer, do any of these attitudes serve the university well? A university is committed to an educational function which is at the very least ambivalent, but one part of which can be referred to as enlightenment, the enhancement of knowledge, and the other part of which we can refer to as 'credentialling,' in which mode, of course, the university becomes the very apex of the vocational school system. So how can we explain the survival of Classics, which has no economic justification? All these sorts of things do not now and may never yield to ascribed quantitative values, weights, and rankings without damage to their essential meaning. Man is not yet totally a machine, although he is getting there. Moreover, better dockets of 'quantitrivia' may stifle intellectual life rather than support and stimulate it as the author doubtless intends.

My last major concern, of course, is that the proposal for new evaluation triggers ancient alarms. Who are going to be the new guardians? Whence their credentials? And what is to prevent their succumbing to the worst kinds of bureaucratic behaviour? Who will guard the guardians?

I would like to end on the promised illustration of the marketplace from my own sub-discipline. In educational administration, we have demands placed upon us to provide programs of rigour at the graduate level. Organizations such as the Ontario Council on Graduate Studies, for example, increasingly want students to engage in thesis-type work and to do rigorous graduate undertakings of various kinds. At the same time, these students come from a marketplace where the demand is for credentials rather than enlightenment, and where within this marketplace, in the profession of teaching, one credential is as good as another.

The upshot is that we have American academic entrepreneurs willing to offer soft-option courses leading to credentials and masters' degrees and even to offer to teach these courses on the very campuses where we are seeking to maintain standards and rigour. So here is a paradox of conflicting demands; and the way things are going the marketplace seems to be winning.

So these are my major concerns: how do you reconcile quantification with quality on the one hand, and qualification on the other?

Several themes emerged in the ensuing discussion.

First, there was some discussion about the assumptions underlying the Cutt paper. The first general point was made in terms of the author's having read the entrails incorrectly, or if he had read them correctly, having perhaps found them in the wrong chicken. Specifically, the point was made that the argument had captured a number of trends which had clearly been in operation over the last 10 or 15 or perhaps 20 years, but that some of these trends might have run their course. In short, the author might be suggesting preparation for a world which would not look like the one we were just leaving. Three illustrations were offered of this problem. First, the argument was made that the last 10 or 15 years had seen an attempt to shift the burden of disclosure, openness, and accountability generally from the private to the public sector, and that universities which were now clearly assimilated to the public sector were bearing a far higher cost of accountability than the private sector would be asked to demonstrate, and run the risk of being subject to a far higher degree of regulation than the private sector would tolerate; the argument was that the time might not be terribly far off when universities and their constituencies would refuse to accept the relatively high levels of accountability and regulation. Second, it was argued that a lot of technocratic management which took credit for whatever passed for economic recovery in the late 1980s was now being carefully scrutinized. People with infallible judgments based on econometric analysis and technical managerial skills and the like had proved as capable of making a botch of things as all the bad old managers who lacked these techniques. Should this same technocratic management be given an opportunity of replicating itself in the public sector? Third, and perhaps most contentiously, it could be held that the inescapable forces of international business, corporate, fiscal considerations and so on had had a lot to do with the reduction in public expenditures in the 1980s. And this had surely been more important in reducing universities' capacities to deal with their mission than the lack of information about how they were discharging that mission. The plight of universities derives, the argument ran, not from their own misdeeds, but from larger events which had come to rest on their heads. And why had they come to rest on universities? Because of a resurgence of populism, consumerism, and faith in the market which was also beginning to run its course. Faith in the invisible hand of market economics which had characterized the last 10 or 15 years had led to difficult times for universities, but was also running its course.

In the discussion of these arguments there was agreement that universities might have been swamped by disclosure requirements with respect to financial accountability, possibly to a greater extent than private sector organizations. But there was also agreement that universities had failed to take the initiative in response to a broader sense of accountability in which they were asked to describe what they do, perhaps qualitatively, perhaps descriptively, with scarce public resources. In short, universities had been asked to demonstrate, perhaps in excessive detail, that they had not stolen or misappropriated public resources, but they had also failed to demonstrate what they had actually done with that money. The discussion with respect to the influence of technocratic management demonstrated broad agreement that universities were not in fact technocratic, not primarily quantitative, but rather were very subtle, complex places with complex missions which might occasionally require them to bite the hands that feed them. But there was also agreement that a willingness by universities to articulate that complex case a bit more than they had in the past might prevent assessment by technocratic managers from public sector departments and legislative auditors. In short, there was agreement that a willingness on the part of universities to articulate the complexities of their objectives and operations might be the price of keeping the technocratic managers at bay. With respect to the pressures on university funding in the 1980s as a consequence of the rise of consumerism, etc., there was agreement that funding constraints had been a problem. But there was also agreement that universities had taken the large increases in funding in the 1960s and 1970s for granted, and had not given any thought to articulating what they had actually done with those resources. Consequently, when the rate of increase in funding was reduced, universities were not ready, and had not managed to articulate their priorities, or to make persuasively the case for more funding.

The second major criticism of the paper was that if decisions about cutting university expenditures in the past had been unrelated to analytical work, then why should it be supposed that analytical work now would either generate more resources or stave off future cuts in the future? The argument was that these determinations were heavily political in their nature, and that universities were losing the struggle to articulate their contribution relative to the health care system and other public priorities. The argument was that universities should not naively assume that if they could but deploy rational well grounded arguments they could stave off the consequences of scarce resources and difficult public priorities. In the discussion on this point, there was agreement that better analytical work and better marketing by universities could not guarantee more resources absolutely or relatively in the future. But it was also argued that if universities did not themselves think about accountability in the broader sense of presenting their case, of marketing their roles in society, then they would certainly lose to other better organized advocates for public funding. In short, there was agreement that universities did face acute competition for scarce resources in the public sector, and that careful articulation of their accountability, broadly defined as marketing, would not guarantee them success, but would certainly serve them better than simply failing to articulate the important tasks they were undertaking for society using scarce public resources.

There was further discussion on whether the so-called technocratic approach could resolve the problems faced by universities. Much of the argument had to do with the complexity of universities. One view was that the future of an organization depended on its internal concept, that is, what it believed itself to be. It was argued that universities have a problem deciding what it was they actually were, and therefore in proving amenable to analysis of any sort using the technocratic approach. It was also argued that universities had a problem of boundary; they did not know what their membership was. For example, was a student a client, or a member of the organization? Another argument was that the technocratic approach was designed to lead to negative feedback, that is, to be a control mechanism, but might result in positive feedback, that is, might exacerbate problems. As an illustration of this last point, it was argued that the vagueness of university mission statements suggested a classic *modus vivendi*. Interrelationships appeared to be working after a fashion, and this delicate fashion might be disrupted if we tried to spell out too clearly the *modus vivendi*. In short, perhaps the increased explicitness which would come from more complete accountability statements would actually redound to the disadvantage of universities.

Another theme which emerged was that the increased demand for information from universities did not reflect a general public demand for more and better information but rather a self-serving demand by bureaucrats in ministries of higher education for masses of information to justify their existence. Discussion of the issue acknowledged that bureaucratic self-interest was alive and well in Canada but that, in general, universities would do well to regard senior bureaucrats in ministries of higher education as their friends and advocates rather than as their enemies. It was observed that bureaucrats had typically given universities an incredible benefit of the doubt, had almost pleaded with them to provide ammunition to make the case for universities to treasury boards and ministries of finance, and had been willing to be advocates and allies of universities in their arguments to maintain or increase their share of public funding. The general sense was that it was the unwillingness of universities to respond to these requests, to allow bureaucrats to be their allies, that was the larger problem. It was observed that in most cases universities produced data internally which, suitably repackaged, could satisfy many of the demands for external accountability. A case in point was faculty appraisal systems which, it was acknowledged, were probably generally more rigorous than in most private sector organizations. The external perception was, of course, that there were no such appraisal systems at all. So again the discussion placed the onus on universities to tell their story. This theme was developed in a discussion of the role of universities in the United States in carefully documenting and marketing their role as part of communities and their effect on society at large. Again the general sense of the discussion was that the benefit of the doubt universities in Canada get from the public at large is enormous. It was felt that the public was essentially on the side of universities, or were certainly not hostile to them, and that with careful attention to marketing, not just to funders but to industry, to the student whether the student was apprentice or customer or a bit of both, to the public which was served in a whole variety of ways, this general goodwill could be harnessed to the advantage of universities. There was extended discussion of the onus on universities to market their missions and activities, and general agreement that marketing, or accountability, to the public, to bureaucrats, and to politicians, was essential if universities were to compete with the other, well-organized demands on scarce public resources.

A final argument, on which there was general agreement, was that the responsibilities of universities to articulate their case to the public, to bureaucrats and to the politicians, went beyond accountability to larger questions of leadership. It was agreed that the success and civility with which societies weathered processes of change—and the 1990s in Canada looked like a particularly difficult process of political, economic, and social change—were heavily influenced by the role of universities, and that the articulation of this subtle, complex, and vital role was the critical component of the external information which universities provided to their various constituents. In short, it was agreed that the qualitative articulation of the vital leadership role of universities was by far and away the most important part of external reporting. This was the part of the role of universities least well-known outside universities, that universities themselves had failed to reflect on and articulate clearly, and that was, ironically, particularly fragile and vulnerable to severe funding restrictions.

IV

University Governance
and Management

Institutional Management: How Should the Governance and Management of Universities in Canada Accommodate Changing Circumstances?

David M. Cameron

Organization is instrumental of values. That is to say, the way in which institutions are organized serves to promote some values and restrain others. Organization is not merely a technical arrangement of work, authority, resources, and relationships. Alternative ways of organizing an institution represent choices among competing values. This applies to all organizations, governmental or non-governmental.[1] It certainly applies to universities.

Organization is instrumental of values in two respects. First, values may be secured or rejected directly, insofar as they are or are not embodied in the organization itself. Values such as participation or professional autonomy, for example, are related directly to the way in which an institution is organized. Second, values may be advanced or retarded indirectly, insofar as the organization is or is not conducive to their attainment. Values such as community service or scholarly excellence are neither secured nor rejected by organization per se, but organization may contribute to their being promoted or eschewed by the institution. In short, values may be organized into or out of an institution, either directly or indirectly. This is what is meant by the statement that organization is instrumental of values.

At least in the case of universities, we are not dealing with simple values, nor are the choices dichotomous. Questions of organization do not hinge so much on selecting appropriate values and seeking to maximize them, as on the appreciation that some values are contending for recognition and that pursuit of one value frequently entails a diminution of others. It is more a question of *optimizing* competing values than of *maximizing* individual values.

What values are at stake in the organization of universities? In the abstract, the possibilities are legion. Within the bounds of the practical, the range is much more limited. The history of Canadian universities suggests that three values have become central to questions of organization. These are: corporate autonomy, state support, and academic self-government. It might be useful at this point to take a closer look at each of these in turn.

Corporate Autonomy

The concept of universities as corporations is as old as the university itself in Canada. The first universities were established by royal charters, acts of incorporation granted by prerogative of the sovereign. This prerogative is now spent, and from the mid-nineteenth century universities have been incorporated by provincial legislation, either through individual charters or under the authority of general university acts. There are a few exceptions to this pattern. The military colleges, for example, were incorporated by federal legislation, although they grant degrees under authority of provincial legislation. Queen's University is in the unique position of having its royal charter subject to amendment by federal legislation.[2]

The authority to govern these corporations is invariably vested in a governing board, variously styled a board of governors, board of trustees, board of regents, or governing council.

The idea of corporate autonomy is not as old as that of the corporation itself. Corporate autonomy means the relative freedom of the university as an institution (i.e., a corporation) to govern and manage itself. Early Canadian universities were hardly autonomous. When King's College in Windsor, N.S., received its royal charter in 1802, for example, it acquired a governing board consisting of members of the Executive Council of Nova Scotia, *ex officio*, with the governor in the chair and with all internal regulations subject to the approval of the Archbishop of Canterbury. Laval was founded in 1852, also by royal charter, but it was governed through the Séminaire de Québec, and was firmly under the control of the Archbishop of Quebec. The early history of Canadian universities is the story of institutions established and controlled by state or church, or both.

The idea of institutional or corporate autonomy began to take hold in the late nineteenth century. It was the product of a new religion, science, and the organizational imperatives of scientific research. The pioneers in this were the leading universities of Germany, whose commitment to academic freedom was to have such a profound effect throughout North America.

The advent of science signalled the end of church control of universities and colleges in Canada. It would take many years for the transition to be completed, but it was well under way by the turn of the century. Science invaded the very sanctuary of the church college, subjecting the study of the Bible itself to the scientific method or, as it came to be dignified, the "higher criticism." More importantly, it created a need for expensive laboratories, equipment, and additional faculty, far beyond the financial capacity of most existing institutions. Moreover, it gave birth to the notion that research could contribute directly to material advantage in an increasingly industrialized economy, a notion which, in turn, invited an entirely new interest in universities on the part of government and business leaders.

A few universities were able to parlay this interest into financial support from individual benefactors. McGill, and to a lesser extent Dalhousie and Queen's, secured their corporate autonomy by means of private endowments. For most universities, however, the more practical alternative was public funding, and thus was confirmed the second of the three values that characterizes university organization: state support.

State Support

Elements of state support were present from the beginning of universities in Canada, but for the most part the support was modest and unreliable. It was also sometimes the object of bitter controversy. In Upper Canada, King's College's monopoly control of revenue from the public endowment of land was resented by the other colleges, and it was the prospect of containing if not eliminating this rivalry that gave rise to the idea of a federated provincial university. The ultimate result, of course, was the University of Toronto.

The major impediment to general public support was the denominational character of most institutions. Immediately after Confederation, for example, Ontario terminated its support of church-controlled colleges. Nova Scotia initially tried the federation route,[3] but when the University of Halifax failed to take hold for lack of support from the participating colleges, it terminated all provincial operating grants.[4]

Public funding emerged in its contemporary form with the establishment of provincial universities in western Canada. Alberta and Saskatchewan led the way in 1906 and 1907 respectively, with British Columbia following suit in 1915.[5] These were state universities in every respect, their boards, and sometimes even their presidents, appointed by government and their funding derived from modest tuition fees and government grants.

Corporate autonomy and state support might be seen as pulling in opposite directions. Such a simple dichotomy has been obviated by the emergence of the third value: academic self-government.

Academic Self-Government

Early Canadian colleges, and even universities, knew little of academic self-government as it is currently understood, although the principal or president usually enjoyed a wide scope of authority over matters academic. The idea of faculty self-government was well established in Britain, however, and it was the incorporation of the Scottish notion of an academic senate in the charters of Queen's, McGill and Dalhousie that gave it its early Canadian roots.

The case of Dalhousie is particularly instructive. It had been established originally in 1818 by the Lieutenant Governor of Nova Scotia, Lord Dalhousie, with a public endowment (from funds confiscated in Maine as customs duties during the War of 1812). Its governing board was constituted similarly to that of King's, however, with several officials serving simultaneously on both boards. The result, despite several efforts to remove King's from Windsor and combine it with Dalhousie in a provincial university, was that Dalhousie did not actually operate for its first 45 years, except for a brief five-year period following the appointment of Thomas McCulloch to the presidency in 1838 (it closed again when he died in 1843). In 1863 a charter not only reorganized the board, giving it a substantial measure of independence from government and changing its designation from college to university, but also established an academic senate. Indeed, the senate was composed of the senior faculty and was given general authority over the internal affairs of the university:

> The internal regulation of the said College shall be committed to the Senatus Academicus formed by the respective chairs or professorships thereof, subject in all case to the approval of the Governors.[6]

All three values, corporate autonomy, state support, and academic self-government, were firmly implanted in Canadian soil by the beginning of the twentieth century. It was the 1906 Royal Commission on the University of Toronto, chaired by Joseph (later Sir Joseph) Flavelle that brought them together in an organizational design which became the model for university government and management through the next half century.

Flavelle and Bicameralism

The Flavelle commission report contained a quite remarkable analysis. Not only did it reflect a thorough understanding of the relationship between values and organization, but it also produced an effective balance between the three values contending for recognition.

The starting point for Flavelle and his colleagues was a clear perception of the university as a state institution. They went further, however, to draw a distinction between state control and partisan interference, the latter a common feature of the existing arrangement.[7] State control was to be balanced against corporate autonomy, the balance secured within a governing board:

> The powers of the Crown in respect to the control and management of the University should be vested in a Board of Governors, chosen by the Lieutenant-Governor-in-Council. . . .[8]

Academic self-government was also to be accommodated. For this, Flavelle took up and adopted the notion of bicameralism:

> The Senate, with . . . legislative and executive powers . . ., should direct the academic interests of the University.[9]

Finally, the key to holding this structure together and facilitating its efficient operation was to be a strengthened presidency, joining senate to board and holding a monopoly on recommendations concerning academic staff.

Flavelle's version of bicameral government of public universities fitted the times perfectly. As a consequence, it was immediately copied, first in the west and subsequently elsewhere. Apart from this, not a great deal changed over the next half century, dominated as that period was by wars and depression. The groundwork, however, was being laid for future tensions.

Calm Before the Storm

At least three developments during the first half of this century are worth noting. First, the idea of faculty self-government took on added meaning, especially with respect to the limits of academic freedom. Sir Robert Falconer of Toronto defined the essential balance between academic freedom and state support in his famous address of 1922. On the one hand, he argued:

> . . . we can measure the rank and stability of a university by the security given to a professor to pursue and expand his investigations without being compelled to justify himself to those who differ from him.[10]

But on the other hand, this freedom was a property of the university, and did not extend to public action or debate. To enjoy academic freedom, at least in a public university, was to refrain from partisan political activity.

A decade later this balance was severely strained by the proclivity of some faculty members to speak out publicly on issues of social and political concern. Chief among them was Frank Underhill of the University of Toronto. Underhill would have been fired by the board of governors, except that the board lacked the power to do so, the president retaining control of academic staff matters as bequeathed by the Flavelle commission. And by the time the president, by then Canon Cody, had had his fill of Underhill's outspokenness, he was blocked by a solid wall of faculty resistance. Faculty self-government was slowly but surely gaining in strength and self-confidence, while it was expanding in scope.

The second development had to do with state support. Here, two things were happening. Although government grants declined as a proportion of total university operating expenditures between 1920 and 1950 (dropping from 50 per cent to just over 40 per cent), this was more than offset by increased tuition, which rose from 20 per cent of operating expenditures in 1920 to 40 per cent in 1950. What is apparent from these figures is that the combination of government grants and fees increased from 70 per cent to 80 per cent of operating expenditures. What is implicit in this change is that other income, and especially endowment income, had shrunk, dropping from 30 per cent to 20 per cent.[11] The clear implication was that universities were becoming increasingly dependent on the combination of government grants and tuition fees.

The second aspect of developments in relation to state support was the entry of the federal government. The first step was taken as early as 1912 with passage of the Agricultural Aid Act and, with it, the introduction of the very first federal-provincial shared-cost program which, among other things, provided federal support to university programs in agriculture and veterinary science. Then, in 1916, the federal government responded to the growing importance of scientific research by establishing the Honorary Advisory Council for Scientific and Industrial Research, soon to be known as the National Research Council. The council quickly embarked on a program of grants to university researchers. With the Second World War, the federal government was drawn even further into the university world, not only dictating priorities with respect to exemption from selective service,[12] but also directly supporting the university education of veterans.[13] Perhaps even more important was the close relationship that was forged during and immediately after the war between senior university officials and the federal government. The legacy of that relationship lasted for a long time.

While the scope of academic self-government was expanding, and universities and government were edging closer to each other, there were signs also that corporate autonomy might not be entirely secure. An incident at the University of Alberta is instructive in this regard. The incident arose in 1941 when the president's invitation to the premier to accept an honorary degree was rejected by the senate on the eve of convocation. The upshot was the appointment by the provincial government of a survey committee to review the university's governing structure. That committee served firm notice that state support, corporate autonomy, and academic self-government had not necessarily been fully and finally reconciled. The survey committee gave early warning that:

> The governing bodies of the institution and the teaching staff should appreciate that the people of the Province are vitally interested in the work of the University— they supply a substantial part of the funds and have the right to scrutinize the actions of the governing bodies and efficiency of the teaching staff.[14]

Post-War Expansion

The phenomenal growth of Canadian universities in the post-war period is well known. More than growth was occurring, however. Two of the traditional values, state support and academic self-government were enhanced while the third, corporate autonomy, was severely constrained.

Universities became almost totally dependent on government grants. By 1960-61, government grants exceeded 60 per cent of university operating expenditures. They hit 70 per cent in 1967-68, and passed the 80 per cent mark in 1975-76. Endowment and other income, meanwhile, had dropped to a mere 6 per cent.[15] Something else was also happening. Provincial governments had moved to control tuition fees, either directly or via operating grant formulas. The result was that fees essentially became government-determined user charges. The true measure of state support, therefore, could be put as high as 95 per cent.

In the course of this transition, and directly related to it, Canadian universities shed almost all of the remaining vestiges of denominationalism. Laval even abandoned its royal charter in favour of provincial incorporation. Almost all universities were now public institutions, in fact if not always in law.

The full impact of provincial government control was masked for a time by the involvement of the federal government. This included direct grants to universities from 1951 to 1966 (with an equivalent fiscal transfer to Quebec after 1960), capital funding through the Canada Council and Central Mortgage and Housing Corporation (CMHC), special grants for the expansion of health programs related directly to the introduction of medicare, and funding of the Canada Student Loan Program. Universities certainly enjoyed this federal patronage, not least because they saw corporate autonomy enhanced by the presence of two paymasters. Federal patronage was not destined to continue, however, except in specific areas. Only two survived: the student loans program, based on an effective marriage of federal and provincial jurisdiction, and research, which most provinces effectively ceded to the federal government. Direct grants gave way to an intergovernmental shared-cost program after 1967, and to a block transfer of tax room and annual cash grants to the provinces after 1977. With that, the federal government gave up all control of university expenditures, except in relation to research.

Provincial governments, meanwhile, had been exploring approaches to the management of their emerging systems of postsecondary education. Initially, most provinces turned either to a royal commission or advisory committee. Some of these produced blueprints for expansion, while others called for rationalization and consolidation. All showed great respect for the value of corporate autonomy. Efforts to reconcile this autonomy with expanding provincial responsibility for financing universities came to rest on two instruments: intermediary agencies and formula financing.

For universities, the model for provincial intermediary agencies was clearly the British University Grants Committee, a body that was frequently misunderstood but was perceived to have maximized corporate autonomy and minimized state control, all the while ensuring adequate state support. Provincial governments almost invariably armed these agencies with authority to rationalize university programs as well as to advise on funding requirements, but equally invariably the agencies backed away from rationalization and emphasized increased funding.

This was facilitated by the adoption in most provinces of formula-based funding, usually incorporating a variation of the Ontario model and its reliance on weighted enrolment. Enrolment-driven formulas obviously encouraged universities to expand, reflecting a brief but happy conjunction of provincial priorities and institutional ambitions. As with the intermediary agency itself, the funding formula represented a very blunt instrument with which to direct university expansion. Not surprisingly, when expansion gave way to restraint, provincial governments began looking for more effective tools.

Something else had changed during the period of expansion. Academic self-government had burst the seams of bicameralism so carefully sewn by Flavelle. Cries for reform and participative governance grew in intensity through the early 1960s. They were embraced and given direction by the Duff-Berdahl report of 1966.[16] The upshot was a veritable revolution in university government and management. Faculty members assumed greater control of senates or equivalent bodies, and greatly expanded the scope of their deliberations. Faculty members were added to boards of governors, and if this privilege had to be shared with students, it nonetheless served to open the business of university government.

Participation transformed university management as well. Flavelle's concentration of managerial authority in the president's office gave way to management by committee, preferably at the departmental level. Then, as the capstone of academic self-government, freedom and security were enshrined in the institution of tenure. Quite suddenly, the management of universities was stripped of its authority. In his typically perceptive and forthright fashion, J.A. Corry, principal of Queen's, summed up as early as 1969 what had happened:

> It is vital to get some things clear. Much of the sub-
> stance of power has been taken out of the president's
> office and away from the board of governors. The
> members of the academic staff now have what has been
> taken out, and they have nearly a veto on the use of
> what is left. They may find this hard to believe, but it is
> true. *That battle is over.*[17]

All of this was to be played out with increasing intensity as the
period of expansion gave way to restraint and a search for new
directions in public policy.

Restraint and Redirection

The bloom went off the university rose in the early 1970s. Demographic projections pointed to declining enrolment after a decade
of extraordinary growth. More significantly, stagflation signalled
the end of unconstrained government spending just at the time
economic analysts began questioning the validity of earlier
estimates of the social rate of return from expenditures on university education. Real growth in government grants stopped and,
in due course, a host of commissions and task forces took up the
challenge of formulating new policy directions. No apparent
consensus emerged, however.

   Matters were made worse by the failure of students to behave
in accordance with demographic projections. Enrolment, after a
very brief pause in the early 1970s, just kept on growing.
Provincial governments were no longer willing to underwrite the
costs of expansion, however, leaving universities to do so through
productivity gains, reflected primarily in higher student-faculty
ratios.

   This, in turn, led to a growing sense of insecurity on the part
of faculty members. Their subsequent search for security led to
collective bargaining, frequently under the rubric of trade union
legislation.[18] This necessarily put boards of governors in the role
of employer and in an adversarial relationship with faculty, a role
for which they were neither prepared nor suited. The result has
been one-sided bargaining in which faculty associations have not
only extended earlier gains but have also secured them in binding
collective agreements.

Provincial governments, meanwhile, have been sharpening their policy instruments. Both the intermediary agency and formula financing have diminished in importance as a consequence. Alberta, Saskatchewan, and British Columbia scrapped their intermediary agencies altogether, preferring to deal with their universities directly. Newfoundland never had such an agency. Nova Scotia has severely weakened the Maritime Provinces Higher Education Commission by creating its own council, one that is positioned much closer to the minister.

At the same time, formula financing is giving way to earmarked or targeted funding, a device by which funds are allocated through specific, provincially defined, policy "envelopes." The effects of this on universities have so far been benign, but targeted funding contains enormous potential for government direction of university programming.

At the federal level as well, government is clearly looking for ways to harness university research more effectively to support economic development or, perhaps more realistically, to avoid economic marginalization. The design of both the matching grants program and the networks of centres of excellence was aimed at drawing university research into partnership with the private sector.

There has been no complementary strengthening of university government and management. The values of state support and academic self-government, as currently manifested, are threatening to squeeze the life out of corporate autonomy. It is true that collective bargaining yields a degree of centralization in university decision making, but it is increasingly routinized decision making. Discretionary managerial authority has been attenuated. This is especially so in unionized universities.

University organization no longer optimizes the three values of corporate autonomy, state support, and academic self-government. A new balance is necessary, or the squeeze on autonomy seems destined to continue and get worse. Increased state control facing collectivized faculties looks like a sure recipe for even greater centralization and routinization. The outcome would almost certainly be a loss of creativity and institutional adaptability.

Are there alternatives? Is it possible to breathe organizational life into the moribund value of corporate autonomy? Is it feasible to strengthen university government and management while preserving state support and academic self-government?

Strengthening University Government and Management

One qualification should be entered at the outset. There can be no single answer to the questions posed above. No matter how much universities in Canada may be motivated by common ideas and values, they are discreet institutions with their own histories, cultures, politics, and provincial contexts. What might work in one university or province could be quite inappropriate in another.

It is also the case that provincial and federal governments could use their support to strengthen university government. For example, the studied refusal of the federal government to cover the indirect costs of research adds mightily to the pressures constraining the research-intensive universities from fully exploiting their comparative advantages. This is a classic case of federal policy constraining its own effectiveness.

The provinces have the major responsibility for university support in Canada. The challenge for provincial governments is to find ways of ensuring that universities do contribute to public policy objectives, and do so efficiently, while at the same time enhancing their capacity to make choices. I have argued elsewhere that this is most likely to occur within a policy framework that fosters institutional competition rather than relying on government regulation.[19] Provincial governments need to be more precise about what they want universities to do and not do, if they expect responsible compliance.

Government can certainly do its part to strengthen universities. But the main challenge faces the universities themselves. What should they be doing? My own conclusion is that the single most important step would be to strengthen governing boards. This is the body most likely to command public (including government) confidence, while at the same time being in a position to understand the true nature and mission of the university. In short, the board can justify state support while respecting academic self-government. It is the critical linchpin.

To avoid making things worse, however, boards must resist the temptation of trying to manage the university themselves, or interfere in its day-to-day operations. Their role is not to manage the university. Their critical contribution is rather to see that it is well-managed. There is a world of difference between the two.

There are at least five areas in which boards could play more effective roles. The first is in relation to strategic planning or, perhaps more realistically, making strategic choices. The concept of strategic planning often conjures up notions of elaborate, deductive exercises involving the specification of objectives, constraints, resources, etc., etc. This may or may not be useful, but I suspect it is mostly a waste of time in a university. What I am suggesting is rather the board's insistence that choices be confronted and made. If current resources are inadequate to continue all existing programs, then some must go. At present, this is just about the most difficult thing for universities even to consider. The issues and choices are rapidly and thoroughly politicized, with the consequence that change is more easily blocked than accepted. In some universities, internal governance has degenerated to the point where the economic self-interest of faculty members has overtaken academic self-government. If universities cannot make these kinds of strategic choices, then sooner or later government will be compelled to do so for them.

The second and closely related area begging for more attention from boards is program evaluation. Most universities already engage in some regular process of program or unit review. What is not so well-developed, however, is the systematic use of such reviews in the allocation of resources, including decisions to continue or terminate programs. The suggestion is not that boards should themselves be involved in reviewing programs. The suggestion is rather that boards should insist that programs are regularly reviewed and, more important, that such reviews lead to deliberate action on the part of the university.

The other side of program evaluation has to do with the evaluation of people. This is the third area requiring attention. The better universities retain procedures for annual performance appraisals and merit-based salary adjustments, but the trend is clearly in the opposite direction. It takes little imagination to appreciate that tenure, combined with lock-step salary structures, has severely truncated the capacity of universities to recognize and reward superior performance, or to respond positively to lack-lustre or deteriorating performance. Boards should be concerned about this, and should be taking steps to see that it is addressed.

For many universities, these issues will have to be addressed within the context of collective bargaining. This raises the fourth area where boards could contribute to a strengthening of university government and management. With very few exceptions, neither boards nor senior academic administrators were prepared for the advent of formal bargaining, and as a result the advantage went to faculty associations. Boards are at an inherent disadvantage in collective bargaining. Unlike private sector employers, they have no direct interest in the outcome, but rather play a trustee role *vis-à-vis* the interests of the university. But unlike most public sector employers, they are, in most provinces at least, unprotected by legislative limits on what may be bargained or on the right to strike.

It is rather late in the day to call for a stronger management role in collective bargaining. The battles are mostly over, and it would be folly to advocate trying to turn the clock back and start again. At the same time, this is the process through which many universities will have to face the critical issues looming on the horizon. If they are to avoid sinking further into routinized mediocrity, management will have to bring more to the table than mere reactions to faculty demands. It is the board's responsibility to ensure that proposals are developed, and that adequate resources are provided to support their development. There is a crying need for increased cooperation among universities in this regard.

Finally, boards are the critical link between universities and the private sector. This relationship is bound to become more important, not only because government grants have stopped growing, but because private support is a key element in securing corporate autonomy. Canadian universities have been making some gains in this arena, but they have a long way to go. This is not to suggest that the privatization of universities is a likely development. The public's investment and interest in universities is too great for that. It does suggest, however, that future institutional success is likely to depend on the forging of part-nerships with *both* public and private sector institutions. This is particularly, but by no means only, so in relation to research.

Such partnerships will require more than cosmetic changes in approach. They will require strategic positioning. They will also require a willingness to consider the interests of the potential partner at the very outset of program planning. Many will see this as a threat to academic self-government and, if not well-managed, that could be so.

The problems facing university government and management promise to be even more challenging and complex than in the past. If universities are to face this challenge successfully, they will need a greater capacity to make strategic choices. There are no doubt many ways in which this capacity could be enhanced. This paper has focused on one: strengthening the governing board. This, in turn, arises from the need to work out a new balance between the three core values that have characterized the organization of universities in Canada: state support, academic self-government, and corporate autonomy.

Notes

1. See, for example, E.E. Schattschneider, *The Semisovereign People*. New York: Holt, Rinehart and Winston, 1960; Arthur Maass, *Area and Power*. Glencoe, Ill.: The Free Press, 1959; W.S. Livingston, *Federalism and Constitutional Change*. Oxford: Clarendon Press, 1956.

2. The problem arose from legislation passed by the parliament of the united Province of Canada concerning the relationship between Queen's and the Presbyterian Church, and a subsequent dispute over whether such legislation could be amended by the Province of Ontario alone. A solution to that dispute was found in federal legislation, with the result that future amendments would have to come from the federal parliament as well.

3. The model for a federation of colleges within a degree-granting university was the University of London. The University of Manitoba initially followed this pattern as well.

4. The legislation creating the University of Halifax in 1876 was intended to last for five years. In 1881 the government introduced legislation to abolish the university and continue funding for the individual colleges. The whole bill, however, was defeated in the Legislative Council, with the result that the non-existent University of Halifax retained its incorporation while the existing colleges (Acadia, Dalhousie, King's, St. Francis Xavier, and St. Mary's) lost their funding.

5. British Columbia had passed enabling legislation as early as 1890, but it failed to get off the ground because of rivalry between Victoria and Vancouver. Between 1899 and 1915, limited university-level programs were offered by McGill University through the Vancouver and subsequently also the Victoria school boards. The University of British Columbia finally assumed responsibility for McGill's Vancouver operation in 1915.

6. 26 Vict., ch.24, S.N.S. This provision has taken an ironic twist over the subsequent 127 years. Dalhousie's senate still includes all full professors, *ex officio*, as well as a number of elected members from the lower ranks, representatives of affiliated institutions, etc. The upshot is that the Senate has more than 400 members.

7. The university was governed by a senate, composed of government appointees, alumni, and representatives of the federated colleges. Decisions of the senate, however, took effect only after receiving government approval. This included faculty appointments, and it was not uncommon for the premier to make an appointment without even consulting the president of the university.

8. Ontario, Royal Commission on the University of Toronto, *Report*. Toronto: King's Printer, 1906, p. xx.

9. *Loc. cit.*

10. James G. Greenlee, *Sir Robert Falconer: A Biography*. Toronto: University of Toronto Press, 1988, p. 280.

11. Figures taken from Dominion Bureau of Statistics, *Survey of Higher Education*.

12. Students in arts and science were treated quite differently. Most science students were exempt from active service, while arts students earned exemption only if they scored in the top half of their class.

13. Veterans received tuition and allowances; their university received a flat $150 per veteran per year.

14. Alberta, University of Alberta Survey Committee, *Interim Report*. Edmonton: Sessional Paper No. 50, 1942, p. 24.

15. Data for 1960-61 and 1967-68 taken from Dominion Bureau of Statistics, *Survey of Education Finance*; data for 1975-76 taken from Statistics Canada, *Financial Statistics of Education*.

16. Sir James Duff and Robert O. Berdahl, *University Government in Canada*. Report of a commission sponsored by the Canadian Association of University Teachers and the Association of Universities and Colleges of Canada. Toronto: University of Toronto Press, 1966.

17. Originally a lecture delivered at the University of British Columbia. Subsequently published in J.A. Corry, *Farewell the Ivory Tower:*

Universities in Transition. Montreal: McGill-Queen's Press, 1970, pp. 111-12. Emphasis in the original.

18. Approximately 60 per cent of Canada's universities have certified unions (29 out of a total of 49, counting federated and affiliated institutions and the multi-campus Université du Québec as single units). This includes a large number of small institutions. Only about 45 per cent of all faculty members belong to certified unions. Both British Columbia and Alberta prohibit certification of faculty unions.

19. See David M. Cameron, "Centralisation or Decentralisation: Alternative Strategies for Public Policy for Universities and Colleges in Canada." In Ron Watts and Jeff Greenberg, eds., *Post-Secondary Education: Preparation for the World of Work.* Aldershot, England: Dartmouth Publishing Company, 1990, pp. 37-47.

Synthesis of Commentary and Discussion on the Cameron Paper

The discussion on the Cameron paper began with a commentary by Dr. Allan Warrack, vice-president of finance at the University of Alberta. Following is a summary of his comments:

> The university governance issue is not a tempest in a teapot; in fact, I fear it is the lull before the storm. Issues of Canadian university governance and accountability are very serious problems. They will not simply go away, so the issues will need to be met. I want to make four points. Two points are about university governance, and the two others relate to university strategies.

Governance

The basic university organization is a dichotomous one. There is a large difference between the academic staffing complement and the non-academic (support) staffing complement. In almost all institutions there are more people in the latter than in the former; in short, there are more support people (servants of the scholars) than scholars themselves.

In the academic component of universities, there is a highly diverse and decentralized organizational governance system of departments and faculties. Leadership is essentially amateur in the sense that specialists in a particular subject are then appointed to administrative roles for which they have no particular training or qualifications. Generally these are shorter-term appointments, commonly for five years, renewable for rather less time than that. In contrast, the university administrative support component tends to be highly corporate; it is hierarchical in nature, its merit system is very rigid, and has less collegiality. The people involved tend to be very professional or technical in their areas of expertise, of which accounting is one. It is a kind of command bureaucratic system. What is essential, of course, in this dichotomy is that the academic priorities must drive the support priorities if the university is to play its appointed role. One of the great challenges of university governance is to succeed with priorities established and managed by leadership based on short-term appointments by people trained for other matters, and essentially amateur in nature. But there is an important and positive implication of this feature of universities. The decentralized, highly informal and collegial nature of university academic governance must surely mean that universities are readily capable of change. If universities were rigidly bureaucratic organizations, like most governments and large corporations, they would be less able to adapt. Universities should therefore recognize their capacities to be flexible, adaptable, and nimble, should recognize their opportunities for dynamic change, and harness their potential more fully and with public accountability.

My second point on governance relates to the matter of leadership style. Leadership is different from management. Management is coping with complexity, or perhaps harnessing complexity. Leadership is coping with change; it is about harnessing change, taking whatever the reality is and harnessing it for future advantage. The difficulty is that academic administrators are kept so busy with what are essentially management activities that they have precious little time left for leadership activity. The right way for a university to operate, to be managed and led, is within the notion that those who govern do so with the consent of those being governed. Only in an environment of trust, collegiality, and thus moral authority, can universities be effectively led and managed. As with most organizations, universities tend to be over-managed and under-led. There is generally too little focus on change, especially internal change to keep congruent with external changes that are happening all the time. Universities which could be adaptive and flexible thus frequently appear insensitive and rigid. Universities need, for instance, to examine why they are generally unpopular. They need to look at that unpopularity and be critics of themselves as well as of society at large.

Strategies

Every entity, be it university, a company, a research centre, or whatever, has a strategy. The strategy is defined by action. We at the University of Alberta make much of the historic fact that we are the university of the province of Alberta; but if you watch us we often act as if we were the University of Edmonton! Strategy must always relate to the external environment, with its vagaries and dynamic changes. Universities in Canada have got into difficulties by overlooking the need to design strategies of adaptation to external environmental changes. A strategic planning exercise—and there are too few of them in Canadian universities—must be focused over a time horizon, with difficult trade-offs between the future and the present. Future planning is about the future of today's decisions, not about future decisions.

My second point relates to strategy for accountability. While I agree with the general need for accountability, I am sceptical about accounting approaches to achieve it. There is an urgency to our accountability agenda. I believe we must press our accountability on the public and their governments, and recognize that if we are popular with the public at large, we will be popular with their governments, no matter what their partisan stripe. This is again the issue of marketing and communicating our story to the public at large and through them to politicians who respond to public pressure. In doing this, we must recognize those prospects of university life which are widely misunderstood by, or not well explained to, the public at large. Issues such as accessibility, research productivity, academic leave, and, perhaps above all, tenure, must be explained to the public, and in many cases changed to accommodate public concerns."

Further commentary on the Cameron paper was provided by Don Yeomans, chairman of the board of Carleton University. Following is a summary of his comments:

I should emphasize that while I am a member of the board of governors of the Canadian Comprehensive Auditing Foundation, I am not, nor have ever been, an auditor. I am at heart a line manager, I have been subjected to a comprehensive audit, and, at least initially, I did not particularly enjoy the experience. The major problem was what norms or standards were to be used by the auditors. Usually translated the problem is, 'Who the hell are these guys to tell us how to run our business?' Let me stress then the importance of the discussion of accountability in the Canadian

Comprehensive Auditing Foundation study on effectiveness, reporting, and auditing completed in 1987. The essential message of that study was that the management of an enterprise should make representations about its objectives and performance, and auditors should attest to these representations. This, of course, amounted to saying that it was up to the management of an enterprise to determine and report in detail on how it should be held to account; and one of the major themes of our discussion today, on which I think we have general agreement, is that the management of universities in Canada should take the initiative in the accountability debate by making management representations to government on their performance. It is then up to the auditors to comment on the adequacy of the accountability process and on these management representations. David Cameron talked about the role of the board of governors of a university, that it is also their role to monitor how the institution is being managed, but not to manage it.

A very clear picture has emerged, in listening to the ensuing discussions, and there would seem to be continuing deference to the independence of universities, and I've no great desire to diminish that independence. But there is also in our society a tremendous increase in the pressure for higher standards of accountability for all public and private business and institutions. There are higher standards of accountability being imposed upon boards of directors of commercial enterprises. I have to challenge Harry Arthurs from York University on that point. The accountability of commercial enterprises now goes beyond simply financial matters to include environmental impact, local community impact, and responsibilities for their employees. So a better informed, better educated public is expecting and imposing this higher standard of accountability on all its institutions, both public and private. It seems to me clear, and there seems to be consensus here, that if universities in Canada want to encourage and maintain the traditional deference to their independence, they must respond vigorously and openly to this heightened public expectation of much greater accountability. Accountability is essentially the price of independence.

We have heard here that there are lots of performance indicators in use in Europe, and the United States, and the time has come in Canada for action. The challenge is now for the

Association of Universities and Colleges of Canada (AUCC) to review what has been done, establish a set of performance indicators for Canadian universities, and then challenge these universities to report publicly, using those management statistics and performance indicators. This would be a major step in the direction of establishing accountability and preserving autonomy. And it would mean, of course, that universities are taking the initiative and not having something imposed on them by bureaucrats and auditors. I believe that the development of performance indicators will encourage an element of competition because each institution will try to bring each of its indicators in line with the best. There is surely no question that conscientious university managers will be monitoring what is happening in other institutions across the country, and I submit that the mere existence of these performance indicators and management statistics—provided, of course, that they are valid and reliable indicators—will, in fact, improve the performance of Canadian institutions.

We have also had discussion on producing a great deal of new and possibly unnecessary data. Surely the management statistics and performance indicators that we develop should be those required by institutions to manage their own affairs, and governments should not expect information or data that are not so required. If we discover that a government ministry is expecting such data, then we can legitimately question the process, because clearly someone is working on conflicting or differing objectives. So if the objectives of the government and institutions are more or less congruent—and I think we are agreed that there is at least a very high degree of overlap—then the data required from dean to deputy minister should be common. Of course, few institutions embark enthusiastically on a program of collecting and publishing performance indicators because initially at least there were a number of warts and lumps. But I believe that provincial auditors and bureaucrats will be reasonable in reacting to these warts and lumps, provided that it is perceived that the institutions are taking action. The perfect set of performance indicators may not exist and probably never will exist, but we have heard that significant improvements have occurred in this area, and the challenge for Canadian universities is to take the best experience to date and get started.

Several themes emerged in the ensuing discussion.

Following David Cameron's analysis of the role of boards of governors of universities in Canada, there was extensive discussion on the nature and role of such boards. First, it was observed that typically members of boards of governors might not have the capacity, and very seldom had the information to provide effective governance. There was agreement that boards could only continue to play their buffer role which was so important to the autonomy of universities in Canada if their members were of high quality and were provided with information of sufficient quality and quantity to discharge their roles. One encouraging sign of a more assertive role by boards of governors in Canada was the formation of an association of board chairs at the national level. The argument was advanced, however, that the role of boards of governors was very different from that of university management, and that boards should not get involved in the detailed management of the university. There was agreement that boards should not be involved in detailed management, but should insist on knowing how well management was doing. For instance, boards should insist on there being processes of evaluation for faculty and for programs, and should insist on assurance that these processes were working well, but should not conduct these evaluations themselves. The view was also expressed that a major responsibility of boards of governors in Canadian universities was to reinvigorate leadership through strengthening the role of the senior management of universities, particularly university presidents who had lost a great deal of authority and capacity to act and lead as a result of the so-called democratization process of universities in the 1960s and 1970s in Canada. There was agreement on this argument, but also agreement on the view that the newer accountability processes under discussion should invigorate, not inhibit, this leadership. There was some discussion of experience in the United Kingdom with university councils, the equivalent of boards of governors in Canada. Reflecting the Jarratt report, which advocated that university councils should become more active, the chairmen of university councils had met in the United Kingdom at six-monthly intervals for about three or four years and an organization called the Committee of Chairmen of University Councils was now in place. Although this had generally been a positive development, there had been some overlap between the activities of this committee and the Committee of Vice-Chancellors and Principals, i.e., the committee of chief executive officers of universities. The roles could obviously be complementary, but the distinction between the two roles and the jurisdiction of each group had to be clearly established. There was some discussion on whether the two bodies could be serviced by the same secretariat, and it was pointed out that the Committee of Chairmen of Ontario University Boards was serviced by the staff of the Council of Ontario Universities. Further, it was pointed out that the chairs of Canadian university boards were just beginning to get themselves organized. They had been meeting for about three years and at their next meeting an item on the agenda would be a proposal to have secretariat services provided by the AUCC. Finally, there was some discussion on whether the many appointment processes to boards of governors of Canadian universities led to the appointment of the appropriate persons. It was acknowledged that government appointments to boards had not always been of the quality warranted by the importance of the position, and that universities that had retained the ability to make appointments to their own boards had retained an enormous advantage. But it was acknowledged that the greatest weakness in the argument that the role of boards of governors should be strengthened in Canada as part of this accountability debate was the wide variety of appointment processes and therefore the wide variety in the quality of people appointed to boards.

The second theme on which there was extended discussion was the sort of information on which governments should insist as a condition of maintaining institutional autonomy. Reflecting again the suggestions of the Jarratt committee in the United Kingdom that accountability should primarily be demonstrated by documenting the existence and proper functioning of management systems and controls, the question was posed as to whether the relationship between governments and universities in Canada would be considered a satisfactory one from the point of view of universities if universities were required to demonstrate to government that they were well-led and well-directed, that they had a mission and a strategic plan, and that they had management systems and controls in place to ensure that their mission and strategic plan were pursued. There was general agreement that this sort of arm's-length approach to accountability was most appropriate but also agreement that from time to time governments would have to insist on information on actual operating results in addition to information of systems, and indeed also insist on the right to limit university autonomy; two examples of areas where this right might be exercised were in relation to major initiatives which reflected a larger public policy agenda, and situations where the basic financial management of universities was deficient. There was also agreement that universities could not get away with providing information on mission statements and strategic plans at such a high level of aggregation that they were essentially useless in explaining what universities were doing or intended to do.

Finally, there was some discussion on the implications of a proposed new accountability procedure, and the strengthening of university management, for the appraisal of staff performance and the question of faculty tenure. There was considerable debate on how effective faculty appraisal schemes had been at Canadian universities, and on the extent to which the democratization of decision making in universities and the unionization of faculties had limited the scope of management initiative in Canadian universities. There was agreement that reasonable job security and fair processes for university staff were essential components of any internal and ultimately external system of accountability, but that these had to be reconciled with public and government concerns over staff appraisal and job security. The position was also advanced that university management could cooperate with faculty unions to strengthen their bargaining position with governments in Canada.

Managing the Relationship: University Relations with Business and Government

Cynthia Hardy

Introduction

This presentation questions some of the basic assumptions that underlie recent changes in the administration of higher education—both those introduced by university administrators and those proposed by external stakeholders, such as government or business. These assumptions hinge on a unitary view of higher education, in which the increased use of rational analysis is believed to improve the effectiveness and efficiency of decision making.

It is argued here that such assumptions fail to provide either an accurate description of how universities operate or of effective managerial prescriptions. As a result, many of the recommendations that have been proposed to improve university administration are counter-productive to the aims of both university administrators and external stakeholders. An alternative perspective will be presented here, which stresses the plurality of higher education systems and the need for a political perspective if internal and external relationships in higher education are to be managed effectively.

The Unitary Perspective

Interest in the "management" of universities has increased in recent years. Sparked by changing enrolment patterns, restrictions in government funding, escalating interest in attracting business support, and demands for increased accountability from public paymasters, university administrators have turned to the business world for management models. As a result, universities have instituted such techniques as strategic planning, program evaluation, value-added and performance indicators (see, for example, Cope, 1978; Miller, 1979; Keller, 1980; Harris & Holdaway, 1983). Similarly, as governments have become more concerned with public sector spending, they have become more interested in how that money is being spent. This interest has been coupled with a growing suspicion that universities are not responding adequately to society's needs (Axelrod, 1986). Such views are, perhaps, best illustrated by the recommendations of the Jarratt report (Committee of Vice-Chancellors and Principals, 1985) which has recommended an industrial "ethos" for U.K. universities (see Jones, 1986; Sizer, 1988b; Lee & Piper, 1988). Similar trends have been noted in Europe, Australia, and New Zealand. Canadian governments have, so far, been reluctant to use specific instruments of control and continue to rely on general funding policies. Nevertheless, there has clearly been a shift in attitude on the part of government and other external stakeholders that has been manifested in questions concerning: universities' value for money; how they can be more closely attuned to societal needs; and the necessity for increased government controls and direction.

Attempts to introduce procedures commonly associated with the private, business sector have been noted elsewhere—for example, the British National Health Service (Hardy, 1986) and in British industrial relations policy (Fox, 1973). Such attempts to adopt an industrial ethos, whether in the form of (external) public or (internal) administrative policy, are predicated on a unitary perspective in which all interested parties are assumed to be bound together by a common goal or purpose. Rational analysis can, as a result, be encouraged (with the right kind of policies, procedures, and managerial techniques) to predominate in decision making with a corresponding improvement in performance. This perspective finds it difficult to deal with the idea that power, competing interests, and either potential or actual conflict may exist. If opposition does occur, it tends to be viewed as some form of aberration, instigated by deviant or emotional individuals (Fox, 1973).

We can see these assumptions in the context of both administrative and public policy. In the case of the former, strategic planning provides a good example. It emphasizes analytic techniques in which organizational strengths and weaknesses and environmental opportunities and threats are assessed. Plans are subsequently formulated to address these factors. The emphasis is clearly on formulation and short shrift is given to implementation. I recall one model presented at a conference of higher education in which 17 formulation steps were identified. Implementation, on the other hand, was dealt with in one step. Clearly the assumption was that once the most rational plan was identified, it would be implemented. The idea that resistance to change might arise did not factor into the analysis and, even if it did, it was consigned to obscurity—irrational resistance to a rational plan by irrational people. Yet, implementation problems are common in strategic planning. When *Business Week* reviewed 33 strategic plans it had reported, it found that 19 had been unsuccessful. It has been estimated that less than 10 per cent of strategic changes recommended by consulting groups like the Boston Consulting Group (BCG) have ever been implemented (see Kiechel, 1982, 1984).

The industrial ethos embodied in such public policies as the Jarratt report also emphasizes the rational/unitary perspective. Proponents of this model have argued that they are advocating an executive management model which can operate under a pluralistic framework, accommodate conflict and disagreement, and in which behavioural and political skills complement management and planning processes (for example, Lee & Piper, 1988). The problem is that while proponents may acknowledge the existence of political factors they focus attention on the rational. The industrial model thus recommends decisive action but offers little advice on how to implement action: it tells you what to do but it does not tell you how to do it. In so doing, it downplays the importance of behavioural and political skills (Lyles & Lenz, 1982). For example, it recommends tough decisions like program closure and radical resource reallocation, but ignores the backlash that such draconian measures are likely to produce (see Hardy, 1990a).

This model thus avoids the issue of conflict other than to pay it lip service. It appears to rest on an implicit assumption that there is a "right" answer out there if only we knew where to find it. As many writers have pointed out, however, what is considered to be "rational" or "true" is socially constructed (for example, Astley, 1985). Knowledge is formulated on the basis of highly selective observations of the world. Sometimes our idea of truth is biased without our knowing, simply by virtue of particular experiences, which lead us to screen in some observations and facts and screen out others. At other times, seemingly "objective" criteria are consciously used to build credibility for some actions at the expense of others (Horowitz, 1970; Majone, 1976/7; Sabatier, 1978; Weiss & Bucuvalas, 1980). Performance evaluation is not neutral and may produce very different pictures, depending on which criteria are used (see Cameron, 1986). In fact, the very use of "objective" measurement tends to focus attention on factors that are easily measurable and quantifiable and immediately cast into doubt the legitimacy of factors that are less tangible (Bowen, 1977).

Clearly, the unitary perspective has limitations that impede its effectiveness in transforming higher education. What is needed is a perspective that more accurately describes the reality of higher education systems and institutions and, in so doing, provides a viable basis for the improvement of university administration. The framework that is proposed here is the pluralist perspective.

The Pluralist Perspective

What does pluralism mean? It means that there is a plurality of groups, inside and outside the organization, which have different world views, backgrounds, objectives, and interests. These groups are, potentially at least, in conflict with each other since they perceive problems, solutions, and goals differently. They are not bound together by any conception of the common interest and, in many circumstances, may be actively working toward mutually exclusive goals. Consequently, if the system (internal or external) is to work, these inevitable tensions must be managed. There must, therefore, be some recognition of who these different groups are, the interests that they represent, the objectives they are pursuing, and the sources of power they can command in their pursuit of them. In addition, skills must be developed that enable actors either to replace vested interests with a common interest thereby avoiding conflict, or to prevail over opposition in the event of conflict.

It is argued here that universities and systems of higher education are obviously pluralist. Diagram 1 shows some of the different groups that have an impact on university decision making. Many decisions involve the input of a variety of external interest groups. Decisions made by professors relating to research and teaching are often influenced by professional affiliations, research agencies, students, users of research, etc. As governments become more concerned with funding, and businesses become more involved in providing financial support, their influence on decision making increases. Inside the universities, most major decisions (and some not so major ones) involve a collection of different groups of professors, administrators, staff and students, and thus fall under the rubric of collective choice. As the diagram indicates, there may be a number of influences in this decision-making arena, but there is no reason to suggest that common interest or analytic process—the assumptions underlying the unitary perspective—will necessarily prevail (Hardy et al., 1983).

The groups that influence decisions in universities are not always bound by common goals and interests. Professors in a faculty of medicine are trained differently, do different work, and operate in a different environment than professors in a faculty of arts. Consequently, these two groups of professors are likely to perceive problems and solutions differently, even if they are not in direct conflict. As soon as resources become scarce, decisions that will benefit the medical school are unlikely to have any immediate pay-off to the arts faculty and vice versa. Similarly, administrators and professors also represent different interests and, the further we go along the continuum of professional administrators, the wider the gap between academics and managers is likely to be.

Once external stakeholders enter the picture, the potential for dissent increases. Those representing a university do not necessarily have the same view of the world, let alone the same objectives, as civil servants, politicians, or business people. And it is naive to think that they do. It has been often suggested that those in governments and businesses have the wrong picture of academia: that they perceive academics as a privileged group of individuals, protected by academic freedom and tenure, who receive large salaries to teach 150 hours a year, write the odd (usually critical) article, and spend the rest of the time consulting or travelling around the world. The implication is that once this misunderstanding is rectified, once communication is improved, once these groups learn how academics spend their time on research, they will be in agreement with the universities. Improved communication is not, however, going to bring about the unity of government, business, and university under a shared conception of common interest. Even if these groups understand each other perfectly, they will continue to view the world differently, define problems and solutions differently, protect different interests and, at times, pursue different objectives.

To make the point clear, let us take a person and move her between the different groups. As a professor, she will demand freedom to pursue research interests in order to secure tenure, which may call into question government policy or business ethics. As a politician she will naturally be interested in re-election, owe loyalty to her party, and support its policies. As a civil servant she will be concerned about the implementation of public policy in the face of ministerial reshuffles, government changes and expenditure cuts. As a business person, she will be held accountable for declining profits or sales in her division and her career will benefit from breakthroughs in productivity, research and development, or new markets.

The pressures inherent in any one of these situations will produce priorities that serve immediate needs but do not necessarily match those of other individuals. Even if we can free ourselves of the more immediate constraints of our environment, we still find ourselves pursuing different—and often conflicting— objectives. For example, when a productive academic assesses public policy, she wants to ensure that it will not hamper her ability, through reduced autonomy or funding, to make a contribution to the research and teaching mandate of her university. When a conscientious civil servant drafts legislation, she is concerned about how to control spending in the universities and ensure better value for money. When an honourable politician helps to develop party policy, she is concerned about how society can benefit from a publicly supported system of higher education. When a caring business person decides to make a donation to a university, she is concerned about how it will ultimately produce better educated employees, or research results that can be translated into new products, production processes, or working methods.

The fact is that even if the groups understand completely the needs and aims of the others, they are still each marching to a different tune. Consequently, if the relationship between universities and external stakeholders is to be effectively managed, we must accept reality—that the different groups involved in this relationship are more likely than not to be in a situation of real or potential conflict. Acting "rationally" does not help because rationality is in the eye of the beholder. Instead, actors have to adopt a pluralist perspective and develop political skills. They must be able to recognize the different interest groups, and the relationships and distribution of power between them, and take action that either substitutes common vision for vested interest or enables them to prevail in spite of conflicting interests.

"Hang Ups" with Power and Politics

There is often considerable ambivalence regarding the explicit adoption of the pluralist framework because it focuses on power and politics. It asks questions like: Who are the interest groups? What are their goals and do they conflict? What sources of power do these groups possess and what political strategies can they use to mobilize them? People are often very uncomfortable with terms like "power" and "politics" because they have connotations of exploitation and manipulation (Hardy, 1989a). The rational model, in contrast, is far more acceptable because it promotes the idea (if not the reality) of objectivity and unity. The symbolism of common goals, a united team, a happy family, is far more seductive. Clinging to the rational model is, however, counter-productive if its underlying assumptions do not apply. It will predispose actors to ignore the existence of potentially competing interest groups, and is unlikely to produce the necessary political acumen and skills that will allow them to overcome this competition and achieve the desired results.

While power and politics are typically equated with the pursuit of individual interests, it has been pointed out that they can also be mobilized to achieve outcomes that have benefits for the larger organization or collectivity. This form of power relates to the Parsonian view of power to achieve system goals (Parsons, 1967) and involves "power to" rather than "power over" (Knights & Willmot, 1982, 1985). Arendt (1986: 64) has spoken of power as the ability to act in concert and people who are "in power" are those empowered by others to act in their name. Habermas (1986: 76) argues that power is not "the instrumentalization of *another's* will, but the formation of a *common* will in a communication directed to reaching agreement." It involves "the consent of the governed that is mobilized for collective goals." Power is not simply repressive, it is also productive (Daudi, 1983). Power is not a zero sum game. It is

> the ability of different parties to achieve something together they could not achieve individually. This power governs a politics concerned with creating new possibilities in a world where resources may be scarce but some interests may be joined and new resources created (Baum, 1989: 195).

"Political" managers are not necessarily evil individuals exploiting sources of power to cater to their own vested interests. They may be trying to employ power to bring about actions that have some benefit for the larger collectivity. The fact that different groups have conflicting goals is not necessarily a product of greed and self-interest. It may be because they come from different backgrounds, experience different pressures and, therefore, have different views of the problems.

> Without perfect, unbounded, rationality it is quite feasible that individuals and groups may agree on ends without agreeing on how they are to be pursued. They are likely to perceive the world in terms of their own interests and see their own contribution to values and ends as especially significant. Thus, there may well be conflict, and the exercise of power, over interests when decisions are to be made (Walsh et al., 1981: 141).

Power and politics should, therefore, be viewed as neutral concepts. They can be put to both "good" and "bad" use in the sense that they can be mobilized for the benefit of the common interest as well as to serve self-interest. Apart from exceptional circumstances, the lines between the two are blurred. Many people act on the basis that power and politics will produce some collective good although they will probably derive some benefit as well. For example, if a dean scores a major coup in hiring a researcher of international stature, it will enhance the research profile of the institution, but it will also enhance her chances of being appointed to a second term. Furthermore, definitions of the "common good" differ according to the orientation of the interest group in question. Many people in the universities sincerely believe that the neglect of the humanities will negatively affect our society. Many people in government and business sincerely believe that more emphasis on professional areas is necessary to ensure global competitiveness and that society simply cannot afford to continue subsidizing the humanities. Both groups may mobilize power in line with these sincere but conflicting beliefs concerning the national interest.

The pluralist model thus includes both "power over" and "power to." In other words, power is not simply power over another individual or group. It is also a capacity or facility to achieve a collaborative outcome. The pluralist model assumes that while conflicts arise, values and norms are not so divergent that workable compromises cannot be achieved. Although society is not a unitary structure, the shifting coalitions of interest groups have to collaborate in some form if any of their goals are to be met. The terms of collaboration are determined by bargaining which, in turn, rests on the possession and use of power sources. Some conflict occurs, but so too do collaboration and consensus. Disagreements are not so great that the underlying system is at risk and, in fact, interest groups are willing to make compromises in order to protect it. In other words, interest groups are sometimes on different teams, sometimes on the same team but pulling in different directions, but they are all playing the same game. The political—or perhaps we should say politic—manager is, as a result, often the more effective because the adoption of the political perspective gives credence to interest groups and incorporates them into the management process instead of merely ignoring them. It also gives some thought to catering to the needs of these stakeholders in attempts to avoid conflict and resistance.

In summary, the pluralist perspective acknowledges that different interest groups with conflicting goals exist. These groups will resort to power to achieve their goals at the expense of other groups but power is also used to manage conflict and secure collaboration among these divergent groups. Power is, as a result, a factor in resolving conflict—whether it is to prevail in the face of opposition, or transform disagreement into consensus.

Pluralism and Practice

What does a pluralist framework mean in practice? There are two arenas that we should examine. The first is the internal arena and the nature of administrative policy. The second concerns the external arena and the links between universities and external stakeholders such as government and business.

The Internal Arena

The internal arena concerns the interest groups inside the institution that are in a position to influence decision making. Typically, they would include such groups as central administrators, boards of governors, senates, deans, professors' associations or unions, non-academic staff associations and unions, student associations, members of key committees, etc. The role played by these groups will, however, differ according to the traditions, history, and structure of the individual institution as well as the distribution of power among these groups.

Collegiality is not inevitable: it must be created

The existence of potentially conflicting interest groups within the university means that collegiality is not an inevitable, or even normal, state of affairs. Disciplinary allegiances tend to produce departmental subcultures (Becher, 1981) rather than institutional identification among academics. Consequently, collegiality has to be *created* by individuals capable of substituting a common vision for parochial interests. This situation has been observed in universities by Burton Clark (1970, 1971, 1972) in his work on saga. University leaders who have created and nurtured collegial cultures have been found (Hardy, 1990b). These leaders act as colleagues. Their focus is on the use of communication, language, and symbols to bind people to the institutional mission (Chaffee, 1984; Chaffee & Tierney, 1988).

A collegial culture means that individuals are willing to sacrifice individual or group interests in favour of an overarching institutional loyalty. This loyalty makes interest groups willing to accept decisions, which do not necessarily have any immediate benefit for them, as long as they have some institutional pay-off. It also makes groups more understanding and receptive to the different circumstances experienced by other groups. It can go a long way to creating excellence in an institution. It means that groups take decisions with reference to the common good rather than their own vested interest. It avoids time-consuming conflict. It builds commitment and institutional loyalty which may keep highly productive individuals—who inevitably have lucrative prospects elsewhere—in the institution. It has been found, for example, that recovery from turnaround is mainly the result of agreement around the institutional mission (Parker, 1987).

The important thing to note is that collegiality has to be created, and it may be difficult to create. It requires leaders who are sensitive and a socialization process that helps people to buy into an institutional saga. Recruitment of people who are likely to "buy into" the saga is important. These kinds of institutions also embody a risk. This type of culture may emphasize conformity to the extent that the organization finds it difficult to make radical change.

Change is not rational: it must be championed

While a particular change may seem rational to some organizational members, it is unlikely to appear rational to everyone. If a common vision has been created, groups that have nothing to gain from a proposal may nevertheless be willing to support it if it can be demonstrated that there is some benefit to the larger institution. But as has already been discussed, since collegiality is not easy to create there are many organizations where such altruism does not prevail. If that is the case, supporters of the change will have to champion its progress through approval structures and subsequent implementation. To do so, they will have to rely on various sources of power at their disposal.

One strategy is to try to prevent resistance by legitimizing the desired change (Hardy, 1985a,b). Sizer (1988b) has talked about how leaders create "on" switches where they build commitment to change, as opposed to "off" switches where organizational members fight the idea of change. Many of the techniques—use of symbols, language, rituals to build commitment—are similar to those used to create collegiality. In this case, however, the ability to create a pervasive collegial culture has proved impossible, and an attempt to create consensus around a specific issue is the goal (see, for example, Hardy & Pettigrew, 1985). Leaders who wish to champion change in this manner must adopt the role of a catalyst whereby they set broad parameters that focus attention and energy but then leave it to the experts—the professors—to determine how that change can be carried out (see Hardy, 1990b).

In some cases, however, it will prove impossible to secure agreement even on a specific issue because the differences between the groups do not allow it or because actors possess insufficient skills to achieve it. In this situation, resistance to change will occur. To overcome it, actors will need to appreciate the political context in which they are operating, possess the relevant power sources, and use them. There is a considerable body of literature in the field of management that has examined the use of power to overcome resistance to organizational change (see, for example, Pettigrew, 1973; Mumford & Pettigrew, 1975; Pfeffer, 1981; Hardy, 1985a).

Culture is not homogenous: it must be comprehended

If administrators are to be successful in both creating culture or championing change they must pay particular attention to the nature of the culture in which they work. University cultures are not all the same. There are significant institutional differences among universities with similar structures. These differences mean that action strategies must be tailored to meet the needs of the particular university. What will be considered legitimate in one university may be perceived as counter-cultural in another. This has implications for the change processes that will work and for the decision outcomes that will ensue. For example, Hardy (1987a, 1988a,b; 1989; 1990c) has found how different retrenchment strategies were adopted in six Canadian universities as a result of cultural differences (also see Hardy, 1990b). In other words, administrators must locate the "on" switches of a particular culture.

> A CEO creating strategic change has to recognize that a key element of the politics of organizational change relates to how the context of strategy can be mobilized to legitimate the content and process of any strategic adjustment. He who understands the political and cultural system of his organization, and the impact of changing economic and social trends on the emergence and dissolution of old issues, values, and priorities, and the rise of new rationalities and priorities is at least beyond the starting gate in formulating, packaging, and influencing the direction of organizational change (Pettigrew, 1985: 70/1).

Understanding culture is related to understanding the particular interest groups that exist in an institution, how power is distributed between them, and how it is used by them (see Hardy, 1988a, 1990b,c). If an assessment is made of the political context, administrators are in a far better position to understand their culture and the levers for change they can use.

Understanding different cultures is also important for public policy makers—any attempt by government to intervene directly in university matters can only occur in a highly standardized fashion. As a result, it is unlikely to be appropriate to and effective in the wide gamut of institutional cultures that seem to exist. It would also seem counter-productive for governments to try to homogenize institutional cultures. Business has recently found that a strong culture is an integral part of excellence (for example, Peters & Waterman, 1982). Watering down individual cultures may have adverse consequences for institutional excellence.

Effective strategy is not planned: it must be crafted

The ability to secure and maintain excellence is unlikely to result from planned strategy. The move to adopt strategic planning in the university context stems from the idea that *planned* change is more likely to result in enhanced performance than change that is unplanned. An example from the business world provides us with an alternative perspective. Honda's highly successful bid to capture the U.S. motorcycle market in the 1960s shows how the company adapted to a series of events and formed a highly effective strategy that defeated rivals on the basis of cost, quality, innovation (Pascale, 1988). What was important in the case of Honda was not its ability to plan but its ability to *learn*. The company was able to respond to events by recognizing them, assessing their potential, and adapting strategy to accommodate them. In fact, had the company stuck to its plans it would have continued to compete in the market for large motorcycles where existing rivals would have probably responded to this new threat. As it was, Honda inadvertently located a new niche in the small (50cc) bikes, which all the planning in the world would not have located nor provided a strategy.

Planning can have major drawbacks, particularly in university settings (Hardy, 1987b). It focuses on the past and extrapolates to the future, thus often ignoring unpredictable new opportunities. It commits resources and makes adaptation difficult. This rigidity produces tunnel vision and pre-empts organizational learning. It focuses on the knowable, the predictable, and the measurable, thus downplaying the importance of intangible factors, which are so important in universities. It separates formulation from implementation and de-emphasizes the latter, which is out of place in a decentralized organization like a university (Hardy, 1987b). Strategic planning has also come up with some "creative" but highly impractical recommendations. One widely read textbook on strategic planning suggests that had buggy whip manufacturers defined their business as self-starters for carriages they would still be in business today. But, as one critic has asked, if that was the case why not transportation accessories, guidance systems, or flagellation (Normann, 1977). The fact of the matter is that, knowing what business you are in or even what business you should be in does not necessarily make you any good at *doing* business (Bennett & Cooper, 1981).

One study of universities and leadership styles (Hardy, 1990b) found that the planner was the least appropriate management style in the context of a research institution. The centralized control and bureaucratic procedures embodied in it were almost totally at odds with the autonomy and freedom needed to stimulate research. The problem is that the planning often neglects people; yet, the key to excellence, particularly in universities, lies in its people. A decision to offer a new program or launch a new research project will not be realized unless the people with the necessary expertise, energy and vision are there to champion it. The key to excellence lies in attracting these types of people to an institution and keeping them there.

Planning may be counter-productive to this aim. It produces homogenized procedures that apply to all academics—both productive and unproductive. It runs the risk of alienating productive professors by curtailing their autonomy, while unproductive faculty will always find a way around the procedures. Planning may prevent the organization from adapting effectively. For example, one lucky—and unplanned—hiring decision can offer enormous potential for a new strategic development. The acquisition of one top researcher (maybe for a seemingly unrelated reason—perhaps she wishes to be nearer aging parents or is moving in conjunction with a dual career family) can bring other researchers, establish a new critical mass in a particular area, and launch a new research direction previously not considered. Conversely, a plan to offer a new program will founder if qualified personnel are not hired. Since initiatives which follow strategic planning exercises are based on market demand, planned developments often revolve around "hot" areas in which the competition for personnel is intense and salaries high. In a world of scarce resources, such initiatives may be doomed to failure or fulfilled only at great cost to other areas that might have benefited (in a more cost-effective way) from those resources.

The External Arena

The second arena concerns the relationship between universities and external stakeholders, notably government and business.

Government cooperation is not natural: it must be cultivated

If there are differences of interest inside the university, there will be even more between the university and external stakeholders. Establishing a common vision is more than just a matter of communication, it requires identifying the relevant interest groups, establishing exactly what their interests are, and framing actions in such a way that they serve these interests (Hardy, 1985b).

As far as government is concerned, the actions and strategies considered by universities will have to be evaluated in terms of their political feasibility.

> Not all the attention of the formulators [should be] on the problem and how to solve it. They must also think ahead to what is feasible ... strategic considerations are directed towards the legitimation process—building support for a proposed course of action, maintaining support held previously, deciding where compromises can be made, calculating when and where to make the strongest play and when and where to retain, controlling information flow to advantage (Jones, 1970: 51-2).

Public or private organizations that depend on external stakeholders have to take their dependency into account when they consider their options. Those that fail to do so may well find their intentions thwarted because they have failed to take into account the needs and power of their stakeholders. An assessment of political feasibility is necessary to bridge the gap between the desirable and the possible (Meltsner, 1972).

It is also important to recognize that government is not monolithic. It consists of its own different interest groups—cabinet members, members of Parliament, civil servants, etc. Each of these groups may have different objectives and may have to accommodate conflicting pressures. Thus, dealing with one group may involve quite different actions than dealing with another (Hardy, 1987c).

Business support is not assured: it must be courted

As far as business is concerned, it is important to recognize that it operates on very different premises to higher education. Support is not automatic and, therefore, universities have to take steps to court it actively. This involves creating legitimacy for the role in society played by universities.

A number of tactics are appropriate in this regard (Hardy, 1987c). First of all, universities must emphasize their visibility by highlighting the way in which they make a contribution to society and how they can make a contribution to business. Part of this process involves the use of public relations to demonstrate the credibility of the university enterprise. Another tactic concerns the control of information. While business is usually well aware of bottom line figures, universities have often been criticized for not knowing basic statistics. Information control is an important source of power and a critical device in creating legitimacy for actions and decisions. Any proposal needs to be couched in terms of the relevant supportive documentation.

> There is nothing intrinsically reprehensible in selecting the particular combination of data, facts, values, and analytic methods which seems to be the most appropriate to convince a particular audience (Majone, 1976-7: 208-9).

Dependence is not healthy: it must be circumscribed

The above strategies are already being employed by universities who have to live in the real world, dealing with government and business. It is, however, important to realize the implications of dependency relations. Universities have been warned about "selling out" to industry by accepting large donations that enable it to dictate the direction of our research; or accepting endowed chairs where the donor has influence (formal or informal) over the selection of candidates. Providing money also provides an opportunity for control. The university sector has also been warned about government visions of a "high-tech" university that has a visible pay-off in terms of the sciences and professions, but which degrades the importance of areas such as the social sciences and humanities and which inhibits the development of critical thought.

Dependency on external stakeholders reduces the power of the universities. Dependency confers power (Emerson, 1972; Astley & Sachdeva, 1984): the more universities are dependent on outside groups, the more power these groups have over the universities. Since these external stakeholders have different interests to the universities, it is reasonable to suggest that they will use that power to further their own interests rather than those of the university community. For example, at a conference on the need for collaboration between the university and business communities, held in 1983 (*Financial Post*, 1983), the chairman of Bell-Northern Research Ltd. is reported as saying (p. C6) that "most of university work is curiosity-oriented and unfortunately pure and not particularly relevant... We fund research but we control the directions it will take..." A university representative, on the other hand, is reported (p. C2) as saying: "I have long believed the research undertaken by the universities should be free, independent and determinately non-utilitarian..."

Difficulties in establishing joint research between universities and business have been attributed to cultural or legal differences. Some writers recommend that various types of "halfway house" (such as joint ventures, partnerships, consortia, or contractual arrangements) be set up to act as a bridge between the two cultures (see, for example, Tatel & Guthrie, 1983; Smith, 1984; Ashworth, 1985; Williams, 1986; Nelkin & Nelson, 1987; Cerych, 1989). These various forms of partnership embody the compromises necessary to sustain a workable relationship. But, as has been argued earlier, differences between the interest groups are not simply a matter of understanding and communication, they are a matter of conflicting interests. When two parties (university and government or university and business) join together to set up any sort of collaborative enterprise, each will be seeking to secure its goals and, while each may be willing to collaborate, the nature of the compromises will be determined by their relative dependency. The more the dependency, the more the need to compromise!

Universities must, therefore, take steps to reduce their dependency on external stakeholders and increase their power relative to these groups. Some of the tactics mentioned above: enhancing visibility, creating credibility, using information, etc., are relevant here, too. Members of the university community must also build coalitions with each other and with other interest groups. Public support can be mustered. There may be some commonality of cause with hospitals, for example. Finally, they must not be seduced by the short-term benefits of securing public and private money by actions which, in the long term, increase their dependency of external stakeholders.

The new reality is here: it must be conceded *and conquered*

While universities can reduce dependency, they cannot eliminate it. They *are* dependent on government and business, which means that these external stakeholders do have power over them. Members of the university community cannot, therefore, act like ostriches and bury their heads in the sand. If they do, government frustration and business disillusionment are likely to cost universities dear in the form of increased controls and reduced corporate sponsorship.

The universities have to negotiate their future with the external constituencies by compromising on some points and holding fast on others (and acquiring the power sources that enable them to hold fast). There appears to be a window of opportunity—so far Canadian universities remain relatively unscathed in comparison to those in some other countries. It would appear that accountability is more acceptable to the universities than direct intervention that constrains university autonomy. If that is the case, universities should start being accountable and building the procedures that are required to satisfy external demands. At the same time, universities must adopt a more pragmatic approach to power—they need it to fulfil their own interests and to ensure productive collaboration with the stakeholders on which they are dependent. In other words, we must both beat and join the new reality.

Conclusions

Pluralism represents a fundamental shift in perception: it means recognizing that the conflicts we experience in the arena of higher education are not the result of miscommunication or misunderstanding, nor are they caused by aberrant individuals. They are the inevitable result of the existence of different interest groups which, while working under the same broad paradigm, are often characterized by incompatible goals. It is, perhaps, not a very attractive framework: we are often reluctant to acknowledge such inherent tensions within our society. Once we do recognize them, however, we are in a position to heal the differences and create some degree of consensus around the functioning of higher education. It is, then, only by recognizing division that we can create a working unity. More to the point, as has been seen in other cases (Hardy, 1986), attempts to introduce administrative and public policy based on the faulty assumptions associated with the unitary approach simply do not work well.

It is the political analysis embodied in the pluralist perspective that is most helpful in this regard. It not only acknowledges the existence of potential conflict as the result of disparate interest groups, but also provides an analysis of why and how it arises by reference to the political context of a particular situation, institution, or issue. It also indicates how power can be used to build consensus. The pluralist perspective thus provides some indication of how competing interests—both inside and outside the institution—can be managed. The unitary perspective neither accurately describes the situation, nor offers useful advice on how to deal with it.

The pluralist perspective draws attention to the relative power of interest groups and places university administrators in a better position to deal with both internal interest groups and external stakeholders. It also injects a note of reality—universities *are* dependent and administrators will have to acknowledge and respond to some of the demands that are being made of them if they are not to lose their existing autonomy.

Representatives of government and industry also need to recognize the plurality of the higher education system and the complexity that is involved in the myriad groups that exist. It is important that business leaders realize that the goals of the university community are different from their own. There are times, however, when those goals are compatible and joint initiatives can be set up that benefit both parties. In setting up any form of partnership, both partners will be seeking to increase their advantages. Thus, the nature of the university-business liaisons will reflect the nature of dependency relations between the two sides.

The realization that universities represent arenas of potentially conflicting groups will also help government to comprehend the difficulties involved in orchestrating change in this sector. Any subsequent inclination to increase the power of central administration at the expense of other groups must be countered with the realization that universities are successful *because* of decentralized power. Moreover, culture is believed to play a key role in organizational success. Any attempt by government to impose standardized systems across the higher education sector is likely to weaken effective cultures and dispel the sagas (Clark, 1970) that make for great institutions. University autonomy may frustrate policy makers because of the abuses they assume take place; but bureaucracy is not the solution because loopholes will always be found. The fact is that neither administrators nor policy makers can afford to hide behind the security of standardized planning mechanisms. Universities (if not many other organizations) require politically astute leaders who can deal with conflict and create consensus; who know how to reward as well as how to control; who can tap the advantages of a strong culture or change an ineffectual culture. They need discriminating management; not across-the-board management that ignores their complexity and diversity.

Bibliography

Ashworth, J.M. "What Price an Ivory Tower? University-Industry Relationships." *Higher Education Review*, 17(2), 31-43, Spring, 1985.

Arendt, Hanna. "Communicative Power." In Lukes, Steven, (ed.) *Power.* Oxford, England: Basil Blackwell, 59-74, 1986.

Astley, W. Graham. "Administrative Science As Socially Constructed Truth." *Administrative Science Quarterly*, 30, 497-513, 1985.

Axelrod, P. "Service or Captivity? Business-University Relations in the Twentieth Century." In Neilson & Gaffield, *op. cit.*, 1986.

Astley, W. Graham, and Sachdeva, Paramjit S. "Structural Sources of Intraorganizational Power: A Theoretical Synthesis." *Academy of Management Review*, 9, (1), 104-113, 1984.

Baum, Howell S. "Organizational Politics Against Organizational Culture: A Psychoanalytic Perspective." *Human Resource Management*, 28, (2), 191-206, Summer 1989.

Becher, T. "Towards a Definition of Disciplinary Cultures." *Studies in Higher Education*, 6, 109-22, 1981.

Bennett, R.C. & Cooper, R.G. "The Misuse of Marketing: An American Tragedy." *Business Horizons*, 51-61, November/December, 1981.

Bowen, H.R. *Investment in Learning*. San Francisco: Jossey Bass, 1977.

Business Week. "The New Breed of Business Planner." *Business Week*, 62-68, 1984.

Cameron, K.S. "Effectiveness as Paradox: Consensus and Conflict in Conceptions of Organizational Effectiveness." *Management Science*, 32 (5), 539-553, 1986.

Cerych, L. "University-Industry Collaboration: A Research Agenda and Some General Impacts on the Development of Higher Education." *European Journal of Education*, 24(3), 309-313, 1989.

Chaffee, E.E. "Successful Strategic Management in Small Private Colleges." *Journal of Higher Education*, 55, (2), 213-241, 1984.

Chaffee, E.E., and Tierney, W.G. *Collegiate Culture and Leadership Strategies*. New York: MacMillan, 1988.

Clark, B.R. *The Distinctive College: Antioch, Reed and Swarthmore*. Chicago: Aldine, 1970.

Clark, Burton R. "Belief and Loyalty in College Organization." *Journal of Higher Education*, 42, 499-520, 1971.

Clark, B.R. "The Organizational Saga in Higher Education." *Administrative Science Quarterly*, 17, 178-184, 1972.

Committee of Vice-Chancellors & Principals. *Report of the Steering Committee for Efficiency Studies in Universities*. United Kingdom: Jarratt report, 1985.

Cope, R.G. *Strategic Policy Planning*. Littleton, Colo.: Ireland Educational Corporation, 1978.

Daudi, Philippe. *Power in the Organisation: The Discourse of Power in Managerial Praxis*. Oxford: Basil Blackwell Limited, 1986.

Emerson, R.M. "Power-Dependence Relations." *American Sociological Review*, 27, (1), 31-41, 1962.

Financial Post. "Conference Report." *Financial Post*, pp. C1-C8, May 14, 1983.

Fox, A. "Industrial Relations: A Social Critique of Pluralist Ideology." In Child, J., (ed.), *Man and Organization*. London: Allen and Unwin, 185-233, 1973.

Habermas, Jurgen. "Hannah Arendt's Communications Concept of Power." In Lukes, Steven, (ed.), *Power*. Oxford, England: Basil Blackwell, 59-93, 1986.

Harris, W.E., and Holdaway, E.A. "Systematic Reviews of University Programs and Units." *Canadian Journal of Higher Education*, 13, 55-76, 1983.

Hardy, C. *Managing Organizational Closure*. Aldershot, England: Gower Press, 1985a.

Hardy, C. "The Nature of Unobtrusive Power." *Journal of Management Studies*, 22, (4), 384-399, 1985b.

Hardy, C. "Management in the National Health Service: Using Politics Effectively." *Public Policy and Administration*, 1, (1), 1-17, 1986.

Hardy, C. "Strategic Planning?" in Paquet, G. & Von Zur-Muehlen M. (eds.), *Education Canada?* Ottawa: Canadian Higher Education Network, 1987a.

Hardy, C. "Using Content, Context and Process to Manage University Cutbacks." *Canadian Journal of Higher Education*, 17, (1), 65-82, 1987b.

Hardy, C. "Turnaround Strategies in Universities." *Planning for Higher Education*, 16, (1), 9-23, 1987c.

Hardy, C. "The Rational Approach to Budget Cuts: One University's Experience." *Higher Education*, 17, 151-73, 1988a.

Hardy, C. "Managing the Interest Groups in University Structures." In Hoy, F., (ed.), *Proceedings of the Academy of Management*. Anaheim, Calif.: Academy of Management, 361-6, 1988b.

Hardy, C. "La Gestion des Restrictions Budgetaires dans les Universites : Deux Experiences Canadiennes," *Sociologie du Travail*, 4, 427-453, 1989a.

Hardy, C. " 'Hard' Decisions and 'Tough' Choices: the Business Approach to University Decline." *Higher Education*, 20, (3), 1-21, 1990a.

Hardy, C. *Managing Strategy in Academic Institutions: Learning from Brazil*. Berlin: De Gruyter, 1990b.

Hardy, C. "Strategy and Context: Retrenchment in Canadian Universities." *Organization Studies*, 11, (2), 207-237, 1990c.

Hardy, C., Langley, A., Mintzberg, H., and Rose, J. "Strategy Formation in the University Setting." *Review of Higher Education*, 6, (4), 407-433, 1983.

Hardy, C., and Pettigrew, A.M. "The Use of Power in Managerial Strategies for Change." In Rosenbloom, R.S., (ed.), *Research on Technological Innovation, Management and Policy*, 2. Greenwich, Conn.: JAI Press, 11-45, 1985.

Horowitz, I.L. "Social Science Mandarins: Policymaking as a Political Formula." *Policy Sciences*, 1, 339-360, 1970.

Jones, C.O. *An Introduction to the Study of Public Policy*. Belmont, California: Wadsworth, 1970.

Keller, G. *Academic Strategy: The Management Revolution in American Higher Education*. Baltimore: John Hopkins University Press, 1983.

Kiechel, W. "Corporate Strategies." *Fortune*, 106, 34-39, 1982.

Kiechel, W. "Sniping at Strategic Planning." *Planning Review*, 8-11, 1984.

Knights, D., and Willmott, H. "Power, Values and Relations: A Comment on Benton." *Sociology*, 16, (4), 578-585, 1982.

Knights, D., and Willmott, H. "Power and Identity in Theory and Practice." *Sociological Review*, 33, (1), 22-46, 1985.

Lee, R.A. & Piper, J.A. "Organizational Control, Differing Perspectives: The Management of Universities." *Financial Accountability & Management*, 4(2), 113-128, 1988.

Lyles, M.A., and Lenz, R.T. "Managing the Planning Process: A Field Study of the Human Side of Planning." *Strategic Management Journal*, 3, (2), 105-118, 1982.

Majone, Giandomenico. "The Uses of Policy Analysis." In Russell Sage Foundation (ed.), *The Future and the Past: Essays on Programs*. 1977.

Meltsner, Arnold. "Political Feasibility and Policy Analysis." *Public Administrative Review*, 32, 859-867, 1972.

Miller, R.I. *The Assessment of College Performance*. San Francisco: Jossey-Bass, 1979.

Miller, R.I. *Evaluation of Quality*. Paper presented at the 8th European Forum of the Association of Institutional Research, Loughborough, England, 1986.

Mumford, E., and Pettigrew, A.M. *Implementing Strategic Decisions.* London: Longman, 1975.

Nelkin, D. & Nelson, R. "Commentary: University-Industry Alliances." *Science, Technology & Human Values,* 12 (1), 65-74, 1987.

Normann, R. *Managing for Growth.* London: Wiley, 1977.

Parker, B. *Discriminants for Recovery from Decline.* Paper presented at the annual meeting of the Association for the Study of Higher Education, San Diego, 1987.

Parsons. *Sociological Theory and Modern Society.* London: Collier-MacMillan, 1967.

Pascale, R.T. "The Honda Effect." In Quinn, J.B., Mintzberg, H. & James, R.M. (eds.), *The Strategy Process,* 104-113. Englewood Cliffs, N.J.: Prentice Hall, 1988.

Peters, T.J., and Waterman, R.H. *In Search of Excellence.* New York: Harper and Row, 1982.

Pettigrew, A.M. *The Politics of Organizational Decision Making.* London, England: Tavistock, 1973.

Pettigrew, A.M. "Contextualist Research and the Study of Organizational Change Processes." In Mumford, E., et al. (eds.), *Research Methods in Information Systems,* 53-77. Holland: Elsevier, 1985.

Pfeffer, Jeffrey. *Power in Organizations.* Marshfield, Mass.: Pitman, 1981.

Sabatier, Paul. "The Acquisition and Utilization of Technical Information by Administrative Agencies." *Administrative Science Quarterly,* 23, 396-47, 1978.

Sizer, J. "The Management of Institutional Adaptation and Change under Conditions of Financial Stringency." In Eggins, H. (ed.) *Restructuring Higher Education: Proceedings of the Annual Conference 1987.* Milton Keynes, England: Society for Research into Higher Education & Open University, 80-92, 1988b.

Smith, K.A. "Industry-University Research Programs." *Physics Today,* 37(2), 24-29, February, 1984.

Tatel, D.S. & Guthrie, R.C. "The Legal Ins and Outs of University-Industry Collaboration." *Educational Record,* 64(2), 19-25, Spring 1984.

Walsh, Kieron, Hinings, Bob, Greenwood, Royston and Ranson, Stewart. "Power and Advantage in Organizations." *Organization Studies,* 2, (2), 131-152, 1981.

Weiss, Carol H., Bucuvalas, Michael J. *Social Science Research and Decision-Making.* New York: Columbia University Press, 1980.

Williams, J.C. "Industry-University Interactions: Finding the Balance." *Engineering Education*, 76(6), 320-325, March 1986.

Discussion following the Hardy Paper

The question was posed whether the two models of the university community—the pluralist and the unitary—could be generalized to other types of organizations and even to systems of government, in particular federal systems; there was broad agreement that the two models did have an application that could be generalized.

There was some discussion of whether the essentially pluralist nature of universities gave them a high degree of flexibility and capacity for adaptation to change. The view was offered that larger and longer-established institutions would be likely to be less flexible and adaptive than smaller and newer institutions, but that, in general, provided university administrators recognized that change occurred primarily at the level of the individual unit or department, and supported that change, universities could indeed be adaptive and resilient at a time of change.

There was some discussion on whether in a pluralist model there was any room for better information systems, strategic planning, and accountability reports of the sort that had been discussed earlier in the workshop. Subject to the various qualifications which had emerged over the workshop about the nature of valid and reliable information about university performance, it was acknowledged that, generally, more information was better than less, and that the pluralist model could and should accommodate the need for more and better information.

The final area of discussion related to strategic planning in universities. The question was posed whether universities should be adopting strategic planning if it was being rejected, at least in its most formal and quantitative sense, in the corporate sector. It was generally agreed that the usefulness of strategic planning in universities depended on how it was used. If strategic planning was adapted to the complexity and subtlety of universities, and was generated from the bottom up rather than imposed from the top down, then it could be used to create vision and collegiality and to improve the management and accountability of universities. It was agreed that the trick was to avoid any notion that there was some sort of magic quantitative wand which could somehow make universities work effectively and efficiently. There was consensus that universities should use strategic planning, like performance indicators, at their own risk, but should also recognize the risk of not using it!

V

How Universities in Canada View the Opportunities and Problems of a Changing Environment: The Perspective of Four Presidents

The University Perspective on Funding, Autonomy and Accountability: A View from Concordia

Patrick Kenniff

Autonomy and accountability are critical issues for our collective futures. As social and cultural institutions, universities do not exist in a vacuum, removed from the exigencies of collective responsibility, and the manner in which we fulfil our obligations may, in a sense, be as important as our obligations themselves.

My perspective this afternoon is twofold: as rector of a relatively young urban institution with much older roots, and as president of the Conférence des recteurs et des principaux des universités du Québec. I shall focus primarily on the Quebec context, but since our experience is not substantially different from that found in most other industrialized countries, I trust my viewpoint will carry some measure of general relevance.

I should like, at the outset, to give a brief historical overview of the major forces that have marked the growth and development of what I shall call "the accessible university" in Quebec in the course of the last 25 years. This quarter-century can be divided into two general periods: from the mid-1960s to the late-1970s, and from the late-1970s to the present.

The early 1960s in Quebec were marked by a profound realignment of educational priorities, which led to an increased involvement of government in the educational sphere. Prior to this period, universities were funded by a combination of tuition fees and some government grants, with tuition fees providing the larger source of revenue. From the mid-1960s through the 1970s and 1980s, however, government grants became an increasingly important component of university funding. By the end of the 1960s, tuition fees in Quebec constituted some 25 per cent of the operating budgets of universities, but by 1989-90, the percentage had dropped to 7 per cent. In Quebec, it is obvious that the process of government involvement in the funding of universities was accelerated by the fact that tuition fees were frozen until this year.

The years from the mid-1960s to the late-1970s were, much like elsewhere, ones of rapid expansion for Quebec universities. Notable features of this period were:

- increased accessibility at the lower level of the educational system, matched with strong pressures in favour of greater accessibility to a university-level education, thereby forming the basis for an important change in the overall profile of university enrolments

- the emergence of a new institutional order in higher education: the government set up new councils and advisory bodies to help shape government policy with respect to universities; new institutions were established (particularly a province-wide university system modelled on some American state university systems—l'Université du Québec); and, most important, a new level of post-secondary education was created between the high schools and the universities: the Collèges enseignement général et professionel (CEGEPs). At the same time, many long-established universities replaced their charters with new acts of the provincial legislature where the principle of active government involvement, especially through the mechanism of appointing government representatives to governing boards, was recognized

- this was also a time of profound social mutations, when students were actively questioning the purpose of education, and collective bargaining by faculty and staff unions became a regular feature of university life. As a result of pressures by the internal constituencies of universities, and in the wake of the Duff-Berdahl report in the mid-1960s, students, faculty and staff sought and obtained representation on the governing boards and senates of most Canadian universities

- in addition, the relative importance of government as a source of operating funds became overwhelming. This led to greater government involvement in policy issues with respect to academic programs, physical facilities and many other aspects of university operations, including the introduction of formula financing. As funds were available in relative abundance, and as autonomy remained basically intact, universities accepted these changes without much outcry

From the late-1970s to the present—a period of slowing economic growth and dwindling government resources—the development of universities in Quebec was marked by four salient characteristics:

1. the advent of government budgetary restrictions without any change to existing policies on accessibility, leading to a dramatic decrease in real per student spending

2. with a scarcity of financial resources at their disposal, universities were forced to take drastic measures: hiring of new full-time faculty was brought to an almost total halt and part-time instructors became an increasingly familiar feature on campus. The resultant stagnation of faculty complements, combined with the inability to renew and upgrade physical facilities and library resources, led to a significant increase of internal tensions and managerial dilemmas

3. a keener awareness of the scarcity of public funds provided an even greater sense of the appropriateness of government involvement in the setting of priorities for universities

4. this final feature translated into universities becoming increasingly encompassed in the regulatory mechanisms developed for the control of public spending, whether through more constraining funding formulas or more sophisticated and apparently more reliable statistical reporting requirements

The foregoing represents a quick overview of the evolution of the Quebec university system over the past three decades. In substance, it is not different from experiences in other Canadian provinces and indeed in many foreign jurisdictions.

Before discussing in more detail the issues of autonomy and accountability, I should like to make a few remarks about where I stand with respect to these concepts in the regulatory environment in which we are required to function at the outset of the 1990s.

I believe strongly in both the autonomy and the accountability of Canadian universities. The notions are not contradictory; they are complementary in exactly the same way that rights and responsibilities go hand in hand. It is part of the accepted pattern of things in Canada that universities will receive important public funding, whether they are private or public. This is, in part, a recognition of the fact that university graduates provide an important benefit to society as a whole. The debate is not about *whether* governments should fund universities, but about the extent to which the source of funding determines the rules of institutional autonomy and accountability.

In this regard, governments have had a tendency to consider that because their role in funding universities is so overpowering, accounts should be rendered only to them, not only with respect to the expenditure of public funds, but also on *all* facets of university administration. I have heard civil servants over the years argue that even if government paid only 50 per cent of the piper, it expected to call 100 per cent of the tune (note that this is the language of control, not of accountability).

Given the tremendous importance of universities in the development of our economy and our society, it is clear that government spending in this area must be even further increased. The disastrous effects of the cuts in government funding in Quebec universities during the 1980s are illustration enough of this need if we are to meet the economic and societal challenges which face us in the decades ahead. What are the implications, therefore, of increased state funding on the autonomy and accountability of universities?

Autonomy

In Canada, universities, whether public or private, have always been considered as autonomous institutions. This has not always been the case for other levels of education. In Quebec, for example, primary, secondary and collegial level institutions are part of the public and para-public sectors for such purposes as collective bargaining, pension plans, benefits and so on. As such, they are subject to regulation under umbrella legislation of the kind which does not exist for the university system.

This being said, government funding constitutes such a major outlay of public funds that it is perfectly understandable that accounts should be rendered, and no one questions the need nor the principle involved. The question is rather one of the type and degree of accountability which satisfy the public, while still remaining compatible with genuine university autonomy.

Let us look at the degree to which this reasonable expectation has resulted in direct changes in the autonomy of universities over the years.

In Quebec, the first half of the last 25 years was marked by minimal government control over universities, apart from the establishment of relatively flexible mechanisms for the accreditation of new academic programs. Neither did the setting up of advisory bodies to government, such as the Conseil des universités in Quebec (created in 1968-69), have much of a constricting effect on our *marge de manoeuvre*.

The shifts which occurred in our internal governance at that time were much more related to such social pressures as student unrest, entrance of an older population into the university and faculty unionization—all factors which forced us to realign our notions of authority and collegiality, while leaving our basic autonomy relatively intact.

It was the second period, from the late 1970s to the present, when government interfered more pointedly with our autonomy, most generally through its control of funding mechanisms. The way was somehow found to pay public lip-service to the sacrosanct principle of accessibility, while cutting resources to universities. We also saw the appearance of a particular phenomenon: different levels of funding by government-defined priority sectors.

Between the end of the 1970s and the middle of the 1980s in Quebec, for example, an important part of the growth of student enrolments was funded by the mechanism of *prélèvement*—better known as "stealing from the poor to give to the poor." Essentially, the monies required to fund the influx of new students were subtracted from the base funding of each university according to the percentage—prorated—of the overall grants, and then redistributed according to each institution's share of the total new enrolments. In 1985-86, therefore, per student funding in real terms was at 70 per cent of its 1978-79 level, even though Quebec universities had welcomed an additional 40,000 students during this same period.

Another clear example of how governmental control of the funding formula has pressed universities into certain orientations and priorities is made evident, in Quebec, by the current policy of funding only 70 per cent of the average cost of new enrolments in the so-called priority sectors, and 50 per cent in the non-priority areas. The priority sectors are generally a reflection of the government's own economic interests: the pure and applied sciences, administration, and graduate levels in only the social sciences and law. This leaves the humanities—to say nothing of the fine arts— in a continued state of underdevelopment.

As disconcerting as such government policies may be, many of the fundamental attributes of autonomy remain unaltered: we are still responsible for hirings and promotions, the internal allocation of resources and modifications to academic programs, or the creation of new ones. In terms of the collective bargaining process, we are the only level of education in Quebec where bargaining is done outside the government framework for the public and para-public sectors.

At the beginning of the 1990s, therefore, what we are facing is not so much a loss of our autonomy per se, as a whole series of contradictory pressures: greater collegiality/less control at the internal level; greater accountability/more control externally. We are also witnessing an increase in the number and seriousness of the constraints affecting our governance, and this is redefining the meaning of autonomy and the choices to which it can realistically be applied. There is a window of opportunity there if we take the lead in shaping the agenda of change, but only if we are successful in making the meaning of autonomy crystal clear—and also abiding by our principles when making our own choices.

The fundamental reason for which autonomy has worked well within our educational system is that Canadian universities, contrary to the other levels in the system, carry out a triple mandate of teaching, research and service to the community. To carry out this mandate in a spirit and a climate that foster critical and creative thinking and inquiry, universities must be protected from external pressures which might threaten the potential for independent thought. To blossom, then, universities, as is the case for knowledge itself, must be able to function with a minimum of outside interference. Obviously, by this I do not mean that universities need not be responsible or responsive to external influences. Such a statement would be absurd, and would only serve to strengthen the tenacious myth that universities are ivory towers where no attempt is made to address the issues and challenges of the communities and societies in which they function.

Rather, my remarks are meant as a reminder that in defining and applying instruments to measure cost effectiveness, as well as in discussing the nature of the services rendered to society by universities, we do not buckle under the tremendous pressures applied to cut the university cloth to fit short-term economic exigencies or ideological trends. Unfortunately, under the guise of legitimate claims of accountability, that line has been crossed on more than one occasion—to such an extent that we now face an uphill struggle if we wish to make the public understand the true meaning of university autonomy and why it is so vital and necessary within our system.

Accountability

In the years of expansion in Quebec, both in enrolments and the infrastructure of universities, the main tool of accountability—and it remains so even today—was the annual financial report which universities had to complete and forward to the government.

Apart from greater sophistication in our financial statements—increasingly made public—and the beginnings of management information systems, accountability during this period was essentially a matter of regular communications between universities and the government ministries concerned, as well as between senior management and the governing bodies of their institutions.

With the appearance of funding cuts, however, the pressure on universities to demonstrate better what it was they did came from new and different sectors: the legislature, the internal university community itself, and, most important, public opinion.

There was, during this period, a qualitative and quantitative jump in the notion of accountability. Even though traditional methods of reporting to government were still in place (and still are), accountability now operated in the public eye. At times, this was because universities themselves were looking for public support; at other times, the legislature, through such forums as commissions of inquiry and parliamentary hearings, was looking for some leverage on university priorities.

Today we can say, on a technical level, that government has all the data which it needs—from numbers of admissions and registrations to research funds, use of space, personnel statistics— to get a complete picture of what universities do and how they do it. Government is as well-informed, if not better, than we some- times are about ourselves. In addition, there have never been so many publications available to the public about and by univer- sities.

The challenge, as I see it today, is not so much accountability per se but rather *what type of accountability, to whom and to what end.*

Universities are and must remain accountable to a wide range of constituencies, *not just to government.* These include stu- dents themselves, society at large, the international academic community, and, increasingly, the peoples of the developing world. As the mission statement from my university puts it: "... we are committed to responsible and innovative leadership in fulfilling the mission of universities to develop and disseminate knowledge and values, and to act as a social critic." The words "social critic" are important to underscore. I hope this is a part of our mission that we consider worth upholding and nourishing. The fact that it becomes an increasingly difficult function to carry out, given our growing dependence on both government and business, as I have mentioned to the university community at Concordia, makes it the more essential that we maintain that function individually and collectively. A community has the right to expect from its universities both intellectual leadership and social criticism based on possession of the facts as well as clear and cogent reasoning. In fact, the vigour with which we carry out these two tasks may provide the strongest argument in favour of our very existence.

Accountability, then, is much more than a matter of acting responsibly in the administration of funds, be they of private or public origin. It is also a matter of taking the lead in providing information required to demonstrate our good stewardship. And, as I have just mentioned, it is also taking a strong and vigorous lead in explaining the role universities must play, the expectations society may reasonably place upon them and the various ways in which we can and must live up to these needs and expectations.

In matters of autonomy and accountability, universities always walk a very fine line, and it is only by respecting our own agenda that we can avoid the attempts at overt control by one interest group or another, be it government, industry, students or opinion leaders within the community. If we owe this to ourselves, we owe it also to our supporters and constituents.

Future Perspectives

In conclusion, I would like to examine some of the trends that are likely to affect the future of higher education in Quebec, in relation to the funding, autonomy, and accountability of universities.

With respect to funding, I see three possibilities:

- at the very best, a levelling off of government support, and perhaps even a decrease, due to the impact of such factors as an aging population needing a greater share of public resources, as well as the imperatives of international economic competition, which will require that public sector spending be less of a burden on the economy

- as the state withdraws more and more from direct support of higher education, a greater reliance upon other sources of revenue—notably tuition fees and private sector support—with the resulting effect of increased competition among universities and even, we should not be afraid to say it, a possible negative impact on accessibility

- quite apart from any debate about EPF transfers and political uncertainties, over which universities have minimal control, the priorities for government spending on universities may shift from an emphasis on basic funding to a desire to finance the end-product or "output" of higher education, which raises yet unsolved methodological problems. If it takes the shape of contractual financing, as in Great Britain for example, it may have a significant impact on our autonomy.

With base funding reduced to bare essentials, we may then find ourselves in the somewhat uncomfortable position of seeking out contracts geared to a very specific market. I need not dwell here upon the severe distortions that already exist between the funding available in certain high-profile disciplines—physics, biochemistry, engineering and electronics being some of the examples that immediately spring to mind—and the underfunding affecting the humanities, fine arts, and the social sciences. Nor need I remind you that "funding the output" will not only dramatically increase those distortions, but it will also seriously alter the balance between fundamental and applied research in those fields attracting the most attention.

We are all generally aware of some of the schemes that governments in other Commonwealth countries, such as the United Kingdom and Australia, and in France, have put in place in order to achieve a measure of more direct control over universities. Whether the policy is one based on "funding by output" or "funding by bidding on contracts," the result is invariably the same: governments tell universities who they educate, at what level, in what numbers and in which sectors. We have not yet experienced government intervention to this degree in Canada, but it behooves us to heed the warning that it could happen here.

Furthermore, our internal manoeuvrability will be greatly reduced by the fact that we will now find ourselves having to engage in very tight and constricting strategic planning, exacerbated by the need to keep up with our competitors. There is no question that universities need to plan, but I doubt seriously if we want to do it without some reference to our fundamental academic mission.

It is clear that universities increasingly have to let the public know what they do, primarily because public support is needed to ensure that government pays attention to our concerns. In many ways, our success at this will determine our capacity to attain our highest level of development. In other words, our autonomy has to be well understood and appreciated, at the same time that we are held increasingly accountable for our actions. For example, the provincial auditor of Ontario has the authority to conduct audits of university accounts and has done so on two occasions (Guelph and Trent). Similar authority exists in the act governing the auditor general of Quebec but has not yet been invoked.

I believe also that we must agree to enter into integrated audit discussions with government, with a view to ensuring that the *collective* concerns as well as the rights of our institutions of higher learning are well understood and respected by the public officials who determine the level of our resources. To refuse to do so would, I suspect, do us significant damage in the long run. I would also submit that this is a collective responsibility shared by all universities, and that collaboration in this area is in the best interests of all.

However, after universities and governments have invested massively in very sophisticated information systems, there is a serious need to determine the type and level of data required by public decision makers. Universities are large and complex organizations and for information to be useful at the central decision-making level, it has to be aggregate data focusing on particular issues. I suspect that the current difficulties in this area are not caused by a dearth of information, but rather by an over-abundance of data combined with a less-than-clear idea of what the facts and figures are saying; in other words, government may well be failing to see the forest for the trees . . . .

These are but some elements of reflection on some very important questions. The manner in which we answer them will undoubtedly profoundly influence the university as we know it. So much more, then, the need for prudence, vigilance and courage in our present and future responses to funding crises, demands for greater accountability, and challenges to our basic autonomy.

There is no doubt that the university must adapt to changing economic and social realities; indeed, I am in a position to observe that we are doing just that and fully intend to continue doing so. But I must also insist that in an age much given to mechanistic models, the university will often continue to baffle with its seemingly contradictory ways, its complex collegial workings and its annoying lack of straightforward responses to complicated problems. Universities have continued to serve society well over the centuries, precisely because they are living entities. As such, they must internalize change and find new, creative balances between traditional needs and contemporary challenges. That is, in fact, our very *raison d'être* which we fully intend to pursue in the years to come.

The University Perspective on Funding, Autonomy and Accountability: A View from Carleton

Robin H. Farquhar

I understand that my role, as with Patrick Kenniff, is to bring to our deliberations the perspective of one who is on the "firing line" of university management. I've enjoyed the opportunity to get away from the "front" for a couple of days and join in these efforts to seek a fresh perspective on the problems and opportunities of Canadian universities in this new decade. By this point in our program, however, there is probably not much left to say about the university perspective on funding, autonomy, and accountability. I could tell you a lot about the impact of financial constraints at my university, or about the global thrust we've been promoting at Carleton and the ambitions we have for our new development corporation which will be a highly entrepreneurial commercial enterprise to market our diverse resources, or about the very productive linkage opportunities with industry, government, and other educational organizations that are unique to the National Capital Region and that we are exploiting rather aggressively. But these are relatively easy topics that I get to address quite often and, with the typical masochism of a university president, I thought I would tackle a somewhat tougher aspect of our subject.

I am going to focus on a topic that I think most university presidents would like to avoid but know that we can't. I'm referring to the inevitable growth of concern for accountability and value for money in Canadian universities. Incidentally, according to my own idiosyncratic definition, accountability requires that a university has a mandate or mission that is clearly understood and agreed upon, knows what it is doing, and can measure, record, and report with reference to its mandate the value that it adds as a consequence of the money that it spends on what it does.

The personal perspective that I bring to this task is shaped by the fact that the field of study for my last degree was administration—specifically, educational administration—and I have been a practitioner of that discipline in five different universities over the past quarter of a century, so I am no stranger to the concept of accountability and I understand and sympathize with the need (especially in publicly funded organizations) to demonstrate value for money as fully and clearly as possible. The fact that educational institutions differ substantially from departments of government or Crown corporations, for example, is no reason to ignore this need. It may make a response to it more difficult, but I view this less as an obstacle than as a challenge. It is a challenge that intrigues me personally because of my professional commitment to the accountability concept; it is also a challenge that cannot be evaded because of political, economic, and societal pressures that have recently become internationally prevalent (as we've been reminded during this workshop). So my inclination is to get on with the task of meeting it, and we're working with our senior board offices at Carleton right now to do just that (including the chairman of our board, Don Yeomans, who is part of this workshop).

As we struggle with this task, we are confronting a number of complexities that characterize the real world of universities which bear directly on the concept of value for money and which differentiate them from most other organizational types to which this concept has typically been applied. We need some professional help to grapple with these complexities and, since there are several professionals here who should have the expertise to help us, I would like to solicit your assistance by sharing with you some of the problems we're facing. First, at the risk of boring you with reminders of the obvious, let me summarize the distinctive nature of universities as organizations.

More than anything else, universities exist as centres of thought. Thinking and learning to think constitute their unique and specialized role. They are devoted to the search for truth, to the discovery, preservation, and transmission of knowledge, and to the analysis of problems. There are other agencies in our society where these activities take place as well—but typically as means to other ends, motivated and constrained by conditions that limit the freedom of thought. Only in universities do we find the essential luxury to pursue the search for truth, the discovery of knowledge and the analysis of problems for their own sake as ends in themselves. This luxury is to be cherished and nourished, because without such freedom our thinking is likely to be sloppy or slanted, our quest may result in half-truths, and the so-called knowledge we discover is likely to remain unconfirmed.

In exercising this freedom, there are typically three ways in which universities go about their work—research and scholarship, teaching, and service. *Research and scholarship* comprise the engine that drives our teaching and service. Research and scholarship are basic to our search for truth, our discovery of knowledge, and our analysis of problems. The purpose of our *teaching* is to pass along the results of our research and scholarship and to help our students learn how to conduct research and scholarship themselves so that, when they graduate, they will know how to seek truth properly, to discover knowledge honestly, and to analyze problems rationally. Ideally, they learn these things by actually doing them under the guidance of a professor who is actively involved in research and scholarship. Our *service* role also derives from research and scholarship. It represents an effort to help the community outside the university make use of whatever truth we find or knowledge we discover. We try to do this in various ways—through continuing education, through consultation and advice, through applied research and development, through technology transfer, through constructive criticism, through social activism, through staff and student voluntarism in the community, and through good corporate citizenship in general (which includes our contributions to the economy of our communities, to their cultural and recreational enrichment, and to their physical beautification). Thus, universities are certainly local institutions, and as you know they are constitutionally provincial; but due to their distinctive nature, they are also at least national and in most cases international resources as well.

In speaking about the distinctive nature of universities, I do not intend to suggest that they are in any way better or more important than other major institutions in our social system. They are, however, different and they must be judged by unique standards—by how well they conduct the search for truth, the discovery and transmission of knowledge, and the analysis of problems. In fairness, then, they must be granted the conditions that are necessary to pursue these functions successfully. Such conditions constitute the fundamental value system of universities, so let me remind you of the three major values without which universities cannot do their job as I have defined it.

The first fundamental value is academic freedom. This means that an individual scholar (in performing his research, teaching, or service) must be free to explore ideas intellectually in whatever directions his thinking takes him, he must be free to look for answers to whatever questions his curiosity gives rise to, and he must be free to criticize the status quo or conventional wisdom whenever rigorous scholarship casts doubt on its validity. The "flip side" of this value, of course, is the scholar's responsibility to exercise this academic freedom according to the most rigorous standards of intellectual logic, research methodology and scholarly ethics, to submit his work for full review by experts in his field of specialization wherever they may be, and to accept a reward system that depends on the results of such external assessment. I can't think of many jobs in which one's performance is subject to evaluation that is as thorough, open, and rigorous as is the case with university scholars. So to give them a fair chance in this highly competitive system, they must be granted the academic freedom necessary to do their job properly (as long as they do it responsibly) without fear of interference on the basis of administrative arbitrariness or political predisposition. Tenure is designed to protect the scholar against such interference; it is not job security (anyone can be fired for just cause after due process, or even laid off for financial reasons), but rather it is a guarantee that the scholar will be allowed the freedom he needs to do the job for which he has been hired.

A second value fundamental to universities is institutional autonomy. This means simply that universities must be free to organize themselves and allocate their resources internally in ways that will optimize the search for truth, the discovery and transmission of knowledge, and the analysis of problems. Because of their unique nature, universities are better able to make such decisions than are external agencies that have other primary purposes, no matter how well-meaning they may be. There is a "flip side" to this one too, of course; it is accountability. Universities must be accountable for absolute honesty, rigour and integrity in their teaching and research; for fair, ethical, and humane treatment of their students and staff; for pertinence in their community service activities, including good corporate citizenship; and for the efficient management of their resources subject to public audit. But as long as they are demonstrably accountable in these ways, they should be allowed the autonomy to make their own decisions about how they will do what they exist to do.

The third value is excellence, which means that universities must strive, and should be expected, to do what they do in the best ways possible. There is no room for compromise in the search for truth or discovery of knowledge, and any university that finds mediocrity acceptable is unworthy of the name.

With this contextual background in mind, let me now sketch out for you a few of the difficulties we confront as we seek to apply the concept of value for money to what we do in our institutions of higher learning. One such difficulty arises from the perception that the application of accountability constitutes a challenge to our essential autonomy. I don't happen to believe that autonomy and accountability are necessarily mutually exclusive and I think people in positions like mine have a duty to ensure that they are not because both are valid, and indeed essential, in publicly funded universities. But the perception is understandable and real, and it must be recognized and addressed directly to reduce the resistance that it naturally generates. Probably the best way to pursue this reconciliation is for university leaders themselves to take the initiative in cooperatively defining their terms of accountability. We could use some help in doing that.

A second difficulty we face arises from the virtual impossibility of separating out the major functions of a university so we can get a manageable "handle" on each one to analyze its components and define the kinds of values that are to be measured. As I have said, the teaching function depends on what we learn through the research function and at times through the service function, and the service function is typically informed by research and often applied through teaching. There is, then, a lot of interaction and interdependence among these basic university functions that makes it extremely difficult to differentiate among them for accountability purposes. Again, we could use some help in doing that.

But let's assume that we do find a way and we are now in a position to try to define value in measurable terms for each of these functions individually. The next step is to determine what is supposed to be achieved through a given function, to what extent a university can reasonably be held accountable for effecting those achievements, and how its contributions toward them can be fairly measured with validity and reliability. Let me approach this subject by taking what is probably the simplest and best understood of our main functions—that of teaching. I'll "chicken out" on research because its goals are so necessarily nebulous that I can't get my head around them in a 20-minute talk: How, for example, do we define and measure value in basic or curiosity-driven research, or in the contribution of particular research efforts to product development, to economic growth, to policy formulation, to social justice and equity, to international relations, to agricultural productivity, to energy conservation, to quality of life, to appreciation of the arts, to environmental improvement, to health enhancement, to cultural understanding, to technological advances, to global competitiveness, to human rights, or to any of the countless other things that could be traced back through an intricate web of events to the scholarship of one or more university faculty members? I'll also "chicken out" on service because by definition it involves the complex interaction of university resources with client systems, and how to sort out the contributions of the former from those of the latter to whatever value is added in the process requires intensive analysis on a case-by-case basis and, since for any major university with a variety of professional schools there is a probably indeterminate number of cases operant at any given time, trying to apply accountability to this function here would turn me into a mental pretzel and give you severe indigestion.

So I'll take the more cowardly route of focusing on what is perhaps the easiest of our functions to analyze—that of teaching. Let's assume that we can all agree on the principle role of teaching to be education, to cause learning to take place on the part of our students. So the task then becomes simply that of defining what we mean by learning, determining the extent to which it occurs, and measuring the value of a university's contribution to that occurrence. I think it may be possible to do this—I earnestly hope that it is—but there are some difficulties we have to resolve in the process.

One such difficulty is that there is much disagreement and uncertainty on the relative priorities among various goals that are held for our teaching function. Is its primary achievement, for example, supposed to be cognitive learning gain, or attitudinal change, communication or quantitative skills, development of taste and judgment, learning to learn, critical and creative thinking skills, analytical or synthetic abilities, peer socialization, values development, vocational preparation, interpersonal relations or leadership, good citizenship, social mobility, or what? Not only can we not agree on what the relative priorities among these various goals are, we can't even agree on who should decide what these relative priorities are.

A second difficulty in applying the concept of accountability to our teaching function is our inability to measure progress toward achieving several of the various goals that I've mentioned. The vast majority of them simply cannot be well-qualified and so it is highly problematic to assess the value we add in pursuing them.

And a third difficulty arises from the facts that the achievement of these goals may require periods that vary up to several years in duration and may be due to many factors other than one's experience in a university—factors such as prior education, family background, work habits, health or disability, peer influences, intelligence and motivation, etc. How do you sort out the impacts of these numerous personal and situational variables in order to identify the value added by what the university itself does, particularly when the evidence of that value may be delayed over many years during which other forces get mixed into one's learning as well?

In other words, cause and effect in education are necessarily loosely coupled rather than tightly linked, and it is important when seeking accountability to ensure that the strengths of loose coupling are not lost in the quest for tight links through close scrutiny and measurement. Otherwise, you run the risk of goal displacement, or what we educators call "teaching to the test." These, then, are some of the complications that we have to sort out very thoroughly in order to develop a realistic approach to applying the value for money concept to the teaching function of universities. As I said, I hope it's doable and we want to try it at Carleton, but here again we could use some help.

If we can get a "handle" on this easier one, then perhaps we can have a go at the research and service functions as well. And then, if we are going to do the job properly, we must recognize that there are important goals of an instrumental type that a university, like other organizations, must also pursue in order that it may operate effectively as it performs its distinctive institutional functions. These include such features as employee morale, school spirit, administrative efficiency, campus maintenance, safety and security, physical accessibility, environmental responsibility, societal criticism, corporate citizenship, knowledge preservation, reputation among students, scholars and the general public, fund raising, public relations, employment equity, and numerous other kinds of grease that keep the wheels of teaching, research, and service turning. Because the achievement of goals such as these are basic to our operation, they too need to be considered in assessing the value gained for the money spent on universities. Ironically, although they are secondary to our major functions, their achievement is probably much more easily measured.

But while we must consider them, we must not let a preoccupation with them divert us from the more important task of trying to apply the value-for-money concept to our major functions of teaching, research, and service. Nor should we allow dangerously time-consuming requirements for masses of obscure data on peripheral input or output factors to masquerade for an authentic effort to identify true performance indicators of the value derived from the money spent on our universities. The former approach can only lead to misspent resources and invalid conclusions. The latter approach presents a challenge that at least some of us feel an obligation to tackle—honestly, fairly, and thoroughly. My own orientation is not to suggest that we cannot do it (I doubt that we really have any choice in the matter); rather, what I'm interested in is identifying the issues we must resolve to do it properly. But, as I've explained, it seems to me a tremendously difficult undertaking and I've told you that we need all the help we can get. If you can advise us on how and where to get it, we'd be most grateful.

The Scope of
University Accountability

David W. Strangway

Before looking at research and the interface of university, government and industry, I would like to address the critical issue of accountability. From my perspective, I would like to say to whom I think I, as a university president, am actually accountable. I listed about 20 major categories of individuals and groups to whom I feel I am accountable. When I got to the end of the list, I realized I hadn't even put government in the list even though they of course are major funders.

Of course I am accountable to the board of governors. Any time the governors wish to fire the president they can. I think that is my ultimate accountability. You are always on the line with them, in fact at every board meeting, and it is the mutual trust that builds up that permits the president to get on with his job of running the university. Boards do not involve themselves in the direct running of the university; rather they exercise their responsibility largely by depending on the chief executive officer (CEO) whom they have appointed.

Although I chair senate, I consider myself to be accountable to its 80 members. The senate consists of members of faculty and the community, students and alumni—many elected, some by virtue of the office they hold. Other members of our senate are appointed by government; so the senate is, in fact, a very widely representative body.

I consider my role to include being accountable to faculty members. Since we have 1,800 of them, I consider myself to be accountable to 1,800 faculty members. They certainly think I'm accountable to them.

The University of British Columbia (UBC) has about 100 academic department heads. Certainly they all consider that I should be accountable to them, and I agree. They deserve to know the information which is used for senior level decision making and they deserve an explanation of the decisions made.

There are 12 deans. I consider myself accountable to them as well.

There are 36,000 students currently enrolled in degree programs. I believe that I have a degree of accountability to them as well. The university must deliver something of use to them and in which they will be interested. I often refer to them as clients because I consider them to be individuals to be treated with the kind of respect that you would give to a client. We must respect them and provide them with quality education and excellent service. It is our product that the students and the public are purchasing, with their tuition and with the taxes that support the provincial grants.

We have 120,000 living alumni. Judging by the letters I get from them, I'm quite convinced they feel that I'm accountable to them; and we are accountable to them. We must continue to run a university that reinforces their pride in their university.

We have a large number of staff members. There are about 6,000 individuals working full- or part-time, but this is very misleading because we have about 100,000 payroll transactions every year. People are appointed, in many cases, for a month, two months, or other short terms. I certainly feel that, to a very large extent, I am accountable to them and once again that they deserve information from the university and explanations of why decisions have been made. They may disagree with any decision but there should be information available to them as to how these decisions were made.

This may seem a little strange, but British Columbia is quite a small province. Much of what we do ends up in the press in one way or another. On this basis, I believe that I have a considerable degree of accountability to our 3,000,000 B.C. residents. Judging by the letters and the open-line radio shows, the president is certainly challenged by the average person in British Columbia. They rightfully believe that this is their university.

As many of you know, I have put a lot of effort into a recent fund-raising campaign. It is still under way. I won't talk much about fund-raising here, but we've now reached the $90-million mark in private sector donations. This is being matched by the provincial government. There are now several thousand donors: corporate, individuals, alumni, and others. I assure you that I feel accountable to them because they make these donations because they believe in the vision that the president has laid out for the institution. As Ron Watts has said, this type of accountability is much more prevalent in the United States than it is in Canada. But the situation in Canada is changing very fast. Our campaign is getting a little tougher these days for two reasons. One is that the economy is not as robust as it was when we started. The other reason that it is getting a little tougher is because there are now many universities engaged in major campaigns. This means there are a lot of presidents of universities who are today much more accountable to their donors. There is a genuine university self-interest in fostering this type of accountability.

I have not added up the number of advisory and visiting committees that we have. There is seldom a week which goes by but that I meet with a committee visiting one department or another or some group reviewing a particular department. We now review every department at least once every five years. These reviewers are the experts in the respective disciplines and deserve our accountability. I consider this to be an extremely important form of accountability since it is to an "expert" public. We not only have such review on a regular basis, we also have a number of standing advisory committees and visiting committees. For example, our Faculty of Commerce and Business Administration has a visiting committee that comes in at least twice a year. This committee has senior people from across the country. Our Faculty of Forestry also has one. We are developing one in the Faculty of Agriculture, in the Faculty of Science and in the Faculty of Applied Science. So again, the president is accountable to these people. They are brought in to give advice and suggestions.

We are in the process of creating an international advisory committee. I will be personally accountable to it because it will be advisory to the president. We will select people from around the world who will come in perhaps once a year to review what we are doing in a broad sense.

We are, of course, through our research grants, accountable to the federal granting agencies as well as to lots of other granting agencies. We are accountable to the provincial granting agencies, the Science Council of British Columbia, as well as others such as foundations that use peer panels. All of these use peer processes, depending on experts who are authorities in the discipline to ensure that only first-rate proposals and first-rate investigations are funded.

Faculty members go through teaching evaluations by students every year. Though these student evaluations may not be as rigorous or as valid as they could be, nevertheless a faculty member does have an annual evaluation by students in his or her classes looking at the teaching in each individual course. Untenured faculty may also have their teaching evaluated by senior colleagues.

This may be stretching it a little bit, but when you think about the people who review the research proposals, and the people who review the publications, and the people around the world who review every promotion that takes place of every faculty member in the university, there are probably several thousand people around the world every year who are asked to pass judgment on one aspect or another of the professional work of UBC's faculty members. This is not an organized, systematic activity by which you could call them all together and get a written audit from them. But every individual is regularly audited with respect to the quality of his or her work.

Another group beginning to emerge, and which carries ever greater significance, is the accrediting body. Some of the professions have always had the responsibility for monitoring and assessing the professions. Bodies such as the Royal College of Physicians and Surgeons, for example, are here once or twice a year with one committee or another deciding whether our particular program in surgery or obstetrics or some other area achieves to the standards set. These are not limited to the undergraduate programs. There are separate reviews, for example, of the residency programs. I think in the Faculty of Medicine every department is reviewed for some aspect of its activities at least annually and we are explicitly accountable to the accrediting bodies. It is not just medicine, of course. There are professional engineering associations for example. In British Columbia we have just created a College of Teachers, and it is developing an accreditation process. There is accreditation in landscape architecture and in many other fields. Anyone who is involved in running a large university knows that there are at least 25 or 30 accreditations taking place regularly.

We are very open to the press. We used to keep press clippings, but we finally stopped clipping them because there was so much of it, relating in one way or another to the university. Every day in the newspapers, there are at least two or three references to something at UBC. These references appear in *The Vancouver Sun*, in *The Province*, in the *Vancouver Courier*, or on radio or television. The press comments are not always flattering. Nevertheless, this is a process that is very much integral to our university. We are a very open system and are prepared to deal with the press openly.

We are accountable to community groups such as the Canadian Council on Animal Care. We have 100,000 animals that are used every year in research on campus and we respond to council requests for information. However, an extremist animal rights group went to the provincial ombudsman and said, "UBC is a public institution and it owes the public an explanation of what it's doing; it owes us a response." The ombudsman said, "The university has full accountability and does not owe any explanation to this group."

I reached this point on my list and realized that I had not even included accountability to the government. But then with all the other forms of accountability, I believe that we have more than satisfied government's need to be sure we are spending money wisely.

Accountability does not end, of course, with what I have described. Accountability exists all the way through the system. There is accountability at the individual level, there is accountability at the departmental level, there is accountability at the faculty level, and there is accountability at the university-wide level. The first year I became a university president, I happened to be in an airport and bought a pocketbook titled *In Search of Excellence*. And I actually read it. What I discovered was that every single chapter in *In Search of Excellence* says that businesses should become more like universities. They did not use those words, of course, but that is exactly what the message was. It said that focus on individuals, focus on decentralization, and focus on excellence were important. There was a chapter on "loose-tight" relationships. At universities we have a very loose relationship in a highly decentralized system but we have a very tight set of constraints in terms of excellence and accountability for actions or decisions. What the whole book really said was that a successful business should be run more like a university. One passage in it even said the most successful companies were the ones that were most campus-like. It has been refreshing to realize that modern management is discovering the very principles that have guided universities and nurtured creativity for decades.

Are we accountable to the public? What most people do not realize is that, at least in British Columbia, every piece of information for every university member with respect to salaries, expense accounts and all business transactions, is published annually in a Blue Book that is available to the public.

Every year, everything is publicly available in this Blue Book. Any member of the public can go through it and figure out how many dollars were spent with any given company, they can figure out how many dollars were spent on individual items, they can figure out what the president's salary is, and they can figure out what the president's expense account is. This requirement was passed into legislation seven or eight years ago. I suspect the people in the universities at that time were really upset with this decision. I even suspect there was a great flurry of news coverage when it first came out. Today when it is released, it doesn't even make a ripple. This year the press decided I was going to be the target. So they went through it and kept calling up the office. They asked how much I actually made? I told them it was already in the newspaper. How much do I spend on expenses? I didn't know what it was, but I simply said, look in the Blue Book. There was no story. They were trying to find something that would make a story. They kept looking through it, and three or four days later, they called back and they said, "We have found something." "We have found a president's grant of $600,000. What did you do with that $600,000? Have you got a slush fund?" It turned out to be the Natural Sciences and Engineering Research Council (NSERC) $600,000 grant which is as accountable as any other money because we award it through a selection process.

We are accountable to government. Government is the one that provides the funds, and I really should have included them in my initial list. I have no qualms in saying that we are accountable to government. I do believe though, as many people said already today, that the things I have just described are key elements in the process. It is through the public, it is through these accreditations and through review processes by experts that we exercise our accountability to government.

I have been president at two universities, in two different provinces, for a total of six years. I thought it would be fun to go back and count up how many premiers and ministers and deputy ministers I had actually been through in this period of time. Over these six years, I have submitted reports to five different premiers, six different ministers and six different deputy ministers. Each one different, each one holding a different view. Very different people in their outlook on universities. Some have been tough, if not hostile toward universities; some very supportive and positive. Bill Vander Zalm has been one of the supporters and he has done remarkable things for the B.C. university system, providing funds for expansion and development, matching grants for campaigns, and new student aid programs. Yet in the not-so-distant past, under a different government leader, but the same political party, universities received quite different attention. Support of the universities is important and it comes from an individual commitment.

Let me share another anecdote which further illustrates this point and reinforces the importance of being facilitative. A few years ago, all three B.C. university presidents were called to meet with the minister of advanced education. It was a wonderful meeting. But then, as we sat there, he looked at us and said, "I was briefed last night and I didn't know it before, but you guys do research." Interestingly enough, this minister turned out to be one of the most supportive of the ministers that I have worked with. He really got fired up about the portfolio, and as he began to understand the issues, he carried them forward effectively. Interestingly, his predecessor was a minister who went into politics directly from the university with an explicit vision of what the university ought to be and a determination that that vision should be followed. On the other hand, the new minister's approach was, "I want to learn what you do; I want to be facilitative; I want to help you" and the rest of the cabinet supported him since they knew he had no preconceived ideas.

Faculty members and universities are under non-stop review. If you believe in the reviewed life, go to a university. I have been a civil servant; I have been in industry; and never in either of those sectors, in my experience, did I go through the kind of scrutiny that I have been describing. In fact, it occurs to me that it wouldn't be bad to start reviewing some of our government departments in much the same way. Could they measure up in the same way as people in the university world must?

I have described a very high degree of accountability. One of the reasons is because of what I consider to be the structure of the university. The first year I was asked to be a president I had to give a speech to the alumni, and I did not know what to say. Finally I decided I would describe my view of the inverted hierarchy of the university system. An instructor is someone who has just finished a Ph.D.—typically instructors are 30 years of age these days. They are subjected to the various reviews that take place. Eventually they get their assistant professorship, tenure, associate professorship, full professorship, and so on. All of this goes on for a long period in their career. Thirty-six or 37 is the typical age for tenure these days. This is the longest apprenticeship system in the world. There isn't any other apprenticeship system I know of that waits until age 36 or 37 to decide whether you are up or out. A lot of people are denied tenure at that point, or have decided to drop out along the tortuous path. Once you are a full professor, you teach and do research. At this point you are the closest to the students, closest to the undergraduates, the graduate students, and the research activity. Then I described the person who becomes a department head. In a sense it means you have moved down a notch because you have moved away a little bit from what the really important mission is. If you become a dean, you have made a really serious move down the hierarchy. If you become a vice-president, you are getting a long way down because you are now far away from what the university really does. And when you become a president, that is it. You are right at the bottom, because you are as far away in the institutional hierarchy as it is possible to be and from what the most senior people, the professors, in the institution actually do; and your role is simply to support those people and to do everything you can to provide the environment. In addressing a meeting of the chairs of governing boards last year, I told this story but then I added, "Think where you are if you are a member of the board of governors or a chairman. You are then right off the scale."

Are we accountable to the public? Let me describe a couple of the things we have done recently at UBC. Somebody said earlier we should bring more people to the campus. This year, in March, we had an open house and we brought 200,000 people to the campus in three days. When you think about it, 7 per cent of all the people of the province of British Columbia walked on the campus of UBC in those three days. Through polling research we have found that 20 per cent of B.C.'s residents had at one time or another taken a course at UBC. Recently, we started inserting the campus newspaper into the local newspaper which is distributed to 25,000 homes in the immediate vicinity of the university. All our warts are there, all our issues and problems and all the rest of it. But we thought that the local community would like to know what is going on.

All of this to me is accountability. We are accountable to individuals, we are accountable to the public, we are accountable to students and their parents, we are accountable to faculty members and others. I want to distinguish between that and what I think some people call accountability. I think this dreaded "A" word has different meanings to different people. I think some people's accountability is not a question of whether we are accountable for what we are doing. I think some people's accountability is, "Are you doing what we want you to?" I am not sure how many people draw the distinction between those two. I can be fully accountable, and people can still disagree with what I do. But in our case, the decisions are all out there for everybody to see. In that sense, we are highly accountable. It seems to me that many people are pushing universities to make them do what they themselves want the universities to do. That, to me, is not accountability, that is an attempt to intervene in decision making. They want us to do the research which they judge to be important. They want us to move the universities to produce more of the kinds of people who they believe they are going to need. They want us to cut back enrolment in the humanities because they don't believe these subjects are as important as other fields of study. In my view, in such a case accountability and intervention have become confused.

This suggests to me that what some people want is something remarkably close to a centrally planned economy. We all know what's happened to centrally planned economies in the last five years. What they are saying to us is, "We want you be accountable to us to do what we have decided we want you to do for our segment of society." We serve many needs. Each person or group looks at the university and one sees only part of the elephant. Few realize the nature of the enormous elephant behind the part that they are interested in.

Let me give you some examples of what I am talking about. We know that it typically takes four to five years for students to go through one of our undergraduate programs. Maybe it takes seven or eight years if you're going all the way through a Ph.D. program. I have only been in a president's office for six years, but let me cite a few experiences I have had. When I arrived in British Columbia only five years ago, I went over to see all the cabinet ministers. They had not seen a university president in years. I made a real effort to get to know some of them, and to say, "I've got an institution to run, and I want you to know what's happening." One of the points raised by almost everyone was, "Why is UBC producing so many teachers? We do not need more teachers in this province. We have far too many now and many are unemployed. We are sending them to California. Why are you producing all these teachers?" That was five years ago. Last year, there was a big royal commission on education and suddenly the province introduced an early retirement scheme for teachers. The teachers are taking retirement in large numbers. Suddenly they came to us and asked, "Why is the university not producing more teachers?" "Where are they when we need them?" We reminded them that we cut back on enrolment because of the pressure. In this case, the government has responded by providing additional funding to permit us to expand the number of teachers. We had not even graduated a cohort of teachers in the time we have gone from the perception that there were too many teachers to a perception that there were too few. We have been through it with nurses. A few years ago nurses were going to California and Texas to get jobs. That was only six or seven years ago. The pressure today is the opposite. Where are the nurses, they ask? Where will they come from? Why are you not producing them? There has only been time for one class to graduate, and we have gone the complete cycle from too many to too few.

Just before I arrived, the former minister decided that not enough doctors were being produced in the province. He came to the university and provided several million dollars to produce more doctors. So we increased the class from 80 a year to 120 a year. By the time I got to UBC, that was all in place. The first expanded class entered the year I arrived. Three years later, the deputy minister came to me and said, "Can you not do something about all these doctors you are producing?" I guess you understand my point. We were chastised for too many scientists and engineers just a few years ago. British Columbia expanded and created two additional engineering schools. The following year the recession hit, and you could not place an engineer or a scientist in a job. Of course now the cycle has reversed and we are being asked if we are producing enough engineers. I emphasize, not even one life cycle of one student passed through the system during the time we went from too many to too few.

Foreign students: In the mid-1980s in British Columbia, UBC responded to the government pressure to keep foreign students out. The fact of the matter is that at UBC today only about 1 per cent of our undergraduate student body is composed of foreign students. I came down on the plane with a man I know. He happened to sit next to me and asked me, "Why does UBC have 30 per cent or 40 per cent foreign students?" He was a little confused. There are increasing numbers of students who are visible minorities including ethnic Indians, Chinese, Japanese, Koreans and so on, but they are all Canadians or permanent residents. This is Canada today. We have decided that at least 5 per cent of our students should be international students. Today we are recognizing that when foreign students return home they will be part of our global network and that they are very valuable to us. Again, one academic cycle and we have gone from thinking we had too many foreign students draining our resources to recognizing that we critically need international students to help build and develop our resources.

I guess the question is accountability. These kinds of rapidly moving short-term pressures and demands are not things to which institutions can or should respond. What we need to know is what the needs will be in five or six years. Students are much smarter than planners. The students are signing up for general science and general arts degrees. The students and their parents know they should keep their options open, thus allowing many choices. Students, who are the clients in this case, are smart because they realize that they can make choices later if they build a broad base at the beginning. Their interest and commitment flies in the face of any pressure to reduce the effort in liberal arts and sciences.

Within 10 years of graduation, Canada employs only 20 per cent of its graduates in science and engineering in the field they were trained. The rest of them go on to other things such as sales, marketing, teaching or other professions. We use only 20 per cent of our university's output to compete in the science and technology world in this country. Is the problem that we are not producing enough scientists and engineers? Or is the problem that they are not being suitably employed in rewarding professions where their skills are really needed? We need to look at where the problem is. If just a slightly larger percentage were employed usefully, we would have no problem. Even a small change in the retention rate in careers would make an immense difference.

Let me just give a few thoughts on research.

It was only 30 years ago when the war cry of North America was that students did not want to get involved with the government-industrial complex. That was the war cry of the 1960s. Students would not get involved in anything that had any obvious government or industrial potential employment at the end of it. Now, a few years later, we are linking them in a much greater way. I believe that there is a lot more room for linkage yet.

Let me give a couple of examples to make a point. Three years ago, the federal government and our provincial government signed an agreement; it was called the Asia Pacific Initiative. It was a very interesting document indeed. It showed that Canada had suddenly awakened to recognize that it is a Pacific nation. The federal government decided that it was going to work with the Province of British Columbia to develop Asia Pacific activities. I read the memorandum of understanding that was signed between the two governments. It was most fortunate, indeed, that the universities had had autonomy. For it was that very autonomy that had led UBC to be committed to Asia Pacific studies, to be committed to Asian languages and culture, to be committed to engineering, to be committed to education, and to all the various kinds of activity that were identified as the new thrusts for the Asia Pacific linkages. Every proposal between Canada and British Columbia and the Asia Pacific built upon the fact that we have been producing the appropriate people for many years. It was these same people who were going to carry out these new Asia Pacific initiatives. Nobody told us to teach Japanese or Chinese or Korean. We were not accountable to anybody when we decided to do it. We believed it was important and challenging. Without our teaching and research over the past decade there would have been nothing to develop under that agreement.

Another example on a slightly different theme. Many years ago, we became very much involved in spin-off activities. I have known for a long time that this was a feature of UBC. Lots of companies spun out of the physics department, out of the chemistry department, and out of electrical engineering and other departments. There are two criteria needed if you are going to have spin-off companies. You must have the source people and the ideas. These come from the freedom of universities to pursue interesting areas. The other is that there has to be a receptive climate within which these companies, having spun out, can take root and flourish. We deal with one side of that equation as a university. Today, we list 70 spin-off companies, doing over $800,000,000 worth of business in Canada. Nobody told us to do this, no one set a mandate. Our people went out there, and they saw opportunities. The activity has accelerated recently, the climate has become a lot better and we are even being supported now for these activities. That activity alone is creating something like 3,000 - 4,000 jobs in British Columbia.

We also bring in annually $100,000,000 in research grants and contracts. This is entirely accountable, because it is all won by individuals who compete. They compete, are assessed and reviewed by peers. Unless people have confidence in them, they don't win any of those grants and contracts. And $100,000,000 is a lot of money. This alone creates 2,000 - 3,000 jobs. And we won this because people have confidence in what the faculty members are doing. They measure up and have been assessed and have passed all of the screens. This is another form of accountability. In fact, there is hardly a piece of research that is done at the university that is not based upon a full peer process assessment.

I want to give one last example. This is not about universities alone but about the origin of the communications revolution. Industry believes that it created the communications revolution. It did not. In fact, it had very little to do with it. The quantum physics and the solid state physics of the 1920s were the start of the communication revolution. Metallurgy and processing of incredibly pure materials so semi-conductors could be made in the 1940s were absolutely crucial elements. None of those developments was based on industry or industry needs. Communications theory was taught in the 1950s. I can remember seeing the textbooks from MIT. They had nothing to do with industry. This incredible subject dealt with how much information could be put into various waves. Digital technology took off in the late 1950s. Again digital technology was not driven by industrial need. But these things came together as one of the necessary conditions for today's communications revolution. None of that was pre-determined; none of it was pre-decided. It was the autonomy of the institutions—not just universities—that was the base for today's communication and transportation revolutions. I like to say these things because when we talk about accountability we must also consider autonomy. There is a lot of accountability, but we must remember that autonomy has served our society much better than intervention.

I think role differentiation is one of the topics that needs to be discussed in groups like this. I think that if we continue to try to force all universities to try to be mirror-images of each other, we will not be successful. I have to hand it again to the Province of British Columbia, because in recognizing that the rates of participation (by people taking courses) were low, the government has decided to expand opportunities for degree-granting programs. All of the colleges have two-year transfer programs at the present time (much like American junior colleges). Three colleges now have four-year degree programs in conjunction with the existing universities. Eventually, they will separate to become free-standing, degree-granting undergraduate universities. A new institution is being built in Prince George. Suddenly the Province of British Columbia has developed a differentiated system. The colleges that could not previously develop two-year programs will now get good two-year programs. Those that had two-year programs in some cases will move to four-year programs. Places like UBC are getting sharp increases in graduate enrolments. We have a unique experiment going on in Canada. A differentiated system is emerging. Within the next four years, the system will be a highly differentiated system and yet closely integrated because the parts will not be working in competition, but with each other.

I hope that I have left you with the sense that I believe that the universities are more accountable in the ways I have described than any societal organization which exists in Canada today. We are more accountable than governments, we are more accountable than industries, we are more accountable than the private sector. I do not know any entity that has more accountability than we do at the present time. Are we centrally planned? No, we are not very centrally planned, but this is our strength. We must be very careful to draw the distinction between accountability and intervention, and we must continue to reinforce autonomy.

Some Concerns about Accountability

Harry Arthurs

While I appreciate most of us would like to press on to some of the practical problems implied by Dr. Cutt's paper, I can't resist lingering for a moment over the assumptions that underlie it. I should have thought that with the overthrow of communism in Eastern Europe we would begin to be a little sceptical about the inexorability of history. I don't see the trends in quite the same terms as Dr. Cutt does. I think there are a number of trends which have clearly predominated in the last 10 or 15 or 20 years which he captures very nicely, but I think it probably worth at least thinking about the possibility that many of them will have run their course and that we may now be preparing for a world which doesn't look like the one we are just leaving. I would just like to offer you a couple of observations which lead me to be somewhat sceptical about the underlying premises of your case.

The first is what I see in the last 10 or 15 years as having been an attempt to shift the burden of disclosure, openness, regulation, and so on from the private to the public sector. It has been characterized on the one side by the whole deregulation movement, on the other side by freedom of information and a number of other things, but the net result of it is that universities now are assimilated to the public sector and are bearing a far higher cost of accountability and run the risk of being subject to a far higher degree of regulation than the private sector itself is prepared to demonstrate. Now it is true that may run on for a while, but at some point people will, I think, begin to scratch their heads and ask why their own institutions should be subject to constraints, to standards of performance and the like which the private sector itself is not prepared to accept. I think that time may not be terribly far off.

The second point is that a lot of technocratic management which took credit for whatever passed for economic recovery in the late 1980s is now probably being carefully scrutinized. The same folks that brought us, say, the triumph of the Toronto real estate market in the last year or so, looked very, very clever three years and six years ago. They don't look terribly clever today. People with infallible judgments based on econometric analysis and technical managerial skills and the like proved as capable of making a botch of things as all of the bad old managers who lacked those techniques. I think technocratic management may be passing through a bad moment, rather than replicating itself in the public and quasi-public sectors. I think the inescapable force of international business, corporate, fiscal considerations, which is powerful, if not inexorable, has a lot to do with the reduction in public expenditures. I can well understand that; it's driven by economics and ideology both. But surely that's been more important in reducing universities' capacities to deal with their mission than the lack of information about how they are discharging that mission. Our plight derives not from our own misdeeds, it seems to me, but from much larger events which have come to rest on our head.

And why have they come to rest on our head? Because all of this has coincided with, I think, a quite understandable resurgence of populism, consumerism, which itself is beginning to run its course. The faith in the unseen hand which has characterized the last 10 or 15 years still is manifest in a lot of political movements today, but I think it's running its course, too. A lot of the forces that converged both on the negative situation for universities and on the proposed solutions for their ills have been running for 10 and 15 and 20 years. But there are signs, at least, that the wheel is swinging round, and that you're designing a university for the 1980s and not for the first decade of the next century as you prescribe what I freely concede you prescribe reluctantly and modestly and in our self-interest. So my first very large concern is that you have read the entrails incorrectly or, if you have read them correctly, you have found them in the wrong chicken.

The second major point that I would like to test you on is this. If, as I think has been true in the past, decisions about cutting university expenditure have been unrelated to analytical work, and I think that must surely be so because there's so little of it being done, then why would one suppose that analytical work will either generate more resources or stave off further cuts in the future? That's a very micro-version of the large point I started out making. Are these determinations not heavily political in their nature? Is it not that we are losing the struggle to articulate the university's contribution relative to the health care system or many others in public priorities? That's a political question. Can the health care system which has claimed larger and larger amounts demonstrate performance? Can it show that all this money that it has been spending has increased the quality of life for the consumers? Is the quality of service improving? We all know those things are not the case, and yet they are able to appropriate larger and larger proportions of what is likely to be a shrinking public pot. So why would we have this naive faith that if we can but deploy rational well-grounded arguments we can stave off what I think is inexorably coming down on our head? I end up on that word that I criticized you for using. I don't see it, it just doesn't make sense to me in terms of what we've been observing.

VI

Common Ground: Perspectives
from Outside the University

Some Observations from a British Perspective

John Farrant

Dr. Cutt has discussed recent developments in Britain almost exclusively in terms of universities, in the sense of institutions receiving government grants through the Universities Funding Council (UFC). These institutions, nearly all called universities, teach fewer than half the bachelor level students in Britain. The slight majority are in institutions called polytechnics, colleges of higher education and a miscellany of other names. Most of the degrees are awarded by the Council for National Academic Awards (CNAA) which has "accredited" the larger institutions so that they have the substantive responsibility for determining curricula and awarding degrees. Most of the students are in the polytechnics which, in the Carnegie classification, would be "comprehensive universities." In Canada they would be members of the AUCC.

In the past 20 years it has been the polytechnics and colleges which have seen closures, mergers, redefinition of roles, substantial innovation in curricula, expansion of access, and large growth in student numbers. They receive government grants, in England, through the Polytechnics and Colleges Funding Council, and in Scotland direct from the Scottish Education Department. The majority which were not already self-governing were, in 1989, removed from the control of local education authorities and constituted under their own boards of governors as "higher education corporations." This move represents a very substantial increase in their procedural autonomy. (The Welsh institutions are still under the local education authorities.)

No institution has moved to the University Grants Committee/Universities Funding Council (UGC/UFC) list in the past 25 years except by merger or assimilation into an existing university. A distinguished elder statesman of higher education, Sir Claus Moser, formerly research director for the Robbins committee, professor at the London School of Economics (LSE), head of the government statistics service and now head of an Oxford college, said in September 1990: "Universities have seemed to be in the governmental doghouse in recent years. For some of this they had themselves to blame. Following the Robbins expansion, they were slow in making the needed internal changes, academic and otherwise; in seeking non-governmental funding; and poor in explaining their achievements. They came over as slow-moving and unresponsive, and for this our collective body, the Committee of Vice-Chancellors and Principals, was much to blame. Inevitably, their high costs ... led to demands for more accountability. No one could object to this."

Dr. LeVasseur identified as a current trend, governments giving institutions greater autonomy along with a more contractual relationship for government funding. That accurately describes the experience of the polytechnics and colleges. Universities consider that they are faced by the second but with an erosion of autonomy. However, the old principle of "deficiency grant" had long since been redundant in practice and may have inhibited universities from diversifying their activities and indeed have encouraged the concentration on a limited number of product lines, particularly the full-time honours degree. If it is clearer what the government is funding, then it is also clear what universities can get on and do, on what financial basis. Diversification of activities and differentiation of institutions are things that the government wishes to encourage.

Professor Watts emphasized that the form of government affects public policy. Federal government leads to dispersal of responsibility and decision taking and is conducive to intrusion in university affairs. The contrast with a unitary state can be developed as follows. In the unitary state, higher education takes a smaller percentage of national budget; the legislature has wider preoccupations of foreign policy, defence, economic management, etc. A provincial legislature is more likely to take pride in some or all of its relatively few universities—of which the politicians may well be alumni. The more intimate connection between presidents and politicians may give rise to the risk of political interference. Cutt cites F. Newman's *Choosing Quality* (Denver, Colo., 1987) which gives amusing and frightening examples from the United States. But it is worth noting one of Newman's conclusions (page 2): U.S. state universities are far more involved in the economic and cultural development of their communities than are the public universities of Europe and the Far East, yet governmental supervision has managed to be both more effective as a force for change, more skilful at preventing an over-focus on institutional self-interest, and more careful about providing the flexibility that we perceive as essential. So the more intimate connection also provides opportunities in skilful hands.

By contrast, the fact of 180 institutions receiving government funding and the presence of buffer bodies stands in the way of British MPs' developing and expressing a commitment to the institutions. As Professor Watts observed, governing bodies are weak in Britain. They are not, even in part, appointed by the providers of funds so there is no direct "delegation of trust." Typically half a university's council is nominated by other bodies, particularly local government authorities; the governing bodies of the new higher education corporations are self-perpetuating. Few are likely to attract figures of national significance who are plugged into appropriate networks through which to advance the institution's interests with government. To the outsider and in the provincial context, Dr. Cameron's advice to strengthen governing bodies is eminently sensible.

The British government's control over higher education is primarily through the allocation of resources rather than the management of institutions. The means of allocation are shaped by, and in the context of, the government's ideology. The Conservative government since 1979 has sought to create the conditions in which markets can function and to remove whatever obstacles exist or may arise in their operation. It is prepared to pressurize every institution to make it supportive of enterprise and capitalism, particularly by using financial leverage, and wants to reduce the power of special interests, particularly of public sector professional employees (see, e.g., A. Gamble, *The free economy and the strong state: the politics of Thatcherism* [1988]).

The various initiatives of government in relation to higher education in the 1980s can be classified with the help of Burton Clark's "triangle of coordination" (*Systems of higher education,* Berkeley, Calif., 1983). Clark's triangle has state authority, academic oligarchy and the market at its three corners, as the three main mechanisms through which a national "system" of higher education is co-ordinated; for him its purpose was to compare several national systems. He placed the British system well toward the academic oligarch corner because of the large role played by "academic notables" in the buffer bodies such as the University Grants Committee (UGC) and the research councils. I have added the providers of resources which may be identified with each corner, and the forces that operate along each side of the triangle. The model is offered tentatively and may not stand up to close scrutiny. In particular, it may make better sense to think in terms of the government establishing a "regularity regime" to ensure that competition flourishes (as it has for privatized utilities and in tackling the restrictive practices of, for example, the stock exchange), rather than imposing regulations on institutions. Also various measures intended to enhance the discretion of "management" in institutions reduce the autonomy of individual academics.

Space does not allow full description of the items in the list that follows: some are mentioned in Cutt's monograph.

Regulation reduced

- polytechnics and colleges incorporated
- accreditation of institutions by CNAA in place of validation of courses
- fewer restrictions on salaries and gradings of academic staff
- weakening of Treasury controls over use of publicly funded capital assets

Regulation increased

- audit requirements greatly increased
- financial reporting standardized

- performance indicators developed and published
- academic audit unit established by Committee of Vice-Chancellors and Principals
- staff appraisal required for academic staff

Privatization

- commercial research should not be subsidized
- loans for students' maintenance partially displace grants
- reiteration of institutions' discretion to charge tuition fees beyond those met from public funds
- fewer subjects restricted by admissions quotas

Surrogate market in the allocation of public funds to institutions

- polytechnics and colleges incorporated (allowing more equal competition with universities)
- separation of funding for teaching and for research in UFC's allocations
- shift of some funds from UFC to research councils
- increased selectivity in UFC's allocation of research funding
- customer/contractor relationship for government research establishments
- publicly funded tuition fees greatly increased at expense of block grant to institutions
- competitive bidding to provide student places

University Accountability and the National Audit Office in the United Kingdom

Patrick O'Keefe

Robin Farquhar's excellent speech underlined my own view that the National Audit Office in the United Kingdom should approach the audit of university accountability with very considerable caution. We do that and we do it quite deliberately. I think what Robin Farquhar was identifying was a move from accountability in a fiscal sense to accountability in a wider sense of what the university is all about. I think that is exactly right, and I truly believe that those sorts of issues will in fact form part of a debate that is going to go on for the next 10 years or so, and perhaps longer. So that's more for the future.

As we see it in the United Kingdom, and speaking purely from an audit office point of view, the issue of university accountability to the taxpayer is not beatable. It is there, Parliament wants it, Parliament expects it. It is therefore a matter of how one processes that view, and I think the opening speech of the workshop on the right balance to be struck between, on the one hand, accountability and, on the other, academic freedom and so on, was absolutely right.

Let me put you into the mind of an auditor acting on behalf of Parliament, not on behalf of the British government. There is a real distinction between the two. From our perspective, looking at whether universities and the buffer body of the university, funding councils and so on, have sound system of controls, can be a bit boring. But what it does bring to mind to most people in universities is a picture of interfering officials in one form or another lacking any sort of sensitive idea of what a university is all about, as Robin Farquhar described. You may feel, for example, that we would be quite capable of coming forward with allegations that a professor of Greek, for example, with poor attendance at his lectures, is cost-inefficient and should be sacked. On the contrary, I think we take an entirely different approach. In 1967, when the predecessor of the National Audit Office gained access to the books and records of universities, our approach then, as it is now, was not to infringe in any way on the academic freedom of what we firmly recognize to be the United Kingdom's autonomous universities. In fact, it was a head of our office at the time who formulated our policy that it was no part of our duty to question policy decisions or decisions reached on academic grounds. That remains the key plank in our audit strategy, and to the best of my knowledge, we put that into practice in our approach.

We are not the appointed auditors of individual universities to certify their accounts. We take an overview of aspects of university activities and report to Parliament as we think appropriate. Our reports essentially focus on fiscal prudence, but can also involve such matters as how the universities reshape and restructure the various sectors to accommodate financial constraints, aged lecturers and so on. Strategically, we are very conscious of the fact that we, like any other auditor, can intrude upon universities, where there are busy people who work 25 hours in every 24. We do take account of the fact that university people are very busy, and it may surprise you to know that we intend to make only one report to Parliament on an aspect of university activity every two years; that is not very burdensome to anybody. And we do in fact seek ways to minimize the disruptions when we call on universities.

Against that sort of background, can I just pick up two points that Kenneth Davies made, and just dwell on those for a moment, because I think there are lessons in them for the British universities and maybe for the Canadian universities and others elsewhere. Kenneth Davies made the point that there were too many audit tiers and there was an emergence of methods designed to evaluate performance. Somebody said that might be burnout.

On the first point of too many audit tiers, there was a heated discussion on the responsibility of the Canadian councils. Against that sort of background, could I just balance with one point what Kenneth Davies was saying. It was the very bad example of one British university that actually added to the multiplicity of audit tiers. It was nothing to do with the central audit organization that I represent.

Very briefly, and I'll now quote from a report of MPs because I think the words are very significant and that they have a message. The words are, "The breakdown of financial control, the attitude of those charged with the proper stewardship of its funds, and the disregard for proper procedures brought a major academic institution to the verge of insolvency." Quite clearly, this sort of situation caused the Department of Education in Britain very reluctantly indeed, and quite exceptionally, to interfere in the affairs of that British university. The department did not want to do so but eventually had to do so because public money was at stake. Within six months of that report, the members of Parliament were considering the finances of the British universities and, like those in Canada, they have suffered from severe financial constraints of one sort and another.

The MPs then made another rather critical comment, and it has an implication, and may I quote it to you? The comment was: "We are especially concerned that some universities have been slow to take action to bring their income and expenditure into balance and we note the view of the Universities Funding Council that this was in some cases because they at universities have simply not been willing to recognize the full seriousness of the situation. We (that is, the MPs) do not accept that their independence and autonomy, although undoubtedly valuable in many respects, is a valid argument against attempts to defend against shortcomings in realistic and effective management and control of the public funds on which universities are dependent." There's a real implication there. The MPs offered a very respectable way out to those very few universities that caused this, by urging them to cooperate more closely with the funding council. The very clear and very, very simple message of that is that universities must continue to keep their houses in order, because if they don't, other people will. And it is as simple and basic as that.

Turning now to the range of performance indicators (PIs) and management information, and all the other things that are going on to evaluate research and teaching quality that Kenneth Davies talked about: it has to be said that the British government saw scope to improve the efficiency of universities. It was the government's comment, nobody else's. The evaluation ethic is quite clearly the flavour of the era. There's no getting away from it. That's reality.

It seems to me that the British universities, through the committee of vice-chancellors and others, have done exactly the right thing in responding to what is essentially a political imperative and are developing all this information and shaping it to the way that they want it. Indisputably, it seems to me, that sort of information, however mechanistic, coupled with the wider values that the universities do certainly add to society, as Robin Farquhar brought into focus, should be able to demonstrate the universities' value to society in the broadest possible sense beyond the mechanistic, and it will most certainly help the negotiators on behalf of the universities to get more funds from the government. By the same token, it allows the government to challenge. It's up to universities to make their point and add to it.

I think all audit philosophy is to let the system settle down. Most certainly, in due course—maybe a year or two years—we will question very closely the extent to which universities and the funding councils use the data, whether there were positive outcomes, did their use facilitate change and improvements? Are the data too mechanistic? Should they be opened up? All those questions are coming your way, I can assure you of that. It is in our strategic approach, and I think Robin Farquhar's points, which I thought were very compelling indeed and struck the right chord, will feature in our strategic approach. We will take note of those comments, because I think they are absolutely valid. So, really to answer the question that somebody raised, there will be an independent scrutiny of all this data to see whether the information is used in a purposeful way, or whether the information is irrelevant.

Another sort of philosophy that we try to adopt is that we want to be very cautious in our approach to universities. We respect the academic skills and autonomy of the universities, and I think the record shows that our touch in the university area has been really quite gentle, compared to the sort of reports we issue on other areas. We do accept and we do recognize the uniqueness of the university field, but other fields have their own specialties. There is something basic, however, to the democratic framework which we do recognize, and we want to approach this with considerable care. So if universities do the work themselves, we will not interfere. And there have been, at a lower fiscal level, very good examples of this.

We were concerned with management structures of universities, with the amount of time spent in committees—I think somebody said they did 26 hours in 24; whether committees are too big, what was the weight, could you quantify, and all those sort of things. And then on a much more practical level, was there good estate management. We had identified and started studies in all of these areas. The British universities, responding essentially to the Jarratt report, which was mentioned earlier, did excellent work in this area, and recognizing that good work, we aborted our studies and chose not to report them to Parliament.

There is a case for saying we ought to report good things to Parliament, and maybe we will do, but we are very cautious in many ways, and we will wait three or four years and check them out again. And if the universities have maintained their excellent record, we will record it as we have recorded good things in the past.

So in looking at all of this, we do recognize your value, we are cautious, we do try to understand universities' problems and, I must say, one of the good things in the United Kingdom from our point of view is the higher profile now taken by the Committee of Vice-Chancellors and Principals. I think that's excellent. They speak with a collective mind, and we can therefore trust them to understand their problems, as we can understand the problem of the Universities Funding Council, which has its own role in monitoring, which must have these systems for public accountability and so on.

So I suppose my view is that it is entirely in the hands of the universities. They have to respond to the imperatives in our countries. If they don't, other people will. I think the universities are doing exactly the right thing. Long way to go yet, but if universities continue to respond to the imperatives, they will put audit where it belongs, on the periphery.

Should Universities View Provincial Public Servants as Regulators or Allies?

Gary Mullins

My comments are personal, rather than those of the office that I hold. I would like to outline three things: one, a summation, as I see it, of the difference between the university and the government worlds in which we respectively operate; two, a little look at the 1990s; and three, from that look a quick summary of the challenges facing universities and governments.

Universities and governments are of very different worlds and very different cultures. The academic culture is a culture of certainty and objectivity. And where certainty is unavailable to you, you create assumptions so you have a form of certainty and work on from that.

Government is a land of uncertainty, where change is the only constant. It is subjective rather than objective in nature, and it is driven primarily by values. I'll talk a little bit about my own values later on because it is critically important for a deputy minister to share some values with the government. It is critically important, in my judgment, for deputy ministers to have absolutely no "tenure." In my own case, cabinet meets every Wednesday, the orders-in-council are published every Thursday, and the deputies look to see if there has been an order-in-council rescinding their appointment.

The challenges facing government are challenges of pattern identification. We can't look at the past. We can't look at detailed studies. We are dealing with uncertainty and the government has to look at patterns out there. The art of politics is the art of the possible, which is guided within those patterns, by the values that the government has.

And the second challenge that government faces is that of expectation management. Satisfaction is all about performance exceeding expectations, and great performance that is accompanied by unrealistic expectations leads to dissatisfaction, whereas relatively good performance with slightly lower expectations leads to satisfaction. Governments are all in the expectation management business, and nowhere is that clearer today than in the kind of work that the government of Premier Rae is doing in Ontario to attempt to lower an unreasonable set of expectations in a variety of policy fields.

I agree with the comments about pluralism. I think a cabinet is best described as a collection of strong egos in which the issues on which they disagree are significantly greater in number than the issues on which they do agree. I worked as a business manager for a law firm where I had 55 partners as my chief executive officers. I had more chief executive officers to work for in Davis and Company in Vancouver than any other executive in the province. And a law firm was a collection of strong egos and the things on which they agreed were smaller in number than the things on which they disagreed. I don't know very much about universities, but I suspect a university is a collection of strong egos and the number of things on which they agree is somewhat smaller than the number of things on which they disagree.

The other thing that should be said about government is that governments do not write the script. They are not script-writers. They are script-readers and script-interpreters. The script is written by an invisible hand. It's not only the invisible hand of Adam Smith, but it's also the invisible hand of demographics, of public opinion, of economics, of business cycles, and of a variety of external interventions. If you don't believe me, think of Meech Lake. Meech Lake is a situation in which the most powerful in this country gathered, in 1986 and 1987, to craft some constitutional amendments. They decided to take leadership, and they decided to try to write the script. Meech Lake ultimately failed because the public of Canada would not accept the premise that the first ministers took, that it was quite acceptable to solve the aspirations of one group and ignore the aspirations of others in that particular round. There the governments thought they wrote the script; they forgot that they are script-interpreters.

Governments are complex organizations; they require good politicians and they require good civil servants. And the two must work together in a variety of constructive ways. The thing that must be remembered in talking about good government, good politicians and good civil servants, is that most major improvements in our society, the quest for excellence in a variety of areas, the important kinds of structural changes that a society makes or an economy makes, are changes that take place over several electoral cycles. None of the fundamentally important things are likely to take place entirely between two elections. And therefore one of the roles of a deputy minister, one of the roles of the civil service in what is a political system of which I am passionately proud, is that the role of the deputy minister and the role of the civil service is, to some extent, to provide stability as change is made over time.

I said earlier that politics and government are areas in which we have values rather than objectivity. And values are driving them. I should therefore share with you some of my personal values because they drive my comments, they drive the way I work as a public servant. My first value is that I have a profound respect for the political process. The overthrow of a vibrant democracy in Chile, where I once lived, tells me volumes about the fragility of the democratic process. Having attended the independence ceremonies of a small African nation and seen what happens when a group of relatively under-educated people take charge of their own responsibility from a group of benefactors, and the importance that gives to the energy of a people, also leaves a deep impression. Having been involved in the process of moving government from civil servants like myself to elected members of the Northwest Territories legislature, gives me an appreciation of the importance of the political role in this country. It is a thing of which I feel very passionately and it is a thing of which I am very proud—to be associated with the democratic process.

My last interview for the job I now have was with the premier. I was living and working in Vancouver at the time, and I knew that his officials had said, "Mullins is the guy for you." What the premier didn't know is that I went to the interview to decide whether I would take the job or not. My purpose was to find out whether my values were compatible with the premier's for this particular role because if they weren't, I wouldn't take the job. The premier had a vision of a competitive economy, a vibrant workforce requiring education and training, and although that is a small subset of the educational role, it is a subset which is compatible with what I saw as being required in British Columbia, which is a significant strengthening of our post-secondary system. So before I talk about the future, and what I see as funding prospects, I should tell you that in the two years that I have worked with our government, we have increased in British Columbia the funding to the post-secondary system over a period of two years by 25 per cent. We have doubled the number of locations at which university degrees are being offered. We are expanding our university capacity by 25 per cent over a period of six years, including the development of a fourth university. We have significantly enhanced student financial assistance, and we have in three years quintupled the capital spending programs at our universities and colleges. I am going to talk a little bit later, in a more pessimistic tone, about what I see as the financial outlook for the post-secondary system, but I thought it fair to share with you the fact that in British Columbia the values are to build, the values are to respect, the autonomy of those institutions.

Governments often talk about the university system as providing a form of professional or career development for individuals. I think I should comment on that just a little bit. The first thing I should say is that—overwhelmingly, the psychologists tell us—people define who they are by their job more than by anything else. I think that's a reality. I think it is also a reality that students who enter our post-secondary education system, more than anything else, see education in terms of the job-enabling potential that advanced education gives them. Finally, I should say that I have a degree in philosophy and geography, and I have found that degree in philosophy and geography to have been tremendously empowering and enabling for me in my professional life. So when I talk, and when politicians talk, about the importance of an advanced education in developing a labour force, I'm not simply talking in narrow technical terms, because I profoundly believe that the kind of education that I had the privilege to get is incredibly enabling and empowering in the workplace, and that the concepts of preparing people for the workforce are not at all incompatible with the curriculum of a general or liberal education.

I'd like now just to outline very quickly three or four things. What is the outlook for the 1990s? I see the outlook for the 1990s as involving dramatically increased student demand. The demand for education, for training and retraining of the existing labour force, will be growing, in my judgment, exponentially. And it is particularly important that we recognize that, depending on the province, something like 70 per cent of the labour force of the year 2000 is already in the labour force today. And that labour force is going to have to be upgraded. Second, government tends to fund access or volume considerations. After all, students and parents of students, and prospective students, vote. But costs per student full-time equivalent (FTE), unit costs, and the other kinds of things that we often associate with educational quality, do not. I expect that governments will consider themselves successful in the future if the proportion of the gross provincial product (GPP) dedicated to advanced education stays relatively constant. And when I take those three things together, dramatically increased student demand, government's preference for funding student numbers, a not particularly virile economy which will have its tax system pressured by the realities of the free trade agreement and by the size of our deficit, I think we are going to be lucky if on average, across Canada—and I emphasize that this is not B.C. government policy—but if, on average across Canada over the next 10 years, the inflation component of the universities' budget is recognized by something like the consumer price index (CPI) minus 2 per cent per year. I think that's a reasonable approximation of long-term budget prospects.

I see the challenge for the universities as one of creating excellent institutions. I am one of those who describes excellence, not in status terms and not in relative terms, but in the ability to be the best you can at what you do with the abilities and resources that you have. The challenge for the universities is to have a well-paid faculty. I would see that the faculty expectations will be that faculty income should go up by the rate of inflation or more. And I see that the challenge for excellent institutions with well-paid faculty is to have good morale and to be involved in a profession which commands the respect of society that it serves.

How can that happen? How can an institution which already has a cost profile of something like CPI plus 2 per cent per year, in an environment in which the resources available are likely to be something like CPI minus 2 per cent per year, meet the challenge of excellence? In my judgment, the answer to that question is that excellence will come by making strategic decisions that involve adjustment to new university models. They will be, as Cynthia Hardy said, pluralistic models and the successful institutions will be those that engage people like Cynthia Hardy to assist them in that process.

Robin Farquhar said very clearly that assistance is required by most universities. That is the kind of assistance that might be necessary. I agree with General Eisenhower on the whole strategic planning process, of which Eisenhower said, "Planning is essential and plans are useless." The process of making decisions strategically, of consultation, of navel-gazing, of setting objectives without the benefit of large back office staff is an essential process. The written word that often comes out in large volumes is not particularly helpful.

What are the tools that universities can use to achieve the challenge of excellence in a period in which financial resources are not likely to be as forthcoming as they have been in the last couple of years? One of the tools, I think, in addition to strategic planning and good visioning, is the reality of an aging faculty. There will be turnover, and there will be an opportunity to look at new models. Second—and we had a passionate speech yesterday about the importance of treating faculty with dignity, etc.—the ability to treat faculty as individuals rather than as resources to be put into a mould will, I think, provide another important key to the resource. What we have learned from the university system in California, which cannot be replicated in Canada, is that you can have a group of people (like those in the University of California system) who have combined roles of research and teaching in relatively equal volumes, and you can have (as in the California State University system) people whose primary goal is teaching and whose academic requirements are to keep themselves current. They do so by engaging in sufficient scholarly activity so their currency is assured but whose status, whose competence, whose performance and whose effectiveness and whose contribution are not measured against other standards. They are recognized for what they are. And I think that if we use the opportunities that present themselves—an aging faculty, an honest recognition of financial prospects, and the ability to openly and collegially determine new models of universities based on what is learnable from experience elsewhere—then each institution will have an opportunity to find its own success.

I think what governments are looking for, at least what the Government of British Columbia is looking for, are vibrant institutions that are autonomous. I have a mandate from my minister to loosen significantly the strings that now bind our colleges to our government and to give our colleges significantly more autonomy than they have had in the past, because my minister and I and others profoundly believe that governments cannot create excellent institutions. Only institutions can create excellence for themselves. Governments have the ability to pull down, but they don't have the ability to push up. But as governments we have to create an environment in which that excellence can thrive. That excellence will take place as a result of being aware of what society needs, being able to respond to those needs, and being able to communicate to that society whose needs are there to respond to and to fulfil.

Universities and Auditors:
Can They Find Common Ground?

Jean-Pierre Boisclair

Cornelius Van Horne, the great railway baron, once said, "Every successful enterprise requires three kinds of people, dreamers, pragmatists and tough sons of bitches." I want to try to approach the question of accountability because I think accountability and engaging accountability require pragmatism, and I want to be pragmatic in my comments to you today. I also want to be pragmatic in recognizing that I am in the "tail-gunner joe" slot, it is late, and I am sure people want to get away.

I have eight points that I would like to touch on, and you may be a little surprised. Only one of those points has to do with audit, and it is the last one. All of the others have to do with a pragmatic view of what it takes to engage the accountability issue.

First of all, a plea. Do not attempt to come at the accountability issue by putting the audit cart in front of the management horse. I subscribe fully to what Robin Farquhar said and how he defined accountability. I could define it even more easily. I think accountability is telling people your story about how you've performed, and telling it with rigour and with fairness, and openly. And that relationship has to be between the people who accepted the responsibility to do something, and the people who gave them that privilege. Audit is an external mechanism, which is imposed from outside. It is meant to be a check and balance and it sits outside of that dialogue. And the moment you take management away from the table and put auditors at the table instead of management and they start to tell the story, you're not going to get at the kinds of issues that Robin Farquhar and other people are talking about. I think that's a pragmatic view. So don't engage notions of accountability in the first instance through the prism of audit. Audit is a useful check and balance in an accountability process, it is not a substitute for management.

My second point is that I think management must accept the challenge to report on its performance, and I say that in a very broad sense, for two reasons. First, I think that failure to do so erodes public confidence which is a large part, I think, of your working capital. And we can look at every kind of public sector institution today and see how public confidence has been eroded, and how that erosion of confidence is making it more and more difficult for institutions to deliver the kinds of services which are so important. Second, I think it is manifestly clear to all of you that in a way you are starting to lose your share of the resource bag. Some of it is through no fault of your own. The demographics of Canada alone suggest that there is a shift in funding over to health care with our aging population, etc. But if ever there was a time that I think the educational sector has to have strong public confidence in what it is doing to preserve its scarce resources, it is now. So for those reasons, management should accept the challenge.

But I think that in accepting the challenge, the first pragmatic step along the way is that it is senior managers in the university community who are going to have to create a new value system, or at least appeal to some different values within their institutions to mobilize people and get them going. In so many ways, Robin Farquhar was right. But it is the people inside the universities who are probably in the best position to deal with all those tough issues he touched on. You can't delegate this thing to a third-rate analyst from outside who is going to approach your institution with a preconceived notion or absolutely no understanding of what you are doing. It is the very same people inside universities who struggle with scholarship, excellence in scholarship, teaching, all of those things, who are going to be able to tackle the issues of accountability. Those people, though, have to be mobilized, they have to be motivated, and they have to subscribe to a value system and they have to start to believe in it themselves. And I think that's the toughest first step in engaging the accountability issue in any sector, perhaps especially so in the educational sector.

Third, from a pragmatic point of view, don't go for the long ball. Every situation we have seen suggests to us that engaging the accountability process in a meaningful and worthwhile way, one that is acceptable to all the constituents to that process, takes time. There has to be a confidence-building exercise that goes on. You can't say, "I'm going to start today, and six months from now I'm going to produce a report for the provincial government or the federal government." I think that process really has to flow internally for quite a while, inside the organization and then ultimately between the chief executive officer of the organization and the senate and the board and they have to be comfortable, and they have to develop a sense of internal confidence in the sense of what's going on, before they are going to want to talk about it outside. I think that's just a pragmatic view, but I think it's an important part of engaging the process.

Next, I think governments who provide funding are eminently capable of responding to initiatives when they take place inside institutions. The best example I can give you is with respect to federal Crown corporations. The Government of Canada did not choose to deploy comprehensive auditing on federal Crown corporations in the same manner as it did with respect to government departments and agencies. Basically what the government said was, "We will pass some legislation that suggests that the board of directors of every corporation has a duty to be informed about value-for-money issues. And we will put in place a system of checks and balances that satisfies us that they are getting the information. However, we respect your need for commercial secrecy, for autonomy, for this, for that, for the other thing. And therefore, we will not demand and drag it out into the public and start a rather fruitless debate with you." So governments are capable of responding to initiative when they see it take place. And I think you should engage the accountability notion with the same thought in mind: if you start doing it for yourselves, governments will recognize that and they will temper themselves accordingly. And that's a pragmatist view.

Next, the only way I think you can engage accountability and make it work, make it beneficial, is if senior managers are personally and directly involved. Some senior managements pay lip service to the issue of accountability: "Oh, yes," they say. "Accountability is a good idea. We must have some . . . we'll have two bags full, please." And you assign it right down the line to the lowest common denominator. What comes back up is the lowest common denominator, and that same CEO will sit there, as will the board, as will the other senior people in the organization, look at the report and say, "That's garbage." I think a bit of what Cynthia Hardy was talking about earlier—strategic plans that somehow don't work, don't seem to have meaning—are too narrow in focus, don't recognize the pluralistic nature of any business. I don't even believe that unitary model exists in the real world. I've never seen it in play. But I think it is key that management can't just talk about accountability; it must be willing to invest time in it, and that's the only way it is going to work from a pragmatist point of view.

Next, accountability cannot in my view be reduced to a set of ratios, performance indicators. Accountability in any kind of institution, be it a university, a health care institution, a social service institution, is multi-dimensional. All of your stakeholders are coming at you from different perspectives, and a simple set of ratios just won't work. They usually tend to encourage exactly what Robin Farquhar said—paralysis by analysis—or focus everybody on the most unimportant things possible, while ignoring the important things. And I think that would be a terrible shame. If anything, I would encourage you, as you engage the accountability process and try to improve it and take specific initiatives in that regard, to go for the tough issues. Don't waste your time going for the simple ones. You can gather that kind of information pretty quickly. It doesn't take a magician to do it. Head for the tough ones. Engage your people, and then maybe something interesting will happen.

My last point has to do with audit. Comprehensive audit will respond to whatever you do as managers and as members of the educational community. There are two ways you can have comprehensive auditing. (Comprehensive auditing, very simply, means looking at something broader than financial matters— looking at value for money, economy, efficiency, effectiveness, etc.)

First, if you are putting in a reasonable effort to report on your own performance as managers, using credible frameworks, putting in credible efforts to do it, I think audit at that point can do what it traditionally does. It can add credibility to your efforts. It is a positive influence at that point. Of audit reports issued in the private sector, 99.9 per cent in effect say that what management said to the board and to the shareholders is something that can be believed. Okay? And if you want to talk about public confidence, that is where audit can help you.

But second, where audit gets all screwy, and where I can see that you get upset and I've heard this many, many times in the educational sector and I've heard it elsewhere, is when management doesn't report, but becomes simply a spectator to the accountability process.

So audit can be two things. It can either support and add credibility to what you say about your performance, or if you're not saying it, you're going to tend to get a negative product, and that's inescapable. So my whole point is that if you want to engage the accountability business, do it from a management point of view, do it from a management information point of view, and try to go at the tough issues. Don't initially try to engage through the audit process, but at some point in time, audit will help you to be more credible once you've developed your information.

Concluding Comments

Rodney Dobell

In many places around the world, relations between governments and universities are in turmoil and ferment. Universities are not simply Crown corporations, they are not simply instruments for economic development and social transformation—though they are indeed both. They have a complex mission that demands a substantial degree of autonomy if it is to be successfully pursued. They also draw insatiably on public financial support, in return for which a degree of accountability must be demanded.

Thus, as instruments of public policy, universities have key roles to play in society. Finding the proper relationship between governments and universities in setting the directions and orientations for these roles these days is a crucial task, much debated. Devising proper structures for institutional governance and effective management in an ungovernable collection of individualistic prima donnas apparently immune to the calls of social responsibilities is also an interesting challenge.

With the very generous support of the Canadian Comprehensive Auditing Foundation (CCAF), the Government of British Columbia, and the Social Sciences and Humanities Research Council, the Institute for Research on Public Policy was able to organize a fascinating review of some of these key challenges and opportunities in the management of the post-secondary education sector—actually the university sector—in Canada today. Professors Jim Cutt and David Cameron prepared major background papers for the purpose, and the participants in the meeting, whose papers are set out in these proceedings, have succeeded in illuminating the many facets of the dilemmas involved in university governance and management.

The motive for organizing the meeting in the first place was the sense that university-government relations are very much under strain, that appropriate structures of accountability are essential but largely absent, and that the vast social investment in post-secondary education, so crucial to our economic and social future, is, in a variety of ways, substantially in jeopardy.

There is obviously no way—and certainly no need—to revisit and recapture all of the intense discussion recorded in the previous papers and transcripts. But a few key conclusions should probably be flagged in closing this volume.

1. Universities have in fact been (or are becoming) extraordinarily answerable to a remarkably wide range of constituencies—but peer review remains a central element of that process. Accountability to the elected representatives charged with articulating the public purpose, or instrumental responsibilities, of universities remains remarkably indirect and imprecise.

2. Enhanced accountability is not in fact (or at least in principle) at odds with autonomy, it is the essential vehicle through which autonomy can be preserved.

3. Autonomy is not at odds with effective functioning of the universities as instruments of public policy, it is the prerequisite to effective pursuit of the social purpose of the university.

4. The key trick will be for the university to define and convey (much more widely, with much greater general understanding) that mission, and the instruments by which its achievement will be measured. Doing so will ensure that auditors—management auditors, comprehensive auditors, value-for-money auditors, and all the others—will be kept where they belong, which is to say, at the margins of the enterprise, attesting to the validity and accuracy and adequacy of the universities' own

reports describing the fulfilment of their mission and the general state of affairs.

5. There is also a big marketing job to be done by universities, and better media relations are crucial.

Thus, in this view it is the role of the president as chief executive officer (CEO) to put forward the mission—and the measures by which its pursuit will be monitored. The role of the comprehensive auditor in university affairs is then to attest to the presence of the systems in place to monitor the pursuit of that mission, and to attest to the representation of performance as captured by the agreed measures.

It seems very clear from the discussion recorded in this volume that the ball is in the university court—the university system itself must take the initiative:

- on the marketing
- on the measures
- on the clearer expression of mission.

It was not so clear with whom the responsibility for animating the next steps should lie. Individual presidents and CEOs, individual boards of governors, or university executives acting collectively through the Association of Universities and Colleges of Canada (AUCC) might all be seen as sources of further action. Or the impetus might come from the Council of Ministers of Education, Canada, or federal-provincial "learning initiatives" reflecting the apprehensions of concerned citizens and advisory bodies.

Probably all have a role to play in initiating a further round of organizational change leading to an institution more responsive in fact, and more effective in telling its story.

Enhanced accountability must be recognized as a response to real and compelling imperatives founded in the concerns of the current clients and customers of the system, not simply a marketing ploy of the accounting profession. It seems clear the primary responsibility probably does not lie with the audit community and the CCAF, although the development of some innovative illustrative systems of output indicators might be a helpful stimulus.

As always, accountability in too many directions, for too many things, may be confusing, constraining, and ultimately paralyzing to executive action. And political "interference" in university affairs will always be suspect. The balancing act is, as always, difficult, but in the sensitive matter of the universities, it is perhaps more delicate than anywhere else.

The discussion summarized in these proceedings struggled with heavy organizational and administrative questions, and ventured answers to some. Accountability of universities to whom, and for what? Accountability established how, and according to what measures? What was notable, however, and could hardly be challenged in these days of trial and transition in social organizations around the world, was the agreement on one basic premise identified in the insightful conference summary by Geraldine Kenney-Wallace, who chaired the meeting. Recasting somewhat the famous observation of Lord Keynes, President Kenney-Wallace captured the meeting's agreement on the fundamental purpose of universities in her observation: "It is the power of ideas embraced by an empowered citizenry that has changed our world."

No one in the room doubted that indeed it is the mission of the university so to change the world, nor that all the apparatus of accountability must ultimately be shaped by—and subordinated to—that purpose.

Contributors

Harry Arthurs
President
York University

Jean-Pierre Boisclair
CCAF

David M. Cameron
Professor, Political Science
Dalhousie University

James Cutt
Professor
School of Public Administration
University of Victoria

Ken Davies
Committee of Vice-Chancellors
  and Principals
London

Rodney Dobell
Winspear Professor of
  Public Policy
University of Victoria

Robin H. Farquhar
President and Vice-Chancellor
Carleton University

John Farrant
Universities Funding Council
London

Stewart Goodings
Assistant Under Secretary of State
Education Support Sector
Department of the Secretary
  of State

Cynthia Hardy
Associate Professor
Faculty of Management
McGill University

Geraldine Kenney-Wallace
President
McMaster University

Patrick Kenniff
President of the Conference of
  Rectors and Principals of Quebec
  Universities, and
  Rector, Concordia University

Paul LeVasseur
Organization for Economic
  Cooperation and Development
Paris

295

Gary Mullins
Deputy Minister of Advanced
  Education, Training and
  Technology
Province of British Columbia

Patrick O'Keefe
National Audit Office, London

Robert H.T. Smith
Vice Chancellor
The University of New England
Armidale, N.S.W.
Australia

David W. Strangway
President
University of British Columbia

Ronald Watts
Director
Institute of Intergovernmental
  Relations
Queen's University

Participants

Canadian Universities:
Problems and Opportunities in the 1990s

November 2-3, 1990
Ottawa, Ontario

Dr. H.W. Arthurs
President
York University
4700 Keele Street
North York, Ontario
M3J 1P3

Mr. J.P. Boisclair
Executive Director
Canadian Comprehensive
  Auditing Foundation
The Carriageway
55 Murray Street
Ottawa, Ontario
K1N 5M3

Professor David Cameron
Department of Political Science
Dalhousie University
Halifax, Nova Scotia
B3H 4H6

Mr. Nigel Chippendale
Executive Coordinator
Policy Review Team
Secretary of State
15 Eddy Street
Ottawa, Ontario
K1A 0M5

Mr. Grant Clark
Council of Ontario Universities
444 Yonge Street, Suite 203
Toronto, Ontario
M5B 2H4

Mr. Ken Clements
Canadian Association for University
  Continuing Education
151 Slater Street
Ottawa, Ontario
K1P 5N1

Mr. John G. Cousineau
Research Consultant
B.C. Research Corporation
3650 Wesbrook Mall
Vancouver, British Columbia
V6S 2L2

Dr. John Cowan
Vice-Rector, Research & Planning
University of Ottawa
Ottawa, Ontario
K1N 6N5

Dr. James Cutt
Professor
School of Public Administration
University of Victoria
Victoria, British Columbia
V8W 2Y2

Ms. Susan D'Antoni
Director R.P.P.
Association of Universities
  and Colleges of Canada
151 Slater Street
Ottawa, Ontario
K1P 5N1

Mr. K.S. Davies
Principal Assistant Secretary
Committee of the Vice-Chancellors
  and Principals of the Universities
  of the UK
29 Tavistock Square
London   WC1H 9EZ
England

Mr. John Dinsmore
President
Corporate-Higher Education Forum
1155, Rene Levesque Blvd. West
Suite 2501
Montreal, Quebec
H3B 2K4

Dr. Rod Dobell
Winspear Professor of Public Policy
University of Victoria
P.O. Box 1700
Victoria, British Columbia
V8W 2Y2

Dr. Robin Farquhar
President
Carleton University
Ottawa, Ontario
K1S 5B6

Mr. John Farrant
Assistant Secretary
Universities Funding Council
14, Park Crescent
London   W1N 4DH
England

Mr. Paul Gallagher
President
Vancouver Community College
P.O. Box 24700, Station C
Vancouver, British Columbia
V5T 4N4

Mr. Donald J. Gillies
Professor of Communications
Ryerson Polytechnical Institute
350 Victoria Street
Toronto, Ontario
M5B 2K3

Mr. Dean Goard
Tri-Universities Presidents Council
University of Victoria
P.O. Box 1700
Victoria, British Columbia
V8W 2Y2

Mr. Stewart Goodings
Assistant Under Secretary of State
Education Support
Secretary of State
Jules Leger Building
15 Eddy Street
Ottawa, Ontario
K1A 0M5

Mr. Jeff Greenberg
Office of the Auditor General
  of Canada
240 Sparks Street
Ottawa, Ontario
K1A 0G6

Dr. Cynthia Hardy
Faculty of Management
McGill University
845 Sherbrooke Street West
Montreal, Quebec
H3A 2T5

Dr. Christopher Hodgkinson
Communication and
  Social Foundations
Faculty of Education
University of Victoria
P.O. Box 1700
Victoria, British Columbia
V8W 2Y2

M. Elaine Isabelle
Director General, Program Branch
Social Sciences and Humanities
  Research Council
255 Albert Street
P.O. Box 1610
Ottawa, Ontario
K1P 6G4

Mr. Glen Jones
Higher Education Research Group
Ontario Institute for Studies in
  Education
252 Bloor Street West
Toronto, Ontario
M5S 1V6

Dr. Geraldine Kenney-Wallace
President
McMaster University
Hamilton, Ontario
L8S 4L8

Dr. Patrick Kenniff
Rector and Vice Chancellor
Concordia University
1463 Bishop Street
Montreal, Quebec
H3G 1M8

Dr. Claude Lajeunesse
President
Association of Universities and
  Colleges of Canada
151 Slater Street
Ottawa, Ontario
K1P 5N1

Dr. D.W. Lang
Assistant Vice-President & Registrar
University of Toronto
Toronto, Ontario
M5S 1A1

Dr. Paul LeVasseur
Head of Programme
Programme on Institutional
  Management in
  Higher Education
Organization for Economic
  Cooperation and Development
2, rue Andre-Pascal
75775 Paris CEDEX 16
France

Dr. Joseph Lloyd-Jones
Assistant Vice Rector
Institutional Research
University of Ottawa
Ottawa, Ontario
K1N 6N5

Mr. Peter McMechan
Director, Pacific Programs
Commonwealth of Learning
Suite 300, 800 Hornby Street
Vancouver, British Columbia
V6Z 1C5

Madam Claire McNicoll
Director General
CREPUQ
CP 952, Succursale Place du Parc
Montreal, Quebec
H2W 2N1

Mr. Gary Mullins
Deputy Minister
Ministry of Advanced Education
  and Job Training
Parliament Buildings
Victoria, British Columbia
V8V 1X4

Mr. P. O'Keefe
Director
National Audit Office
Buckingham Palace Road
Victoria
London SW1W 9SP
England

Monsieur Pierre Robert
Vice-recteur à la planification
Université de Montréal
C.P. 6128, Succursale A
Montréal, Québec
H3C 3J7

Prof. Donald C. Savage
Executive Secretary
Canadian Association of
  University Teachers
294 Albert Street, Suite 308
Ottawa, Ontario
K1P 6E6

Dr. Har Singh
Executive Director
Policy, Planning and Program
  Evaluation
Ministry of Advanced Education,
  Training and Technology
3rd Floor, 818 Broughton Street
Victoria, British Columbia
V8V 1X4

Dr. Robert H.T. Smith
Vice Chancellor
The University of New England
Armidale, N.S.W.
Australia

Dr. Guy Steed
Director of Programs
Science Council of Canada
100 Metcalfe Street
Ottawa, Ontario
K1P 5M1

Dr. David W. Strangway
President
University of British Columbia
2075 Wesbrook Mall
Vancouver, British Columbia
V6T 1W5

Dr. Allan Warrack
Vice-President (Administration)
University of Alberta
3-20 University Hall
Edmonton, Alberta
T6G 2J9

Dr. R.L. Watts
Department of Political Studies
Queen's University
Kingston, Ontario
K7L 3N6

Prof. Fred Wilson
Vice-President of CAUT
Department of Philosophy
University of Toronto
Suite 419, 720 Spadina Avenue
Toronto, Ontario
M5S 2T9

Mr. D.R. Yeomans
310 Clemow Avenue
Ottawa, Ontario
K1S 2B8